FINDING WAYS THROUGH EUROSPACE

Edited by Noel B. Salazar, KU Leuven, in collaboration with AnthroMob, the EASA Anthropology and Mobility Network

This transdisciplinary book series features empirically grounded studies from around the world that disentangle how people, objects and ideas move across the planet. With a special focus on advancing theory as well as methodology, the series considers movement as both an object and a method of study.

Volume 7
FINDING WAYS THROUGH EUROSPACE
West African Movers Re-viewing Europe from the Inside
Joris Schapendonk

Volume 6
BOURDIEU AND SOCIAL SPACE
Mobilities, Trajectories, Emplacements
Deborah Reed-Danahay

Volume 5
HEALTHCARE IN MOTION
Immobilities in Health Service Delivery and Access
Edited by Cecilia Vindrola-Padros, Ginger A. Johnson and Anne E. Pfister

Volume 4
MOMENTOUS MOBILITIES
Anthropological Musings on the Meanings of Travel
Noel B. Salazar

Volume 3
INTIMATE MOBILITIES
Sexual Economies, Marriage and Migration in a Disparate World
Edited by Christian Groes and Nadine T. Fernandez

Volume 2
METHODOLOGIES OF MOBILITY
Ethnography and Experiment
Edited by Roger Norum, Alice Elliot and Noel B. Salazar

Volume 1
KEYWORDS OF MOBILITY
Critical Engagements
Edited by Noel B. Salazar and Kiran Jayaram

Finding Ways through Eurospace
West African Movers Re-viewing Europe from the Inside

Joris Schapendonk

berghahn
NEW YORK · OXFORD
www.berghahnbooks.com

First published in 2020 by
Berghahn Books
www.berghahnbooks.com

© 2020, 2026 Joris Schapendonk
First paperback edition published in 2026

All rights reserved. Except for the quotation of short passages
for the purposes of criticism and review, no part of this book
may be reproduced in any form or by any means, electronic or
mechanical, including photocopying, recording, or any information
storage and retrieval system now known or to be invented,
without written permission of the publisher.

Library of Congress Cataloging-in-Publication Data
Names: Schapendonk, Joris, author.
Title: Finding ways through Eurospace : West African movers re-viewing Europe from the inside / Joris Schapendonk.
Description: New York : Berghahn Books, 2020. | Series: Worlds in motion ; volume 7 | Includes bibliographical references and index.
Identifiers: LCCN 2020006095 (print) | LCCN 2020006096 (ebook) | ISBN 9781789206807 (hardback) | ISBN 9781789206814 (ebook)
Subjects: LCSH: West Africans--European Union countries--Social conditions. | West Africans--Cultural assimilation--European Union countries. | Immigrants--European Union countries--Social conditions. | Transnationalism--European Union countries. | European Union countries--Boundaries--Social aspects. | Africa, West--Emigration and immigration. | European Union countries--Emigration and immigration.
Classification: LCC D1056.2.A38 S35 2020 (print) | LCC D1056.2.A38 (ebook) | DDC 305.896/604--dc23
LC record available at https://lccn.loc.gov/2020006095
LC ebook record available at https://lccn.loc.gov/2020006096

British Library Cataloguing in Publication Data
A catalogue record for this book is available from the British Library

EU GPSR Authorized Representative
LOGOS EUROPE, 9 rue Nicolas Poussin, 17000, LA ROCHELLE, France
Email: Contact@logoseurope.eu

ISBN 978-1-78920-680-7 hardback
ISBN 978-1-83695-687-7 paperback
ISBN 978-1-80758-933-2 epub
ISBN 978-1-78920-681-4 web pdf

https://doi.org/10.3167/9781789206807

Contents

Acknowledgements vi
List of Abbreviations viii

Introduction 1

Part I. Navigations 13

  Chapter 1 Worlding Departures 17
  Chapter 2 Moving through Affective Circuits 52
  Chapter 3 Navigating Webs of Facilitation/Control 89
  Chapter 4 'The System' 109

Part II. Re-viewing Europe 141

  Chapter 5 In Place/Out of Place 145
  Chapter 6 The Multiple 178

Conclusion 194

Glossary 200
References 201
Index 215

Acknowledgements

In this book you will probably get lost at some point. The storyline frequently moves between settings and places and often shifts in time and between people. I have long doubted whether I should provide more cartographic hints on where you are in space and time. In the end, I decided not to do so. The main reason is that there is a world out there that cannot be pinned down, that lacks a clear scale and that does not follow pregiven maps. Thus, when you do get lost, you should not worry. It is part of the argument and soon a new passage will follow that will give you new directions.

This book is based on dialogues and engagements with multiple people whose real names are not used. You will know when it is about you. First and foremost, I am grateful for your time and energy, your trust and guidance, your questions, reflections and stories. May your pathways unfold in ways you like.

The book is a collection of findings from my Veni grant by the Netherlands Organisation for Scientific Research (NWO). I express my gratitude to my close colleagues at the Radboud University Nijmegen, and in particular to Kolar Aparna (my critical sister) and Roos Hoekstra-Pijpers, who commented on an early version of this manuscript. I am grateful to Marisha Maas for her incredibly close readings and careful language editing that continued in very hectic times. Without you, this book would not have been published the way it is. In addition, I value very much the input and reflections on my work of other 'Nijmegen people', most notably Lothar Smith, Olivier Kramsch, Henk van Houtum, Martin van der Velde, Tine Davids, Tineke Strik, Rianne van Melik, Ton van Naerssen, Cesar Merlin, Federico Alagna and Mirjam Wajsberg (although the last two are not often in Nijmegen). I owe special thanks to Huib Ernste for his continuous support within the Department of Human Geography, but also for inviting key scholars to our borderland for engaged discussions and thought-provoking lectures. Moreover, it was a real privilege to work in this research with talented students including Michelle Brugman, Saskia van Ooijen, Peter Teunissen, Iris Poelen, Marieke Ekenhorst, Bram Bos, Carla Longares, Thomas Noten, Laura Guenther, Johanna Longerich and, last but not least,

Fransesco Branchi, who sadly lost his life before he could finish his project. Fransesco's thoughts, however, resonate in the chapters to come.

Outside Nijmegen, I am grateful to Janine Dahinden, Matthieu Bolay, Sophie Cranston, Derek Gregory, Adrian Favell, Daniela de Bono, Charles Heller, Xavier Ferrer Gallardo, Griet Steel, Inga Schwarz and Bruno Riccio, for their insightful comments on my work and/or our recent inspiring dialogues. I would like to thank the Helping Hand Research Network, coordinated by Marie Sandberg and Dorte Andersen, for raising new questions that helped me to explore other fields, thoughts and places. I am grateful as well to the wonderful people (most notably Maggi Leung, Ilse van Liempt, Annelies Zoomers and Gery Nijenhuis) of the Transmobilities Network, which keeps the dialogues on mobility going. I also value very much my recent discussions with Valentina Mazzucato, Joan van Geel and others from the Globalisation, Transnationalism and Development research group of Maastricht University. All these people have directly and indirectly left their traces in this book.

Finally, I owe my thanks to my lovely family whom I have left behind so many times on my field trips in the past four years. Thank you, Joëlle, for absolutely everything. And thank you both, Polle Mo and Noes, for bringing even more movement into our lives.

Abbreviations

CAS	Centri Accoglienza Straordinaria (Extraordinary Reception Centres, Italy)
CDA	Centri di Accoglienza (Collective Reception Centres, Italy)
CPSA	Centri di Primo Soccorso e Accoglienza (First Aid and Reception Centres, Italy)
CTRPI	Commissioni Territoriali per il Riconoscimento della Protezione Internazionale (Territorial Commissions for International Protection, Italy)
DT&V	Dienst Terugkeer en Vertrek (Repatriation and Departure Service, the Netherlands)
ECOWAS	Economic Community of West African States
IND	Immigratie- en Naturalisatiedienst (Immigration and Naturalisation Services, the Netherlands)
IOM	International Organization for Migration
JJC	Journey Just Come
MVV	Machtiging Voorlopig Verblijf (authorization for a temporary stay, the Netherlands)
NIE	Número de Identificación de Extranjeros (identification number for foreigners, Spain)
SPRAR	Sistema di Protezione per Richiedenti Asilo e Refugiati (Protection System for Refugees and Asylum Seekers, Italy)

Introduction

In September 2015, I entered a relatively empty apartment in the heart of the Bijlmer area of Amsterdam. I brought some cookies with me as a ridiculously Dutch sign of appreciation that I was welcomed in somebody's home. George, an intelligent 34-year-old Ghanaian man, was the one who welcomed me. I got to know him through my informant Cedric, a Nigerian man living in Nijmegen (the Netherlands). While George made tea, I looked around in the living room and saw some piled boxes, a large TV screen, a couch, a small coffee table and a family photo on the wall. 'Is this your family?' was the – what I thought to be – simple question I raised when I saw the photo. The answer, however, was more complicated than I expected, as George responded: 'Well actually I am renting this house from someone who is now in Africa. That is this man and his wife [pointing at the woman on the photo]. So, he is all the time in Africa, and once in a while he comes back. But until that time I can rent this house from him. But I think it won't take long for him to return, so I move again soon'. The temporary sojourn of George explained that the house reflected a kind of preparedness for movement.

Some five months earlier (April 2015), I visited Pape, a good friend of George. He lives in Lleida – a Catalan city not far from Barcelona. Pape is a Gambian man who emphasized that he was among the first Africans who reached Spain through Ceuta in the mid 1990s. At the time of my visit, Pape shared the apartment with two fellow Gambians: Moustapha and Babacar. Their living space had some strikingly similar characteristics to the apartment in the Bijlmer. The large TV screen and a comfortable couch were among the few furnishings in the living room. This place was, as I learned later, also full of mobility as the three inhabitants had all left the building by September 2015. Moustapha moved to a small village in the neighbouring Huesca region to work in the *frutta* (fruit) sector, Babacar moved back to the Gambia to spend some months with his family and Pape himself made a 'European tour' and travelled to the Netherlands (to also meet up with George) and Germany, respectively. After his tour, which lasted a few weeks, he returned to Spain, and from there he left for the Gambia as well.

This book is about migrants, but it is not about migration. It discusses transnational movements, asylum, belonging and borders, but it is not about migration. There are two interrelated arguments to abandon the term migration in the context of the African movements that are central to this book. First, a migration perspective creates significant analytical discomforts as the terminology related to it is so closely intertwined with the normative logics of the nation state (Wimmer and Glick Schiller 2002; Dahinden 2016). As we will see, the 'African movers' that I aim to portray can actually be best approached as 'experts' in transcending the norms and expectations deriving from the same political entity, especially when we take into account their lifeworlds from the time they have entered Europe. That is not to say that my informants destabilize societal structures through their mobility and informal practices. Certainly, many of them are pushed to the margins of 'Eurospace' due to severe politics of exclusion and discriminatory structures of European labour markets. Consequently, many of them manoeuvre in informal circuits and a few even end up being involved in illicit economic activities. In fact, George and Pape first met in a French prison. That is where they became friends, and from that point on they kept each other up to date about their whereabouts. Despite the fact that I acknowledge these dynamics related to the marginalized socio-economic position of migrants in Europe today, the arguments made in this book rather hint at a different logic. That is to say that the African movers transgress the norms and values of the nation state because they do not necessarily reground in a national space after they have left their places of origin.

Like the 'Eurostars' who are so vividly portrayed by Favell (2008) as the pioneers of an integrated Europe, the African movers in this study position themselves in a postnational Europe. They are not bound to national belongings, and they navigate Europe as a truly integrated socio-economic space. Moreover, like the mobility of the Eurostars, the diverse mobility processes of the African movers connect different places, within and beyond Europe. Through these practices, they actively contribute to a further 'integration' of European spaces as well as to a further 'worlding' of Europe (Simone 2001; Loftsdóttir 2018). Through their movements, formal and informal businesses, religious networks, money transfers, communications and, above all, their imaginations (e.g. Salazar 2011), they connect Milan with Barcelona, Barcelona with El Ejido, El Ejido with Serekunda, Serekunda with Nijmegen, Nijmegen with Athens, and Athens with Istanbul. Likewise, this book does not only add to the lively academic debate on African mobility and the social, economic and political dynamics that are produced by these movements,[1] it is equally about Europe – and ultimately it is about re-viewing Europe's place in the world through the lens of African mobility. As Giglioli, Hawthorne and Tiberio (2017: 338) write: we need to reframe migrants not as 'external bearers of "difference" but as active creators of European-ness'.

The second reason to abandon a migration framework is because of its reductionist and sedentarist understanding of migrants' mobility. That is to say that migration studies usually take mobility into account as an in-between phase between a place of origin and a place of destination (Cresswell 2006). If at all, when studies with a migration lens do notice that people do not stay in their places of (previous) arrival, they tend to frame the emerging dynamics as 'transit migration', 'onward migration' (e.g. Lindley and Van Hear 2007; Ahrens, Kelly and Van Liempt 2016; Ortensi and Barbiano di Belgiojoso 2018; Ramos 2018) or – in the case of EU policymaking – 'secondary movements' of 'third-country nationals' (EMN 2013). The use of this rather specific terminology reveals that the authors somehow acknowledge that migration processes can be lengthy, fragmented and flexible, but it also shows the persistent practice of analysing these movements from the classical notion of a residential relocation: a move from one home place to the next. An emerging body of critical literature on migrant journeys and trajectories attempts to move further away from this linear relocation logic of departure – movement – arrival by highlighting that the beginning and end points of migratory journeys are often very hard to pinpoint (e.g. Collyer 2007; Mainwaring and Brigden 2016; Schapendonk and Steel 2014; Kleist 2018; Moret 2017; Zhang 2018). With this observation, however, we reach the boundaries of what migration studies as an academic field can bring us in our understanding of mobility. As Allison Hui (2016: 75) tellingly outlines: 'But if migration does not stop after moving to another country, when does it stop? Or more precisely, when do "migrant" practices give way to other types of practices, making migration no longer of primary relevance when orienting research?'

Hui challenges us to interrogate the basis on which we differentiate migrant journeys from pre-migration and post-migration mobility. What makes a migration process really different from other mobility processes? The self-evident response of 'migration involves a change of residence' is unconvincing since we know from transnational migration studies that people may have multiple belongings, and may be present in two or more 'homes' at the same time. We also know that a considerable number of people maintain highly mobile lifestyles,[2] and we are aware that processes of inclusion are often accompanied with new forms of mobility and circulations (Moret 2017). In this context, even return migration as a permanent form of resettlement is considered a myth since it involves circulations as well as new attempts to reach previous destinations (Sinatti 2011; King and Christou 2011; Kleist 2018). Thus, instead of being about a single destination-oriented movement towards a destination – migration – this book is rather about mobilities in the plural form (e.g. Adey 2010; Cresswell 2010).

With these dynamics in mind, this book aims to put forward a de-migranticized view on African mobility within Europe. In other words, and in line with Dahinden (2016), I consider 'migration' and its related ontological foundations of stasis not necessarily the best analytical starting point to understand the lifeworlds of African movers in Europe today. Rather than seeing 'migrancy' as the primary marker of my informants' lives, I aim to understand how flexible mobilities relate to migratory projects, and how relations and notions of belonging change along pathways of movements.[3] Instead of seeing the term 'migrant' as an existential category of life, I seek to understand how my informants got 'migranticized' through state-led bureaucracies as well as the expectations that circulate through their affective circuits (Cole and Groes 2016a). At the same time, the chapters show how mobility remains central to their being in Europe, *despite* the existence of harsh mobility regimes that aim to hamper, stop or control their mobilities (Glick Schiller and Salazar 2013). This book dives into the ways African movers navigate Eurospace – defined as an imagined geography of Europe that, in potential, facilitates cross-border mobility.[4] It discusses how they encounter migration bureaucracies, and how they invert the logics of the rules and regulations of these bureaucracies; how they are confronted with borders, but also how they manage to transgress and circumvent them. It attempts to unpack the ways they incorporate the common labels of migration, such as asylum seeker, refugee and illegal migrant, but also the ways they keep away from them or actively reinvent them. It discusses how they feel lost and have lost in Europe as well as the ways they 'just manage' or 'get by' in Europe. Such a de-migranticized view on the im/mobility of people who are generally viewed as migrants sounds like a contradiction in terms, but I argue that it is highly needed to move from the 'master narrative of migration', as Favell (2008: 101) outlines:

> Above all, it is important not to see these aspects of spatial and temporal volatility in a negative light, as is often the case when they are looked at from the classical nation-state centred perspective of 'integration'. This is the master narrative of immigration, wielded by receiving societies, which assumes that all legally welcome 'immigrants' must be

on some kind of track to full integration: to inclusion, incorporation, permanent settlement, and one day becoming a citizen among others.

In sum, the analytical contribution of this book lies at the multiple crossroads of movement *and* stability, everyday mobility *and* migration, European policy *and* so-called 'African cultures of mobility', borders *and* transgressions and ultimately – as it is so cleverly addressed by Kleist and Thorsen (2017) – hopes *and* despairs. Although I highly appreciate the work of critical scholars who emphasize the precarious positions of migrants in Europe, and their analyses of the ways this precarity is actively produced by mobility regimes and their related industries (e.g. Verstraete 2001; De Genova and Peutz 2010), I am deliberately not focusing merely on situations that reinforce the image of the African migrant as homo sacer (e.g. Rajaram and Grundy-Warr 2004). I actually seek ways to link the multiple restrictions and barriers they face in Europe with their creativity and improvisation skills that help them to navigate these uncertain terrains (e.g. Vigh 2009). It follows that I – in line with Kothari's (2008) work on street vendors in Barcelona and Riccio's (2001, 2004) work on Senegalese transnational Mouride networks – refute the notion that cosmopolitan imaginations and mobile lifestyles are reserved for a selected few – as if these only matter in the lifeworlds of white and elitist voyageurs.

Following Im/mobility Trajectories: A Methodological Entry

As a foundation for this book I use a research that aimed to capture the dynamics of African im/mobility in an integrated Europe by means of a trajectory ethnography (e.g. Schapendonk et al. 2018). In methodological sense, this trajectory approach is closely linked to Marcus's (1995) seminal work, which can be understood as a pioneering attempt to make the methods of social science more sensitive to relationalities and mobilities (see, for instance, Büscher and Urry 2009; Salazar and Smart 2011; Merriman 2014). Marcus (1995: 96) encourages researchers to move away from 'single site designs' in order to 'examine the circulation of cultural meanings, objects and identities in diffuse time–space'. My research started with three broadly defined access points from where I attempted to follow im/mobility trajectories: Lombardy (Italy), Catalonia (Spain) and Randstad (the Netherlands). In these regions, I met many, but certainly not all, of my informants for the first time. In places like Bergamo, Lleida, Barcelona and Rotterdam I managed – however oftentimes did not manage – to build social relations with people who gradually granted me access to their lifewords. However, even more so, this research relied on my previously built social connections. Some of these relations have been established more than ten years ago in Morocco and Turkey, which have constituted the EU's external borderlands or 'transit spaces' for about two decades now. Others have grown over the years in my hometown, the city of Nijmegen in the eastern part of the Netherlands.

The stories in this book are based on my fieldwork notes, recorded interviews, reconstructed travel stories and countless informal conversations (face-to-face as well as by telephone or through social media). I primarily approach these stories as products of relations and hence they are not so much phenomenological representations of *their* worlds. The ethnographic details of this book are based on my encounters and engagements with the lifeworlds of my interlocutors. Only through these relations was I able to construct an alternative worldview regarding mobility in contemporary Europe. En passant, these relations served mobility, both for me and my interlocutors. They gave us insights about possible travel destinations and led to new connections. At the same time, our encounters included many situations and confrontations where any ground for relatedness between me and my interlocutors was difficult to find because – as the typical white male EU citizen/scholar – I am not confronted with Europe's racialized mobility regime and its politics of exclusion in my daily life (Cabot 2016; Khosravi 2018; see also Chapter 5).

The book mainly discusses the trajectories of Gambian men, but it also includes stories of people (including a few women) from other African countries, including Senegal, Nigeria and Cameroon. While the central arguments are somewhat biased to the ways Eurospaces expand for those who have recently arrived in Europe through unauthorized channels, it also includes the im/mobility of individuals who have lived in the same space for over twenty years.

The use of the three access points in Europe indicates that a trajectory ethnography is not placeless. Although I find the idea from Feldman (2012) of a nonlocal ethnographer very appealing and convincing in the light of migration apparatuses, there is still a local component to my research activities. In the same way mobilities ground in place (e.g. Favell 2008; Dahinden 2010a), the research activities that aim to study mobility may start from specific 'anchor points' in the field. For example, my fieldwork in Barcelona usually started in a laundry in the middle of the bustling, and centrally located, Raval neighbourhood. In this laundry, I always met the Gambian man called Ebou, doing his daily job – washing, drying, ironing and folding clothes, mattress covers, tablecloths and other textiles coming from individuals, families or neighbouring restaurants. It is from this place that I saw the world moving around us (see for a methodological argument Gielis 2009). The world was in motion through Ebou's stories about his life in the Gambia and the lively illustrations of his journey to Europe that brought him all the way to Syria and Turkey from where he reached Greece and later Italy – the country where he spent some seven years of his life, be it in a highly mobile way. When we 'chopped food' in his workplace, we intermingled discussions on his ongoing struggle of getting regularized through his labour contract with everyday chitchats about football, development, tourists and politics. While I helped him fold some of the clothes that were still warm from the dryer, we informed each other about the whereabouts of some of our contacts and we discussed life in the nearby city of Lleida. Ebou considered Lleida (or Lerida in Spanish) 'his place' since that is the place where he received his 'paper'. Not only Ebou's dynamic storylines hinted at lives in motion. So too did the informal conversations I had with the many Senegalese and Gambian 'brothers'[5] of Ebou who came to visit him. So too did the way his Nigerian ex-girlfriend, who worked as a sex worker close by and who ran into the laundry now and then, usually when there were police interventions. From this specific place, I saw 'the stuff' Ebou was buying from waste collectors who wander through the streets of Barcelona day in, day out, to look for some value in the things that people throw away. Underneath the dinner table (which was also the table to fold clothes), Ebou stored, among other things, bicycle lights, shoes, heads, music boxes, shavers and belts. Many of these materials – or 'stuff' as Simone (2014) would call it – waited underneath his table to be repaired, if necessary, in order to trade them soon again in the urban environment of Barcelona. Other 'stuff' was gathered by Ebou to be put in a container in order to be shipped to the harbour of Banjul, the capital of his country of origin. Next to this laundry, other anchor points from where I started my research were a public square in Bergamo, a shared apartment and an African grocery shop in Lleida, an asylum centre in the Italian region of Liguria and a house of a Ghanaian pastor in the Bijlmer area of Amsterdam.

These places are insightful access points to study mobility; however, they tell us little about the ways mobility trajectories evolve in expected and unexpected ways. For this reason, the trajectory approach I put forward here is not meant to stick to places. In other words, to capture the navigation of Eurospace by African movers, the researcher is challenged to be flexible, to be prepared to switch gears and also to change places. The researcher is asked to develop mobility capital (Moret 2017) and to find ways to connect with informants through the use of mobile devices and social media[6] (which raises new questions regarding ethics and the researcher's positionality). Over the years, I have remained in contact with many of my informants, and this allowed me to keep track of people's changing, and sometimes remarkably *unchanging*, situations. More fundamentally, this trajectory approach enabled me to revisit my informants in the places they grounded for different periods of time, including Athens, Naples, Tenerife, Leiden, Vevey, Bern, Bremen and smaller places in Italy, the Netherlands, Germany, Switzerland and Spain. I also visited places and people in the Gambia that were most meaningful to some of my Gambian interlocutors. This mobile and translocal design runs the risk of being a 'shallow jet-set ethnography' (Olwig 2007: 22, cited by Khosravi 2018) as less knowledge is produced on local sites (see also Elliot, Norum and Salazar 2017). I indeed have been hopping places, meaning that I spent only limited time in each of them. Consequently, I have collected only limited information regarding place histories, local regulatory frameworks and migrants' engagements with local communities. Some 'thick descriptions' of localities are thus sacrificed for the sake of grasping how my informants move through, within and across places.

The method of following trajectories adds empirical and analytical value to our understanding of im/mobility processes since it goes beyond ex post reconstructions of movement.[7] It is predominantly built on the idea that we can understand im/mobility processes better at times they are actually unfolding (BenEzer and Zetter 2015; Schapendonk et al. 2018). The value added not only lies in the fact that it puts emphasis on the evolvement of a certain pathway and the experiences attached to this. A trajectory approach is particularly insightful since it is able to unpack some of the inherent aspects of mobility that tend to be left out, or which become 'rationalized', by ex-post reconstructions of travel stories. This includes the multiple aspirations people have in mind, the shifting of destinations and renavigations, the multiple moments of breakthrough, the eventual failed attempts and inconsistencies as well as the unforeseen and unexpected ruptures of mobility. That is not to say that everything should be told. As Shahram Khosravi (2018) so powerfully argues in his reflection on the trajectory approach, movers, migrants and asylum seekers have a fundamental right to opacity.[8] This particularly applies in the framework of the tactics attached to unauthorized border crossings and the skills and techniques of my informants to circumvent state control. The ethnographer, then, constantly needs to balance his or her search for the specific, the detailed, the untold – in sum the 'thickness' of mobility illustrations – with the informants' fundamental right to opacity. In the chapters to come, I do not provide a separate section with my methodological and ethical reflections. Instead, I discuss some of the dilemmas, failures, awkward situations and ethical boundaries when I actually encountered these during my research practices.

A Guide For the Reader

As with the trajectories of African movers, the storyline of this book is also fragmented, dynamic and nonlinear. It emphasizes process and movement, but at times it stands still. The stories of my most important interlocutors are spread over the book and are deliberately interwoven with the pathways of other people. In each chapter, we meet new movers who lead us to new places. Although the entire book is based on ethnographic insights, I use vignettes to further zoom in on specific details that deepen our understanding of the im/mobility involved. These vignettes appear at the beginning of the two parts of the book.

The first part, 'Navigations', focuses on the wayfinding practices of the African movers. It consists of four chapters. Chapter 1, 'Worlding Departures', starts from the notion of 'worlding', a concept coined by the urban theorist AbdouMaliq Simone (2001, 2004) in order to understand the multiple ways African movers link up with processes of globalization and how these processes result in multiple departures. Chapter 2, entitled 'Moving through Affective Circuits', dives into the complex relation between mobility and affective relations. It starts from Vigh's (2006, 2009) notion of 'social navigation'. Whereas most migration studies frame social connectivity as automatically beneficial to mobility processes, I actually approach it as an uncertain terrain that requires careful navigation by the movers in question. Instead of the 'strong and weak ties' thesis of social networks, I start from the notion of 'affective circuits', being constructed by the myriad exchanges of goods, people, money, emotions and ideas across borders (Cole and Groes 2016b). By navigating these circuits, movers negotiate individual aspirations and social expectations synchronically. The same circuits help them to create new openings and new directions in their mobility processes. However, these circuits are regulated, performed and kept under surveillance, leading to considerable financial, social and emotional losses. The subsequent chapter, 'Navigating Webs of Facilitation/Control' (Chapter 3), focuses on a second uncertain terrain that is navigated by my informants: the complex web of mobility facilitators and mobility controllers. While realms of mobility facilitation and realms of mobility control are usually separated from each other in discussions on migration industries (e.g. Gammeltoft-Hansen and Nyberg Sørenson 2013; Cranston, Schapendonk and Spaan 2018), I actually start from the opaque boundaries between, and shifting roles of, actors that are present in this relational force field. This discussion continues in Chapter 4 in which I elaborate on 'The System' – an expression that my interlocutors used not only to articulate the migration apparatus with which they are confronted, but also to indicate their confrontation with othering, ordering and bordering processes in Eurospace (Van Houtum and Van Naerssen 2002). Although the system is omnipresent and powerful, it is seldom seen as a determining force. This chapter thus shows how movers escape the system, find ways to live with it, or invert its logics. This final chapter of Part I ends with some concluding notes on the ways people find ways.

The title of the second part, 'Re-viewing Europe', holds a double connotation. First, it points to the processes and moments whereby my interlocutors seem to reconsider their position in Eurospace. Chapter 5, entitled 'In Place/Out of Place', therefore focuses on the mobility/locality configurations that are inherent parts of the trajectories under research. From a relational politics of im/mobility (e.g. Adey 2006; Cresswell 2010; Schapendonk and Steel 2014; Bolay 2017), it discusses how the African movers relate and belong to specific places in Eurospace as well as the ways they at times feel excluded and isolated from the very same places (Lems 2018). Being a human geographer, I feel less equipped to write about people's shifting identities and social becoming in these processes (e.g. Wilson Janssens 2018) and instead focus more on the various attachments to place involved. The second connotation attached to the title of 'Re-viewing Europe' points to the way the African movers help us to rethink the role of cross-border mobility in processes of European integration. Hence, Chapter 6, entitled 'The Multiple', sheds a more positive and diffuse light on the margins of Eurospace by pointing to mundane processes of circulation, informality and flexibility, especially in economic circuits. This helps us to destabilize dualities of core/periphery, success/failure, vulnerability/resourcefulness, here/there and inside/outside. Through their mobility and related circuits, African movers redefine the ways presumed margins relate to self-defined centres and, in doing so, they coproduce a worlding and multiple Europe.

In the Conclusion, I reflect on the position of im/mobility in migration studies and herewith offer new openings for framing and studying trajectories.

NOTES

1. There is a very rich field of literature that discusses the diverse cultures of mobility in various settings across West Africa. The *Mobile Africa* book, edited by De Bruijn, Van Dijk and Foeken (2001), is an important point of reference in this respect. Other compelling ethnographies include: Prothmann (2018) for a Senegalese case, Piot (2010) for a Togolese case, Gaibazzi (2015) for a Gambian countercase on sedentary lives, Alpes (2011) for a Cameroonian case and Bolay (2017) for a case on

itinerant miners. Next to this anglophone field of literature, there is an equally rich francophone field of literature on mobility (Choplin and Lombard 2010; Bredeloup 2008), transmigration and circulation (Alioua 2008; Carnet et al. 2012).

2. These mobile groups include privileged movers like Favell's (2008) Eurostars, Ong's (1999) astronauts, elitist travellers (e.g. Camenisch and Müller 2017) as well as less privileged movers (see Tarrius 1995 on Maghrebi commercants in Europe, Engbersen et al. 2013 on Polish workers in the EU, Bolay 2017 on itinerant miners, Meeus 2012 on Romanian workers in the EU, Dahinden 2010a on cabaret dancers in Switzerland and beyond and Kalir 2013 on Chinese workers in Israel).

3. In that sense, I indeed follow an Ingoldian approach to mobility and consider my informants as *wayfarers* (Ingold 2007, 2011). In all his essays, Ingold prioritizes dynamics over statics, process over product and entanglement over classification. See Schapendonk (2018b) for an elaborative discussion on Ingold's conceptual distinction of wayfaring versus transporting and how this relates to the field of migrant trajectories.

4. The notion of Eurospace overlaps to a large extent with Europe's Schengen zone, but as we will see throughout the book, there are many 'internal externalities' (Schapendonk 2017b) in this Eurospace. It can best be considered a borderless zone with borders (see Chapter 4). At the same time, through people's movements and imaginations Eurospace might expand to other places outside the Schengen zone. It is a travelling entity in itself.

5. The terms 'brother' and 'sister' – as well as the French terms *frère* and *soeur* – are commonly used by my informants to indicate a relatively strong social bonding with somebody. It often does not refer to a family relation (see also Andrikopoulos 2017).

6. These research practices partly rely on the methods and reflections of other scholars aiming to understand mobile populations, including Meeus (2012) and Elliot, Norum and Salazar (2017).

7. Ex-post reconstructions can still lead to highly informative contributions, which unsurprisingly come from gifted anthropologists like Michael Jackson (2013), Annika Lems (2018), Shahram Khosravi (2011) Hans Lucht (2012) and Jonny Steinberg (2015). Despite their different writing and research techniques, all these authors nonetheless manage to construct a multilayered portrayal of what it means to be on the move in a world full of political, social and racial borders. In my view, the work of Steinberg deserves special attention for its deeply touching description of the journey across Africa of a Somali man called Asad. The writings of these anthropologists go naturally beyond the analytical points of departure of mainstream migration studies that start from binary thinking such as departure versus arrival, legal versus illegal and push versus pull (King 2002). At the same time, these books cannot easily be subsumed under the interdisciplinary field of mobility studies (Sheller and Urry 2006; Cresswell 2010) since they hardly fit the framing of 'new mobilities' that hint at technology-driven mobilities and elitist and borderless movements of global nomads (see also Cresswell 2011).

8. Khosravi relates his argument to the work of the postcolonial scholar Édouard Glissant.

PART I

Navigations

Milan, May 2017

Doudou had a bad night. In the smallest sleeping room of the apartment that he shared with one other Gambian man, he got up several times at night to search with the torch of his mobile phone for something that was missing. He checked again a small pile of papers that was placed underneath the tablecloth and again opened a suitcase that was stored in the only closet of the room. He went out of his bed again to have another look inside the pockets of his jacket. From my bed – that stood so close in line with his bed that our feet could easily touch each other when we both lay down on our mattresses – I saw him scratching his head, and I heard him say, 'Ohh, this makes trouble'. He did not say this loudly, apparently, he thought that I was sleeping.

It was the first night that I spent in his place in Milan. On our way from the bus stop to this apartment, Doudou had kept on stressing that he lived in a place that was far from comfortable, and not at all clean. He did not dare to invite his wife – who was living in Leiden (the Netherlands) at that moment, and whom he had not yet officially married – to this 'African house'. However, since I was there to understand 'the African experience' it was the best sojourn for me he could think of. He was right. It enabled me to understand that this specific apartment in Milan can be best considered a guest house. There were two main renters of the place, but they were seldom the only two people around. Doudou could not even count the number of travellers originating from the same area in the Gambia who had stayed at some point in time in his apartment. He commented, 'They come and contact me. I say, "I cannot help you with money, I cannot help you with your travel, but I can offer you a place for the night, so you can leave the next day"'.

The guest house basically distinguishes three types of visitors: first, those who stay for only a few days, without being charged; second, those who stay for longer periods of time, and who are asked for a financial compensation; and third, special guests who also contribute to the house rent, and whose sleeping places are guaranteed. In this week in May, I belonged to the first category of travellers. But I was not the only visitor. Babacar – one of my main informants whom I first met in the Catalan city of Lleida – also came to Milan and stayed in the same place. Babacar was a very good friend of Doudou and a privileged guest. He even held the house key of Doudou's apartment – a valuable gift in the light of his mobility dynamics in and beyond Europe. He could come in at any moment and ground in Doudou's guest house for a while.

However, running a guest house also comes with an administrative burden – and this is why Doudou had slept badly that night. One 'young boy from the village' was about to arrive all the way from Germany to collect the papers that he had handed over to Doudou some two years ago. Doudou showed me the Gambian passport of this boy but he could not find his *permesso di soggiorno* – the residence permit. This was crucial, however, as the boy was coming to Italy to actually renew his residence permit. When the boy would be unable to show his documents to the Italian authorities, he would most likely fall into a period in which his stay in Italy was unauthorized.

After vainly searching his apartment, in Doudou's mind there was only one option left as to where this particular document could be: in his previous apartment in Milan, which was inhabited by other Gambians after he had left. Here, as he explained to me, he had stored some of his belongings. This made me think of the scattered geography of his life in Europe, having stuff spread over two apartments in Milan, a wife in the Netherlands and feeling moral duties towards 'his village'; located not far from the city of Bassé in the eastern part of the Gambia. With this scattered geography comes a careful navigation. He called one of his 'brothers' who owned a car and who could easily go to Doudou's former apartment to search for the paper there. In the meantime, Doudou and I went for breakfast in a nearby café and then wandered the city. Doudou loves to move through the urban environment by foot. I had walked for hours with him through Amsterdam and Leiden before – which finally made me name him 'giroman', a nickname he seemed to embrace.

Late afternoon Doudou received a phone call – the young boy had arrived at the central station of Milan. Doudou, however, still had no news from the driver concerning the whereabouts of the missing residence permit. His first reaction indicated he had hoped for more time, as he said to me: 'Agh, I thought it would take a long time, but he is here now in Milano'. He decided to go home quickly and leave me in the same place we had eaten breakfast. He returned in fifteen minutes with a smile of relief on his face and told me: 'There is a big confusion. The boy who is coming is not the boy of the paper. His papers are at the other side, my brother found them. The passport and the soggiorno!'

It appeared that Doudou looked after the papers of three young boys from his village at the same time, and he had simply mixed up two of them. Having left his place of origin many years ago, he barely knows the next generation of travellers from his village who are moving to Europe through the 'backway'. Due to his own 'incomplete' documents, he has not been able to visit his place of origin for years now. To make me understand his confusion, he explained that this young boy was about four to six years old at the time he himself had left: 'He was like this [holding his hand at knee-level to indicate the length of the boy]. So I don't know this boy, but I know his family'.

To hand over the documents, Doudou, the driver and the young boy decided to meet each other in an African restaurant, not far from central station. On our way, I started wondering about the economy behind this. Was there some transaction involved? During the meeting in the restaurant there was no sign of an economic dimension. The young boy ordered food and paid for it himself. Guilelessly, the driver handed over the plastic bag with the passport and the residence permit. The boy took a brief look at his papers, without any expression of mistrust. After this occasion, I checked with Doudou and I checked with the boy and both stated that there was no money involved. But the altruistic role of Doudou is not without risk, as he explained:

> I had a problem some years ago. I carried the papers of one boy who left. But I put this paper in my jacket. So, because it is a jacket, I put it somewhere, and I forgot about this. So, I carried it for days. But one day, police searched me, and they saw the paper, and they brought me to court ... They thought I had stolen this document and I used it for maybe travelling or working, you see? It is like that ... I explained to them that I kept this paper for somebody who is travelling in Europe, so I don't get any money [for this], but they still brought me to court ... Yes yes, the people think like this, if you hold the document of a different person, they think that you steal it and that you use it.

A little later, the four of us went by car to a different part of town. We still had a few hours left before the young boy's train would depart for his next destination – Sicily, where the renewal procedure would start. Doudou and the driver left the boy and me at a café, which was located in a little square where a dozen African men were gathering. When we entered, the young boy in a split second recognized somebody sitting at a table. It was his former roommate with whom he had spent about one week in Rome.

Some twenty minutes later, another young Gambian entered the café. Being even more surprised, the young boy gave a big hug to the newcomer, who appeared to be his brother (from the same father, but a different mother). The young boy had had no idea that his brother would be around in Milan. Unexpected encounters in specific meeting places seem to be the norm in mobility wonderland.

We went to the train station quite early – one hour before the train would depart. Doudou did his very best to remain in charge of arranging the passage of the young boy. He held the young boy's ticket, he informed us about the timetables, however he repeatedly made mistakes due to the fact that the trains and times on the electronic board shifted continuously. Instead of direction, Doudou created confusion with his authority. The young boy, however, was patient with him. It seemed that he directed his docile smile to me to tell me: 'There is no need to worry – I will find my way'.

CHAPTER
1

Worlding Departures

When one walks through the bustling market of Serekunda in the Gambia one gets a glimpse of the worlding views of some of the young men from Senegambia whom I encountered in the course of my project. If one makes one's way through this lively environment, one begins to comprehend that any attempt to explain the root causes of irregular migration from this particular location will be incomplete at best, and will miss the point at worst. Evidently, a geohistorical context of colonialism and the devastating effects of structural adjustment programmes, the latter having affected household forms in the Gambia profoundly since the mid-1980s (Kea 2013), need to be taken into account to understand these outward movements. Moreover, the suffocating political regime of the West African equivalent of Ghadaffi – as some of my informants called the former Gambian President Jammeh – has created very limited pathways for the Gambian youth to further their social and economic careers (e.g. Kea 2016; Gaibazzi 2015).[1] Especially during the last period of the more than two decades his political regime has been in power, opponents and critics of Jammeh have had very good political reasons to leave their country of origin, including escaping the risk of imprisonment without trial, torture and death (Hultin et al. 2017). For many Gambian citizens, and especially Mandinkas, this suffocating regime was omnipresent.[2] For the tourists enjoying the smiling coast of Africa after their charter flights, however, the regime seldom revealed itself.

Lamin – an intelligent young man who was raised by the streets of Serekunda – explained to me during different encounters in three different countries (Switzerland, Italy, the Netherlands) how the political oppression entered the daily lives of the urban youth. He described in great detail his pre-college period in which he and his group of four friends were used to hanging around on the streets of the Jewsang district of Serekunda. They were killing time, hoping for petty jobs, listening to Gambian radio DJs and smoking *ganja* (marijuana). During many of these occasions, the group of friends collectively and repeatedly mocked and criticized the president. They, for instance, discussed and further spread the popular rumours that Jammeh did not emanate from a Jola family, but was born as an extramarital child. At some point, Lamin expected that his constant on-the-ground criticism would get him into serious trouble, as Jammeh's spies were spread all over the same quarter. When these critical words would be caught by the wrong person, he could easily be woken up at night by police forces taking him to prison. For this reason, his mother kept on warning him about this careless conduct. However, from Lamin's standpoint, he had very little to lose and he replied to his mother that he was ready to go to prison. This feeling, in combination with the stubbornness of 'the ghetto youth' (his words),[3] was the main reason that the mocking continued. Lamin's situation became more precarious, however, when one of the four friends joined the president's armed forces. This not only broke down the strong bond between the young men, but also provided the new authority agent with a lot of in-depth information about who said what and about their daily activities and whereabouts. Lamin remembered very well how this created an uncomfortable encounter not long after his friend joined the armed forces:

> Once he saw us smoking *ganja*, he threatened one of us to arrest him. But he knows we do this all the time, it is normal for us, he used to smoke with us. But now he is in the military he thinks he has strong powers. That also made us think – maybe we should join the military too, because it makes you a strong man.

Indeed, the persistent political oppression seemed to create two options for Lamin and other young men in Serekunda – either join the regime or move out.

However, as argued above, such an explanation concentrating on root causes is incomplete since it omits inherent aspects of the African mobility here under study. It omits the persistent wish among the African youth to transcend borders and it ignores the multiple ways in which mobility becomes interlinked with lifestyle and social becoming. Desires (Collins 2018), imaginaries (Salazar 2011) and social worth (Prothmann 2018) are indeed expressed through mobility, and mobility is indeed central to the multiple roles and activities in the everyday lives in many African settings (e.g. De Bruijn, Van Dijk and Foeken 2001; Hahn and Klute 2007).[4] To articulate these processes, this chapter takes the notion of worlding as its main starting point to understand the mobility of African movers, towards and within Europe. Worlding, as noted by AbdouMaliq Simone (2004), inherently relates to the informal and the mobile. It is not to be considered a by-product of socio-economic implosions of African urban economies, it rather points to 'the production of orientations to, and sensibilities about, the urban that seemed to posit that the salient features of urban life and its accomplishments were always also taking place somewhere else besides the particular city occupied' (Simone 2001: 18). Worlding processes bring with them a constant state of preparedness to 'switch gears', as he writes: 'Indeed, if you take the life stories of many households across the region, people have been prepared to migrate at a moment's notice, to change jobs, residences, and social networks with little apparent hesitation' (ibid.).

From this notion of worlding, this chapter starts with a brief discussion of notions of immobility, desire and *hustling* that have started to resonate in migration studies recently (e.g. Belloni 2016b; Alpes 2011; Gaibazzi 2014; Collins 2018). While these social dimensions are mostly applied in the context of departures from the African continent, I will particularly elaborate on the various ways these notions continue to make sense in the context of the im/mobility processes towards and inside Europe. Thereby the focus is on the im/mobility trajectories of six young men from Senegambia (five Gambians, one Senegalese) who entered Italy by embarking on the same boat that departed from the Libyan coastline in the second half of 2013. Lamin is one of these men.

During the nerve-racking journey across the Mediterranean, the captain initially lost direction and was redirected to Italy by the crew of a Maltese ship. After two days of drifting, the boat – with approximately eighty other passengers – encountered a border guard ship. When the border guards asked for someone who spoke English, Lamin was appointed by his co-passengers as 'spokesman' to coordinate the risky shift of people from the inflatable boat to the much safer ship deck of the border guards. A lot of people have seen their co-travellers die at similar moments when they thought themselves in reach of safe hands. After long days of fear, panic and exhaustion, they just cannot stand the relatively time-consuming process of this transfer and make their way to the rescue ship by a combination of swimming, writhing, scrimmaging and fighting. Often this leads to another capsize, another border tragedy in which people die on their way to better futures. In this case of the shift that Lamin coordinated, however, all the people on the boat survived and were shipped to the Italian island of Lampedusa. From there, most of the eighty boat passengers were sent to a small place nearby Naples where their asylum procedures started. This was the place where the friendship between the six Senegambian young men grew. This was also the place from which their trajectories evolved in different directions across Europe. In the following three chapters, the divergent storylines of this small group will gradually intertwine with those of movers who departed from other West African regions.

Sitting, Gambling, Moving

When you enter the main market building of the Serekunda Market in the Gambia, you hear multiple voices echo from all possible directions. Soon the smell of fresh and not-so-fresh food mingles and starts to dominate over the smell of exhaust gas coming from the continuously stagnant traffic. Upon entering you need to meander through the narrow and shady alleys where retailers do their best to establish a better income than yesterday. When you take one of the stairs to the first floor, the daily cacophony of the 'black market' reaches you before your eyes can actually see what is going on. The black market is an epicentral place where countless young men and women mingle to market second-hand mobile phones, SIM cards, groundnuts, buckets, clothes, textiles and other stuff – day in, day out. If you manage to find your way back to the outside world, you come across numerous other women and men that work as vendors in one of the most important urban economies of the Gambia. The Serekunda Market is a node of informality, business, daily movement and encounters – having many such equivalents in West Africa and beyond.

During my first visit to this worlding place, I made my way through by the means of two worlding connections. First, there was Alagie, a Gambian man whom I first met in the city of Nijmegen, the Netherlands (my hometown). Our mutual friend – another Gambian man named Dawda – has held a stable socio-economic position in the Netherlands for several years, which helped Alagie to obtain a three-month-valid tourist visa to enter this European country and visit his friend. When we met, he assured me he would be my 'guide' when I would visit the Gambia – so here he was. My second worlding connection came from my WhatsApp communication with Lamin who was in Italy at the time of my stay in Serekunda. With a series of voice messages he tried to guide me to the exact locations where he had spent so much time hustling – a common way to navigate precarious urban environments (Thieme 2018).[5] Through these two worlding connections and the people I met here, I learned how the Serekunda Market is an intermediate place where urban actors express their capacity to make something of and with the city on an everyday basis (Simone 2004: 133; see also Hahn 2010). Besides that, I learned how the Serekunda Market is a node of incoming movement, daydreaming, desiring, discussing with friends your pathway to a better future, your pathway to somewhere – elsewhere in the world. However, departure from this place should not be considered to be a rupture per se. It is rather a continuation of mobility rhythms and practices whereby some movements cover longer distances and take more time than others. From this standpoint, departures are – as we will see – almost always multiple.

Saihou

Of all my informants, Saihou probably fits best the term *Afrostar* that I once coined as the African version of Favell's 'Eurostar' (Schapendonk 2017a). In his book *Eurostars in Eurocities,* Favell (2008: xii) creates a highly informative portrayal of the Eurostars that 'stepped off the national path to follow an uncertain future in an integrating Europe'. The reader of this book gains first-hand knowledge regarding the experiences and politics attached to the mobility processes of EU's pioneers of cross-border movements. Favell powerfully illustrates how his informants learn to adapt and change while crossing intra-EU borders. Like Favell's Eurostars, Lamin and Saihou live mobility, and any EU citizen may learn from the ways they have navigated and co-created the postnational Europe we are living in.

I first met Saihou in Naples (May 2015). He is a slim and talkative Mandinka young man just over twenty years old. In the days of our encounters in Naples he was accompanied by his close friend Amat, who embarked the same boat in Libya. Amat originates from the Senegalese region Casamance and has a Jola background. His physical appearance much resembles that of a professional Senegalese wrestler. Saihou was actually visiting his friend Amat in the region where they both entered the asylum system of Italy, after they had been transferred from Lampedusa to mainland Italy. There they were housed in a large asylum centre not far from Naples for about six months. After this, Saihou was transferred to Milan, whereas Amat was sent to the city of Naples. The southern spheres of Naples were definitely preferred over the more controlled urban space of Milan. According to the young men, Naples is the European capital of *raba raba,* a term that has a mixed connotation of hustling, struggling, rapidity and business. Raba raba is very central to the informal activities of the Serekunda Market described above. The phrase '*raba raba*' was made popular in Senegambia by reggae/rap artist Dro Kylah, and has since then evolved into a 'household term' in the Gambia and beyond. As Lamin once explained to me with a kind of hip-hop rhyme:

> My mom always told me, 'Oh I go to the market to do raba raba'. Or she could say, 'Let me clean the kitchin the raba raba way'. It is meaning like quick ... The same as the ghetto youth would just say, 'Boy let me just do this kind of thing in order to finance something or to adopt something or to earn something'. We think the *move,* we can define it as raba raba.

In the period he lived in the region of Naples, Saihou created something out of the raba raba system by working in the neighbouring agricultural fields, by doing some street vending activities, by using public transport without paying for it, by connecting to the many Italian friends he had made through his informal activities (see Lucht 2012 for a detailed description of such lives in the margins of southern Italy). In the view of Saihou, the Neapolitan environment fits him better than the Milanese as he is the kind of young man that cannot just 'sit' and wait for better days – an attitude that is so clearly reflected in his movements across European borders. Whereas his Senegalese friend Amat waited for the outcome of the asylum procedure, Saihou decided to 'try his luck somewhere else' just a few weeks after his transfer to Milan. From the migrant accommodation centre in Milan, he went to Switzerland irregularly and applied for asylum there. Soon after, the authorities recognized him as a 'Dublin case' and they started the process of removal. The Dublin regulations have been invented by the European Commission (EC) to reduce cross-border movements of asylum seekers by generally making the EU member states in which the asylum seeker first arrives responsible for their asylum procedures. The EU, thus, is a mobility regime that aims to 'normalise the movements of some travellers, while criminalising and entrapping the ventures of others' (Glick Schiller and Salazar 2013: 189; see also Chapter 3). The screening and separation of different travellers is crucial to this politics of im/mobility; asylum seekers are to be separated from economic migrants, irregular from regular migrants, knowledge migrants from other labour migrants, etc. Bordering practices are indeed also ordering practices (Van Houtum and Van Naerssen 2002).

But Saihou decided to run away from 'the camp' and went underground in a Swiss middle-sized city. In this place, he entered into a relationship with a Swiss girl for some months. As Saihou commented, he was hoping for 'strong love' that could lead to marriage and, ultimately, regularization. But this was in the end not the case. Instead, he was apprehended for being 'illegally' in the country during an unexpected control of the Swiss authorities. He was put in detention and transferred to Rome by plane soon after. This bad experience, however, did not stop him from dreaming of another movement. As he stated when I met him in Naples:

> Saihou: I am a human being that loves to travel, you know. My next stop is maybe Germany, but I also come to Amsterdam. I love Amsterdam! I even have one Holland friend there, I know him from my time in Gambia. I also have black friends in Germany. I want to go to Hamburg or Bremen.
> I: Bremen?
> Saihou: Yea! I love too much Bremen. Bremen is a good life! I know, because my friend tells me, he is married there, so you have good chance there!

After I returned to the Netherlands, Saihou started to prepare his next move. It was when concerns about the so-called 'EU refugee reception crisis' had begun to swell. Through telephone conversations and voice messages Saihou kept me up to date with his travel plans. At the end of the same month, he indicated his readiness to take a train to Austria. I started to worry when the communication fell silent for a few days, but then a comforting voice message arrived:

> Hi brother, good morning, how are you, how are you doing? So right now I am in Germany, I arrived in Germany now. So I left Italy yesterday, because Friday and Saturday it was not possible to travel, because these days the border was very, very hard to cross, you know. So I came by car, yesterday at night, so right now [I am] in Germany. When I take a number, I give it to you ... Have a nice day.

His means of travel struck me. He had attempted to cross the Italian–Austrian border by train, but this attempt failed due to the intensified border controls. He explained to me that he had travelled by car because there was 'too much control' at the train stations. He had 'ordered' this car on the internet for only twenty or twenty-five euros. A pleasant journey followed, with two German women taking him, and another traveller, to Germany. Saihou stated with joy: 'We were drinking, we were doing music, and after we were running [driving] for maybe one hour or two hours we stopped and we started drinking, making music. It was a very nice journey!' Thus, while I was a bit worried about Saihou, he found his way by making use of a hitch-hiking website (which was at that time a rather anonymous and by default cash-only service) and had a wonderful travel experience. For me, it was a time of scholarly reflection on my own prejudiced assumptions regarding unauthorized journeys – as if they are always hectic, fearful and turbulent.

During his first weeks in Germany, Saihou kept me updated about his situations and transfers to different asylum spaces. He finally ended up in an asylum centre in southwest Germany, not far from the French border. I was able to visit him there some two and a half months after he arrived in Germany. When I actually arrived at the train station of his place of asylum, I called him several times, but he did not pick up his phone. Later I learned he suffered from a bad hangover from the dancing night that ended a few hours before my arrival. When I told him that I was still looking for a place to spend the nights, he insisted that I would stay in his place – in the *Asylheim* that was, as so often, located in the periphery of this middle-sized German town. The Asylheim was an old villa that, given the desperate state of the facilities, had probably been abandoned a long time ago. When I entered this typical refugee emergency building, I dropped my travel bag at the lower end of a bunk bed in the 'Nigerian room'. As there was no space left in the Gambian room on the third floor, Saihou had to share a room with two Nigerian men. All the socializing in which Saihou partook, however, occurred on the third floor with other movers from Senegambia. The particular 'Senegambian room' in this Asylheim was a 'thrown-togetherness' (Massey 2005) of different mobility trajectories with various spatial-temporal stretches. The youngest boy, about nineteen years old, had lived in Spain for three years where he was reunited with his grandmother before he moved to Germany. Mr Sweden, a Gambian man who had passed the age of forty, had stayed in the UK for nine years where he had studied. While studying he had to work long hours to finance his study programme. After getting his master's degree, life became worse for him as he lost his job and soon after his study-based papers expired. He moved to Sweden (where his brother lived) and next to Denmark, where he stayed only short periods of time. He decided to return to the Gambia. From there, however, he applied for a visa to visit Germany as a tourist. Because of 'his record' (having been in the UK for a long time without violating his residence conditions), he encountered little difficulty in this process. Once he arrived in Germany, he simply overstayed and asked for asylum. Another Gambian man had lived in Italy for about thirteen years and just recently tried his luck in Germany. The shared dinner in this particular room was a collective story of travel dynamics that went beyond my imagination.

My 'first asylum night', as Saihou called it, was not very convenient. There were boys playing football at night. There was Nigerian music coming from the other side of the room. I was constantly disturbed by a congregation of bleeping, ringing and buzzing of mobile telephones, and the light of the room was switched on and off every time somebody was entering the place. How on earth could one find rest in this place? Besides the restlessness of this place, the peripheral location – which can be seen as a sedimentation of the general deterrence paradigm of EU's migration and asylum policy (Gammeltoft-Hansen and Tan 2017) – had a direct effect on the mental well-being of Saihou:

> So the first day I came here, I did like this [puts his hands before his eyes] and told myself: 'Oh, what are they doing! They put me in this far-away place, and even now this house, it is faaar away from the town'. So. They make us bored, you know. Me, I am really tired of *Asyl*.

Knowing his current location and situation – and in particular the mismatch between this asylum location and his outgoing attitude – I understood very well his relief when he heard from his lawyer back in Italy that his Italian refugee documents would very soon arrive. This relief is inherently related to a sense of overcoming one's involuntary immobility. Over the years, Saihou regularly told me how he was not a person that could 'sit in one place'. Interestingly, many Gambians refer to the notion of 'sitting' when they describe their motivation to start their adventure by moving northwards. Sitting refers to non-movement, but also to social stagnation, to situations in which individual and collective lifeworlds do not make any progress. This form of involuntary immobility is very widely present across West Africa (Carling 2002; Jónsson 2008). It is closely related to a general notion of abjection (Ferguson 2006) regarding the positionality of Africa in processes of globalization. This positionality implies that most African youths are directly affected by processes of globalization. However, they are seldom in the position to actually have a say in the very same processes. In this context, the 'backway' and other forms of irregular pathways become important replacements for other paths of upward social mobility, such as educational and professional careers (e.g. Ludl 2008). The backway – like the exit strategy of visa lotteries (Piot 2010) – can then best be framed as a lived and firm critique concerning Africa's position in the world (Lucht 2012).

Saihou profoundly disliked the idea of 'sitting' in the German system any longer. The fact that he was sent to this remote location contributed to his feeling of stagnation. During our time in Germany I asked him about his future horizons after he would have obtained the paper in Italy, and he told me:

> Saihou: Yea, that is open for now. But I think I come back to Switzerland again. It is a very, very nice country. Ah, I like Zurich too much. My friend in Zurich told me some day that he was going to party, and ahg, I miss that time, you know. Zurich, even people in Asyl have a good house. They don't put people in these kind of houses like this. No they have a good house.
> I: Really? Switzerland? When I met you in Napoli you were really negative about Switzerland, I remember you were saying it is a racist country.
> Saihou: The police is racist, but the country is very, very nice. Zurich. They control you too much, but now with the paper, I can be there without problem. They cannot make problems with me anymore, because then I have the paper. With the five-year paper, I can stay there for three months ... But first I go back to Italy, and see what I can expect there.

Unpacking a Sociocultural Displeasure

There is a parallel between Saihou's notion of sitting and the way involuntary immobility is framed as a positionality of abjection or impotence in times of globalization (Bauman 1998; Ferguson 2006). Saihou's allergic reaction towards sitting is related to a cultural notion that successful Gambian men (and to a lesser extent women) reflect an outgoing and proactive attitude (Gaibazzi 2015; see Prothmann 2018 for a Senegalese/Wolof context). This cultural notion is the reason that mobility is so central to the aspirations of Gambian youth – as Gaibazzi (2013: 262) writes of the Soninke context: 'Youths are expected to go and look for the means to support their parents in their old age and to better their own lives'. To further explain this it is important to know that Mandinka young men – such as Saihou and Lamin – are raised with two central intergenerational moralities shaping their becoming within the context of family and community: *badingya* (or *badenya*) and *fadingya* (or *fadenya*) (Bolay 2017; Kea 2013, 2016). Whereas badingya (maternal lineages) points to a sense of closeness, locality, group cohesion and stability, fadingya (paternal lineages) implies change, conflict, innovation, self-promotion, competition and 'anything tending to spin the actor out of his established social force field' (Bird and Kendall 1980: 15, cited by Bolay 2017: 27). Badingya and fadingya are understood as 'twin concepts' (Bolay 2017: 26–8) or 'complementary forces' (Kea 2016: 82–5) that position many youngsters in ambivalent positions. They are expected to move out with fadingya-oriented practices in order to become a 'somebody' – at the same time, they need to balance this behaviour with badingya-based duties in the communities of origin. This double morality requires careful navigation, which often translates into mobile livelihoods and circulations. Thus, young Mandinka men – similar to many youths in other parts of the world – remain submissive to intergenerational authority while at the same time needing to find ways to become autonomous actors (Gaibazzi 2015). In this context, 'sitting'[6] – whether it is in a Gambian town or a German asylum centre – is the undesirable antinode of fadingya.

The experience of sitting is often persistent and might reappear in the daily lives of Gambian youth. This was underlined by two young Gambian men whom I both met, on different occasions, during my brief stay in the city of Bansang (the Gambia) where I visited the family of one of my Gambian informants living in Spain. They had both returned from their backway experience – this return movement is usually coordinated by the International Organization for Migration (IOM; see Brachet 2016). The first returnee was a young man sitting at one of the lower walls around the Bansang *garage* (bus station). He told me how he had been exposed to the horrific reality of a Libyan detention centre for three months to be deported in stages to the Gambia. From Tripoli he was brought back to Sabha (Libya), from Sabha he was directed to a plain that flew to Agadez (Niger). There he was put on a bus to Niamey (Niger) and from Niamey he boarded a flight to Bamako (Mali) – the turmoil after the 2016 elections having made it impossible to land in the Gambia. Now he was back in the place of sitting – the garage of Bansang that he once had left with high hopes. In this place, he shared his frustration with me: 'You can only sit here, there are no jobs, I am a driver but I have no car, so how can I make money?'

I met the second deportee in the compound of one of my informants who lived in Spain. This young man spoke English fluently with the tongue of an American rapper. He just had no luck, he explained. Once he reached Libya, he simply encountered the wrong *coxeur* – the bus boy responsible for transfers at transport nodes (Brachet 2005). Instead of helping him with the next connection, this fraudulent middleman of the mobility industry brought him directly to the Libyan authorities. After a period of detention, this led to his forced return to Agadez. In this trans-Saharan mobility hub, he tried to connect again to his friends in Libya to send him some money that would enable him to continue his journey northwards. But all attempts failed, and he went back to the Gambia instead. His frustrations with sitting intensified, and with that the urge to try the backway again re-emerged. During our conversations he repeatedly referred to the paradise-like Europe as 'Babylon', and he called those who had reached paradise the Babylonners. In his mind there was one escape route out of the pathway of irregular movement: having his own mode of mobility. In line with the centrifugal and entrepreneurial spirit of fadingya, he believed that a motorbike or a car would allow him to start a business and move ahead in life. For him, however, saving money for this investment would take ages. Instead he directed his hopes towards the Babylonners in Europe:

> I ask my brothers many times if they can help me to get a motorbike, so I can make business, or a Benz. With a Benz, you can make good business as a driver. But until now the motorbike has not come! So I tell them, 'If there is no motorbike I am forced to take the backway again'.

Thus, through processes of moral chantage of Babylonners, this returnee tried to overcome his daily reality of sitting.

Hustlers and Gamblers of Connectivity

Considering West Africa's positionality as a form of abjection, it is no surprise that many African youngsters, and certainly not only youngsters, seek alternative ways to link up with processes of globalization. Next to the multiple exit strategies of people (e.g. Piot 2010) and the processes of moral chantage that derive from these, other ways to link up include engaging with informal trade circuits (e.g. Schmoll and Semi 2013), finding European spouses in the hospitality sector (e.g. Ceesay 2016; Wagner and Yamba 1986), becoming involved in 'Four One Nine' online scams (e.g. Ellis 2016), working as or connecting to a migration broker (e.g. Piot 2010; Alpes 2011) and claiming spaces of artisanal mining in the light of exploitative mineral industries (e.g. Bolay 2017). These *hustling* practices – which my informants call raba raba – can be regarded as the socio-economic equivalent of what Stephen Ellis (2012) has termed 'political ju-jitsu'. It is a process in which a weaker actor uses the weight of a stronger actor in such a way that it actually increases the former's own strength. These tactics of hustling – which in francophone contexts are oftentimes called *débrouillardise* (Waage 2006) – reflect a 'de Certeauian' approach, displaying the art of the marginalized to invert the logics of an oppressive political economy or to create space to manoeuvre within a setting of precarity and uncertainty (Homaifar 2008; Vigh 2009; Schapendonk 2018a). As Thieme (2018: 537) frames it, hustling 'infers a constant pragmatic search for alternative structures of opportunity outside formal education, employment and service provision'.

In the Gambian context, hustling has a broad connotation of 'getting by' and it may refer to all kinds of off-farm work as well as to the process of moving abroad (Gaibazzi 2015; Van Nieuwenhuyze 2009). Thus, the scenery of Serekunda Market, as described above, is all hustling. However, whereas many hustling practices are limited to everyday interactions between urban actors, other practices are tactics to link up by design – these are what I call the *hustling tactics of connectivity*. A compelling ethnography on two different hustling tactics of connectivity in the Gambia comes from Ceesay (2016), describing the lives of two groups of hustlers. The first group consists of people who are popularly known as 'bumsters'. They are the 'beach boys' who are looking for 'a connection' with tourists from the Global North in Gambia's tourist spaces.[7] Bumsters engage in a variety of connecting tactics and are usually hinting at the provision of sexual services to Western female tourists (see also Nyanzi et al. 2005). Next to instant economic or material profit, they often hope to cultivate a long-lasting relationship that brings in a substantial and stable inflow of overseas money or an opening concerning travel opportunities to the north. While walking through the Gambia's coastal tourist areas of Bakau and Senegambia, Alagie – who had a long history in the tourism economy himself – repeatedly called this area 'the industry side'. This term emphasizes that in his eyes tourist spaces are spaces for labour. Alagie's observation resonates in Ceesay's (2016) work as the latter describes how bumsters operate in multiple locations, how they classify different tourists 'first-timers' versus 'repeaters', and how they align their daily schedules to the rhythms of the tourism industry. Some of my informants in Europe shared some of their bumster practices with me. In different places, I met young men who easily combined a stylish English tongue with some basic greetings in Swedish, German or Dutch. They usually took up the role as informal tourist guide in the coastal area of the Gambia and found ways to connect to tourists beyond merely economic spheres.

The second group in Ceesay's study are the 'online hustlers', locally known as 'chanters', who look for opportunities to establish online relationships with people elsewhere in the world. The online hustlers have different 'itineraries of accumulation' through their 'love methods' (2016: 49). While the first type of hustlers have a concrete geographical space to look for global connectivity (the industry side), the second group of hustlers find their ways through virtual space. In his pre-college period, Lamin and some of his friends were also involved in online hustling. He once told me how one of his friends taught him how to find, seduce and win the trust of people elsewhere in the world who are in pursuit of love and/or sex through the Internet. Like the chanters in Ceesay's study, Lamin (at that time aged around eighteen) had to overcome many cultural and social barriers, especially when it concerned the eventuality of contact with gay men. The Gambian society is tremendously homophobic, and the hustling practices of these young men are therefore not free from risk as they can easily lead to stigmatization and other situation of social conflict (Ceesay 2016).

It did not take long before Lamin had found a promising connection with a man from Switzerland who had worked for UN organizations and NGOs and had spent substantial periods of time in different African countries. Ironically, this particular man worked for the immigration authorities of Switzerland at the time they connected. The online encounter developed in a patronized form of friendship that Lamin highly respected. For him, the Swiss man was a replacement of his biological father who had paid very little attention to him as a son, as he was just one of the many children of his extended family. Lamin simply lost count of how many children were delivered by the four wives his father had married, there were at least more than twenty. Contrary to his father, this Swiss man had the will and the means to invest in his education, which allowed Lamin to enter college and study tourism and hospitality management. The trust relationship solidified when Lamin – unlike the other young Africans the Swiss man had supported over time – handed over proofs of school fees and exam results. Every time Lamin received some money from his 'foster parent', he carefully calculated the small leftovers that would remain after school fees were paid. This 'pocket money' was partly used for daily expenses, but also for gambling related to football. Through his gambling activities he wished to push his luck further and 'double the money', which could either mean a fast track to social success in the streets of Serekunda or a fast track to a ticket to Europe. His gambling activities are the reason why he so well knew the performances of the Dutch football clubs whose stadiums we passed during his brief stay in the Netherlands, in early 2018. Unsurprisingly, once Gambians reach Europe, their gambling practices do not necessarily stop. When I accompanied some of my informants to the sport cafés in Rome and Lleida (Spain), among others, I noticed how gambling was not limited to football alone. I saw acquaintances and friends of my informants try their luck on futsal matches, dog and horse running, as well as at roulette tables (see also Belloni 2016c).

Several comprehensive studies on Africa's positionality in times of globalization point to the similarity between gambling and the visa system processed by European and American embassies. For the Togolese context, Charles Piot (2010: 78) describes this visa lottery as 'an enormously inventive, entrepreneurial border practice, which has generated its own scales of value and pricing, and has produced far-reaching networks of debt, rank and clientage'. It is a migration industry (e.g. Cranston, Schapendonk and Spaan 2018; Gammeltoft-Hansen and Nyberg Sørenson 2013; see also Chapter 3) based on the 'paperwork' and 'networking' of different types of brokers. These brokers vary from well-established offices specialized in the facilitation of study migration or procedures shaping family reunification, to individual agents who are considered to have 'just the right contacts' or have a long track record in terms of bribing government officials. This migration brokerage sector, as Alpes (2011) so clearly illustrates in the Cameroonian context, does not work outside the domain of the state. Rather, it is characterized by its connectivity with local government officials, embassies and consulates, which makes it a lottery that sometimes pays out. As Drotbohm (2017: 35) argues, visa lotteries, consulates and migration brokers distribute hope as a crucial mobility resource.

Like in other situations of gambling, however, people have contrasting and ambivalent attitudes regarding this visa system. Some would say that the lottery is a system of hope and you can always 'try your luck', whilst others would conclude beforehand that the chances are so limited that it is not worth any financial investment. During conversations with Alagie and his friends in front of their gym in Serekunda, the moneymaking aspect of the European visa system was the central topic for debate. The reason for this ongoing discussion was that Alagie had just entered another visa application to visit the Netherlands for a second time. This time, he did not only rely on the connection with Dawda to facilitate this procedure. In fact, during his previous three-month stay in the Netherlands, he had started a love relationship with a Dutch woman – which had created high hopes for Alagie that he would come to the Netherlands again soon. Next to this relationship, he had already anticipated his future steps in the Netherlands by contacting one of his former clients when he was still active as a tour guide in the Gambia. This Dutchman is the director of a small roofing company – and by visiting him during this brief stay in the Netherlands, Alagie explored the opportunities to work for this company. The Dutchman was said to have a place for him when all papers for a long stay, guaranteeing the right to work, were set. Thus, all the conditions for a promising future in the Netherlands appeared to be prepared. Alagie only had to pass the threshold of the embassy – and therefore he needed luck. At the time of my stay in the Gambia, Alagie's documents were just sent to Ghana 'because all these things are sold to the Dutch embassy in Ghana'. The notion of selling is interesting here, as it emphasizes the lottery as a lucrative business model. In general, Alagie was rather pessimistic about his chances as he felt that his application came too soon. It was just over three months after his return – which is the minimum period of immobility before one is entitled to apply for another visa. During the continuous discussions on his chances, one of his friends made the explicit link with the notion of gambling, by saying: 'You can try thirty times without no luck, but you can also get it after one shot. But if you don't get it, they don't give you back your money. So they make business, it is a gambling business'. About two weeks after I left the Gambia, Alagie sent me a text message: 'Unlucky, I can't make it this October bcos they rejected me'. The embassy informed Alagie that there was not enough evidence for the purpose of the visit and they also indicated that Alagie had insufficient economic power to be eligible to visit the Netherlands for a second time.

As a consequence of the business model, some would-be movers draw the conclusion that chances are too limited only after they have experienced considerable losses in the game. Lamin belongs to this latter group. He had himself tried the visa lottery in 2009. He approached a migration broker who had arranged the visa application for France, including flight tickets, accommodation and an invitation letter of a Gambian family living in France. To complete the application, Lamin had to travel to Senegal, find accommodation there and find his way to the French embassy. He wasted more than 600 euros on this application. Besides this failed attempt, he had contacted the Dutch immigration authorities – the 'Immigratie- en Naturalisatiedienst' or Immigration and Naturalisation Service (IND) – and he had written a letter to the German embassy. He himself did not hold very high hopes that these institutes would respond to his writings – which indeed did not happen. As an alternative, he turned to his online hustling activities that in the end appeared to be more effective, also – as we will learn later – in the light of his wayfaring to Europe.

Multiple Departures

In the light of the overall de-migranticized view on African mobility that is central to this book, the stories of Saihou and Lamin bring important dynamics to the fore that deviate from the standard notion of the migratory process as a process of uprooting and regrounding. When we take this observation into account, we should rather position their mobility practices towards and inside Europe as a continuation of past im/mobile lives in and out of the urban economy of the Gambia. Similarly, Alagie's anticipation of a longer stay in the Netherlands profoundly questions the beginning of a migratory move. With his move to the Netherlands, he certainly did not settle in a new place. At the same time, he really used this short-term visit to massage his social relations in such a way that it would create better opportunities for him to ground in the Netherlands at a later stage. As Gaibazzi (2015: 108) writes in his compelling ethnography of im/mobility in the Gambian context: 'Any attempt to reduce [hustlers'] trajectories to neat patterns and modes of mobility would fail to do justice to the spatial complexity and lived dimension of hustling'. To understand this further, the next section dives deeper into the multiplicity of departures that is so central to the im/mobility trajectories of my informants.

Omar

'Life is good but Oslo is better,' Omar joked on this pleasant spring day in May 2015. We sat down in front of his asylum shelter in the Italian region of Liguria. Next to him sat a young man from Central Asia who stayed in the same 'camp' that was run by the aid organization Caritas. Omar started to nickname him Oslo once he heard that he had lived in the Norwegian capital for a considerable period of time. Giving names to people according to the places they have crossed seemed to be a common practice for him. In January 2016, for example, I revisited Omar in the emergency camp in southern Germany after he had departed from Italy. In this emergency camp, he introduced me to an Eritrean man who was commonly known as Frankfurt in this asylum space. Apparently, this particular man was full of frustrations after his transfer from inner-city Frankfurt to this former military base in the forests in southern Germany – a remote place some 300 km away from his former place of residence. Omar explained:

> This boy from Eritrea, oohh, the first day he came to the camp, I saw him entering, and he yelled: 'Why did they put me in this place, I was *inside* Frankfurt!' With this he said that he liked the city more, and that he don't understand why they put him so far. He was *inside* Frankfurt [laughs]! That is why I call this boy Frankfurt now.

While we sat down in front of the Italian asylum shelter in May 2015, Omar pointed at Oslo and gave me a first glimpse of the long trajectory of his friend: 'This man, he has been in so many countries, he was in Norway, in Libya, in Turkey, in India. He travelled through three continents! Three!

For us he is a teacher of the travel'. From this moment, Oslo started to illustrate his worlding travels by showing us some pictures on his mobile phone, and these pictures were taken in various locations. He started with pictures from an atypical individual asylum room (spacious, with furniture and TV). 'This was the Sicilia side,' he said, and then continued by showing us two dogs: 'They were my dogs in the camp, I love them too much!' 'So you had dogs in every country?' I asked him, and his reply could have not been more illustrative for a life lived across asylum spaces: 'Yes. In Turkey, Iran, Norway, Italy, yes. Without animals around me, time is not going'. At that moment, I noticed for the very first time that he wore a t-shirt with a world map. When I pointed at it, Omar screamed out of joy: 'Yo Oslooo, you carry the world! You carry the world! You are a traveller; you carry the world!'

Oslo's worlding asylum history stimulated Omar to navigate his next departure. From the very start of his European project, Omar has had multiple departures. In the Gambia he worked as a retailer at an equivalent of the Serekunda Market – the Albert Market – located in Banjul, some 20 km further eastwards in the West African country. He tried to reach Europe in four different ways. In 2008, he tried to reach the Canary Islands (Spain) from the Senegalese coast. One of his neighbours arranged his boat journey but due to some 'boat problems' he ended up in Mauritania. In 2009, he tried the same way, but his 'connection man ran with the money'. In 2011 he tried the backway (the trans-Saharan journey to Libya) for the first time and he moved from Senegal all the way up to Agadez – the famous carrefour of Niger that is seen as the main port for trans-Saharan mobility. There he was stranded due to the outbreak of the Libyan civil war. He decided to return again to the Gambia. Only the fourth time, in 2013, did he manage to reach European grounds by following the same trans-Saharan pathway to Libya. These multiple attempts to move out are reflected in many im/mobility trajectories that I have come across. Mariama for example – a Mauritanian woman whom I first met in Nijmegen some ten years ago – also had a period of trial and error at the time she moved out of Mauritania. She first tried Spain but returned to Mauritania after a relatively short period of time. She subsequently departed to France from where she reached the Netherlands later.

When I sat down with Omar later on that spring day in Italy, I asked him about his future plans. His plans depended heavily on the outcome of his asylum commission, but they were strongly hinting at another departure:

> Omar: [After the decision of the commission] I decide what I do. If they give me a paper, I will stay, and wait for a stable paper. If I get a negative, then, as I say, I have three options: sign to go back to my country, sign for staying in Italy, or sign to go to another European country. I will go to another European country.

I: To Oslo?
Omar: No! I hear from Oslo that Oslo is like working from hand to mouth. You may earn 1000 euros a month, but then 700 goes to an apartment. No, me, I try Austria.
I: Austria?
Omar: Yes!
I: Why Austria?
Omar: It is close to Italy, you can just reach it straight from Italy.
...
I: But do you have a contact in Austria?
Omar: No, but I hear that you may try your luck there. That sometimes they give you papers.
I: But this is not easy, because you have your fingerprints here.
Omar: Yes, I know, that is the problem with European system. If they find out, they send you back to Italy. But they never send you back home. They always send you back to Italy.
I: But you have to be careful. One of my Nigerian friends tried it. He failed in Austria and Switzerland, and they threatened him to bring him back to Africa.
Omar: Is it!? Agh...
I: Yes. But he escaped.
Omar: And where is he now?
I: He is back in Roma now. I am going to meet him tomorrow.
Omar: You see!? If you fail, you can just come to Roma.
I: And if you stay in Italy, where do you go?
Omar: I would go to Napoli!
I: To Napoli?
Omar: Yes. Napoli is the raba raba capital of Europe.

Omar's travel aspirations can best be described as a multiple 'what-if scenario'. If he would obtain his paper, he would probably stay in Italy; if not, then he would try his luck somewhere else. And if he would fail, there is always the option of living a life in the informal economy of Naples – which in his view is a continuation of his former practices in the Albert Market of Banjul. Deportation within the Schengen zone, in this context, can still be very painful, but is not a severe risk as it creates just a different window of opportunity.

However, in the end, his next destination turned out to be different from all the above scenarios. After Omar had obtained a two-year residence status (humanitarian-protection-based) in Italy, he actually moved to Germany to enter the asylum system there. He used his raba raba skills to navigate borders in the heyday of Europe's refugee reception crisis (the winter of 2015). Similar to the young boy in the opening vignette of this part of the book who moved across Europe and left his papers with Doudou (the owner of the guest house), Omar left his documents behind in Italy and tried his luck in Germany. Like other documents, such as the pink card in Greece, the humanitarian protection status in Italy has acquired 'various lives' (i.e. diverse meanings and uses) (Cabot 2014: 42) by the engagement of asylum bureaucracies and people in the asylum procedures. Like the anthropologist Cabot in Greece, I also had many difficulties with understanding the history and logics of people's acquired documentation and related paperwork. What is more, as in Omar's situation, the humanitarian protection status induces mobility. In this light, Borri (2017) argues that this particular status contributes to the creation of im/mobile subjects across Europe. Those who are granted humanitarian protection move to other EU member states, but need to be back in Italy after a short period of time to start the procedure to renew the documents.

For Omar, the tactics behind his undocumented move were related to gambling. Like many others, he was fully aware that he was likely to be controlled during his undocumented journey by train, and he knew very well that his fingerprints were 'in the system' and that according to the Dublin regulations he could soon be returned to Italy. But this did not prevent him from trying – as, in his mind, you can always be lucky. Interestingly, like in Saihou's case above, I expected Omar to have a nervous journey, in which he felt the risk of being caught at the border or being controlled in the train. This was not at all the case. Omar was calm and felt comfortable. In fact, once he had embarked the train in Milan, he soon fell asleep and did not wake up until he reached Bavaria (Germany). During a telephone conversation, he reflected on his travel to Germany by saying that 'nothing really happened'.

Omar ended up in an asylum emergency camp. This camp was located some 3 km away from a German village of no more than 4,000 inhabitants. The Gambian young men I met there referred to the camp as 'bush life', or 'living in the forest'. The camp – a deserted military terrain – was indeed located in the middle of a forest. It takes a thirty-minute walk from the nearest train station to get to the fenced terrain. During my visit to this place in 2016, the trees and earth's surface were covered by a package of fresh snow – a very different setting compared to the last time I met Omar in springtime Liguria. Occasionally, willing car drivers offer the young men a ride to the forest area to drop them at the gate. At the camp's entrance, there was a place for one or two security guards, but there was no control at the moment I first entered. A long barrack-like building was located to the right. The long corridor with dozens of rooms seemed to be a purely masculine space. Some men maintained a family life through the weak telephone connection that could only be accessed at the very end of the corridor, close to the Gambian rooms. The two Gambian rooms were perpendicular to the other rooms, all being organized by nationality. Small cardboard plates, being torn off from boxes, functioned as signposts to indicate which part of the world were located behind the white doors. There were Pakistani, Togolese/Cameroonian, Bangladeshi, Nigerian and Eritrean rooms. On each signpost, there were dashes set counting the number of people sleeping in the room. According to the plate, Omar's room counted sixteen Gambian people. Behind the door I found a lively atmosphere. Some men were praying, others were listening to music or staring at their phones. Upon entering, Omar yelled 'Amaaaaat!' The signpost at the door was actually wrong – as among the sixteen assumed Gambians there was at least one Senegalese man. Amat – the wrestler type whom I had met in Naples as the close friend of Saihou – was staying in the same room as Omar. He stood up from his bed, still a bit sleepy, and gave me a firm hug.

After sharing time and space together in the region of Naples, the trajectories of Omar and Amat diverged. In the time that Omar was transferred to Liguria and Amat to downtown Naples, they were only updated about their well-beings and whereabouts via mutual friends. They were themselves surprised to see each other again at a main emergency camp in southern Germany. From the group of six young men whom I got to know over time, they were not particularly close 'brothers'. In different settings, I even noticed that they had their personal frictions and tensions. However, the fact that they shared the same travel experience from the time they embarked the same boat for Libya to the period in the asylum centre in southern Italy, created a kind of social bond. They shared breakfasts and dinners with a few other people. This smaller segment of this Senegambian asylum community also divided their funds and the tasks of cooking and grocery shopping. Interestingly, the two men had departed from Italy exactly the same day. Omar crossed Switzerland, and Amat travelled through Austria, from where they both reached Munich. Germany's public position of welcoming refugees during the European crisis of migration management, in combination with its structured asylum system, was why diverged im/mobility trajectories became once more intertwined for a considerable period of time.

During my first stay with Omar in this typical German village (January 2016), I had many questions in mind. Why had he moved to Germany and not to Austria – as he had been hinting at during our time together in Italy? Why had he moved to Germany even though he had just received his Italian papers? Why had he moved without documents, while the short-lived Italian residence permit granted him the right to move across EU borders? Omar was always very willing to provide me the answers, but the answers were never one-sided, and they seldom appeared to me as clear-cut answers to direct questions. At one specific moment, we reached a deadlock. I was curious why he had decided to leave his documents behind. His short answer was that there was the risk that people would take your paper during a border control. Thereupon, my puzzling face must have given him sufficient information that his answer was not satisfying. He burst out laughing, and gave me his explanation later:

> People come here and they leave their paper in Italy. If you bring your paper, they don't accept you in the camp. And you need to go to the camp because many people don't have a good connection here in Germany. They don't have anybody who can take care of them ... Germany would never give you a paper to stay, not even after ten years, we know that. Only if you marry or make a baby, you get a paper. But the system gives you some working document, a permit to work. But you need to speak the language first. To find a job, you need to speak the language first. Then with the paper and the language you can find a stable job.

Thus, following his logic, the documented status in Italy of Omar and Amat provided some stable ground for onward mobility. However, in order to profit from Europe's cross-border opportunities these men had to enter the German asylum system in disguise. After all, the short-lived Italian residence permits did not allow them to work in another European member state. Consequently, Omar and Amat sensed that the asylum route through Germany created quicker and better economic opportunities compared to the scenario in which they could only slowly climb the socio-economic ladder in Italian society. Thus, whereas Saihou, on the basis of his aversion to 'sitting', had decided not to stay in asylum procedures anymore, these two men actually regarded the same asylum procedure as an opportunity. In terms of timing, there is a significant difference between the moves as well. Saihou explored the opportunities in Switzerland and later Germany when his asylum procedure in Italy was *not* yet decided on, while Omar and Amat both travelled after they had obtained a legal status in Italy.

The travels of these young men indicate that all attempts to harmonize the EU's asylum system have not washed away the unequal social and economic terrains within the same political space. Omar, Saihou, Amat and Lamin all position themselves in a postnational EU, while the EU member states do their best to tie down the social and economic rights to the national containers. Although the journeys of Omar, Saihou and Amat were all directed to Germany, it would be misleading to argue that this mobility follows a clear South–North logic – as if African movers living in southern Europe necessarily move further up north. During the four-year period of this research project, I have seen informants move from Italy to Malta, from Catalonia to the Canary Islands, from Italy to Greece and from Dortmund to Marseille. In a way the overall picture is saturated in irony.

With European-wide programmes such as the 2006 Year of Labour Mobility programme as well as Erasmus programmes, which promotes student mobility across EU borders, policymakers in Brussels put a lot of energy into the quest to mobilize the EU citizen in order to get them moving across borders. From their viewpoint, there is too little mobility to construct a fully integrated European space – despite the fact that this mobility is freed from most institutional hurdles. At the same time, EU policymakers regard the mobilities central to this book as not so desirable. This is rather ironic since these movers are actually free from any national identity that might create mental thresholds to cross-border EU mobility. They are in fact *living* postnational lives through mobility *despite* the many institutional hurdles they face. In this context, it is interesting to return to the case of Oslo – Omar's friend from Central Asia whom he met in the asylum shelter in Liguria. On the first day of my stay at Omar's place in Germany, Omar informed me about the whereabouts of Oslo. According to Omar, Oslo was in Sweden now, and he had obtained his five-year residence paper. And with that document he was allowed to work in Sweden. When we called him, however, this information was already out of date, or false from the beginning – Oslo actually found himself again in … Oslo.

Multiple Departures as 'More or Less Holiday'

The ways the Gambian young men, and other informants, have positioned themselves in a postnational Europe are particularly reflected in the way horizons shift during the processes of movement. Their movements affect their longings and belongings. In the processes of moving through Eurospace, being 'here' might increase the longing to reach 'there' since new opportunities appear on the horizon. Once one has arrived 'there', another 'there' might emerge – or the wish to return 'here' might again become prominent. This dynamic of longing for an 'elsewhere' is powerfully described by Eric J. Leed's (1991: 22) book *The Mind of the Traveller* that deals with all sorts of travel:

> Needs are a product of situations, and each of these events, through many repetitions, produces and serves a particular set of needs. Departure may serve the need for detachment, purification, liberty, 'individuality', escape, self-definition. Passage serves and generates a need for motion but may, in turn, generate other longings: for stability in a condition of disequilibrium, for fixed orientation in a world of flux, for immutability in the midst of transience … In any one place and moment, these needs may be perceived as opposed and conflictual, but they are not when sequenced in the form of the journey. Here may lie the eternal appeal of travel – it resolves a logic of contradiction, a logic

of place, into a logic of sequence, an order of change and transformation which serves and fosters a variety of human longings: for motion and rest, liberty and confinement, indeterminacy and definition.

The manifold or contradictory logics of mobility – of being a logic of place as well as sequence and motion – affect the ways horizons shift. In this respect, Vigh's (2009) notion of social navigation is related to both near and distant futures. There is an interesting parallel here with the way the phenomenologist philosopher Edward Casey thinks about the horizon as constantly evading fiction. For him, the lived body in motion requires for its very movement 'the notion of an ever-expanding range of action' (1993: 62). In this way, 'moving in the near and into the far is always done *in regard to the horizon*' (ibid.).

With regard to the horizon, movers might experience new ranges of action as a result of their movements. Mobility, however, is also primarily used to shift places and explore new horizons. Soon after Lamin received his Italian refugee papers, for instance, he moved to Switzerland to visit Pappy – his Swiss foster dad – for the very first time. I visited Lamin in Bern just a few days after he had arrived there. He had not only used this first visit to become familiar with Switzerland, he in fact also took his presence as an opportunity to explore new places. Some two months after my visit in Switzerland, he planned to go to Germany for the second time during his stay in Switzerland:

> Lamin: Yea … I am thinking, like maybe next Monday I am [going to be] in Germany, Monday evening, for visiting a friend for two or three days.
> I: Is it? So you go to Germany again?
> Lamin: Yes, I want to visit and to analyse the situation down there, I want to really understand what is going on there … Because people are just making people to travel. They say, 'OK you have to come here or you have to make here asylum'.

With 'analysing the situation', Lamin referred to a form of exploring opportunities beyond the current place of residence that was quite common among my informants – regardless of the legal situations in which they found themselves. Exploring places here implies that one evaluates the place according to one's aspirations for a daily living. One interlocutor phrased it as going for 'more or less holiday' and explained this expression as follows: 'More or less holiday is like you go to see, you go for holidays but at the same time you also want to inquire or have an experience how it works [in that place] … just to see also how things go that way'. 'More or less holiday' trips appear to be rather important for my informants to find potential places to live that meet people's aspirations. Doudou (the owner of the guest house in Milan), for example, made several trips to the Netherlands to visit his soon-to-be-married Gambian wife there. During his trips he gradually looked for work opportunities and explored his potential living environment. Another illustrative example of how these 'more or less holiday' trips work comes from July – a Nigerian woman living in the Netherlands.

In the period I got to know her well, July was preparing her future move to the UK. She aimed to work at a UK-based university, and I assisted her with several applications. July literally used her holiday breaks to explore the consequences of her intended move to London. The reason for her leaving the Netherlands was basically that she felt stuck in her socio-economic career there. Interestingly, during one of our multiple recorded conversations, she told me she had actually attempted to reach the UK by unauthorized means a long time ago – in the early 2000s. This was the time she first entered Europe on a study visa. Her studies, however, did not go as planned. Her situation soon deteriorated after she found out that her 'uncle' who was supposed to financially arrange her stay and take care of her enrolment in the higher vocational training programme did not provide the promised support. In fact, he ran away with the money July had sent to him from Nigeria. Consequently, once in the Netherlands, July could not afford the school fees and dropped out. After a brief period in Germany, she returned to the Netherlands and started to work as a strawberry picker to make ends meet. In the meantime, she explored other directions. She considered applying for asylum in the Netherlands, but then 'You have to completely change who you are'. This would not only involve the spreading of untruths to construct a legally effective story (Berger 2015), it would also affect her identity deeply, as she noted: 'When I tell these lies, I am totally not educated any more. I thought: "No! You pretend you are not knowing".' Instead, she decided to try her luck and move to the UK by unauthorized means. She deliberately did not move with the lookalike strategy – a form of document lending to access one's travel destination – but moved with 'somebody'. She never wanted to explain what exactly happened that day, but she clarified that a border guard noticed her attempt of an unauthorized entry and that she was returned to the Netherlands the very same day. After this failed attempt, she actually felt that the Netherlands was her fated destination, as she stated: 'After the UK I said, "No. I have to go home or I have to stay here." The experience was horrible, so I felt [she hesitates] so little. I felt little for myself ... I had to go through that. It was then either go back [to Nigeria], or staying [in the Netherlands]'.

This indicates that explorative moves may fail and redirect some movers to their previous destinations. In other words, horizons may shift back to previous places. In the subsequent years, July gradually built up a stable socio-economic life. She married a Dutchman, gave birth to their son and obtained a master's degree at a Dutch university – which functioned as the foundation for her applications for various Ph.D. positions at UK universities. In the end, one of her applications was successful, which was the start of her move to London, involving a lot of mobility in holiday breaks. The first trip to London was in October 2015, the second in February 2016 and the third was a three-week-long trip during the summer holidays of 2016. These pre-relocation holiday visits did not only have a practical function (she arranged housing as well as the subscription of her son to a school), they were also a way of seeking comfort: 'I take it step by step, otherwise I will lose my mind, and I am too much thinking, "Ohhh, am I doing the right thing?"'

The 'more or less holiday' type of movement destabilizes the harsh distinction between migration movements as relocation processes to a new place to live on the one hand, and flexible mobilities related to tourism, transnational businesses and the visiting of friends and family members on the other hand. In fact, many flexible spatial–temporal movements are inherently related to the migratory relocation to a new place of residence. A short-term visit might trigger a long stay, and a long stay might provoke new flexible movements. This observation further destabilizes the exceptionalized mobility category of the 'migrant journey', as indicated in the Introduction.

Multiple Departures as Visa Trouble

It would be misleading to relate the multiplicity of departures only to the narrative of Omar, Saihou and Lamin, who all three resemble the image of a self-made Gambian man. The risk of such narrative is that one tends to romanticize mobility as a source of empowerment only, thereby ignoring issues of power in border crossings (Hyndman 1997). For this reason, I return to the issue of visa applications. As stated before, many West Africans who want to enter Europe through the visa lottery need to travel to a European embassy located in another African country to apply for their desired travel papers. Once they find themselves lucky and they are allowed to move to Europe, their sojourns in Europe are usually limited to a period of three months in case of tourist visas. Temporal restrictions and visa conditions thus produce movements that are often turbulent in terms of the motions as well as the emotions involved. The visa troubles of a Cameroonian/Dutch couple presented below are characterized by the multiple im/mobilities involved in this entire process.

Eugene originates from a coastal town in western Cameroon. In 2009 he met Caroline, a medical doctor in training originating from the Netherlands.

Caroline moved to Cameroon in order to join a voluntary internship programme to gain medical experience in a different setting. When the couple fell in love, they well knew that Caroline's internship would only last for a limited period of time. She actually had to return to the Netherlands a few weeks after their first encounter. They created their own transnational affective circuit (Cole and Groes 2016a) through numerous telephone calls and Facebook interactions. However, the challenging question was how to find a way to physically live together, how to create the conditions for being co-present? The first two visa applications for Eugene to come to the Netherlands, in 2010 and 2011, were rejected by the Dutch embassy. Meanwhile Caroline had already travelled four times to Cameroon to spend as much time as possible with Eugene (she travelled twice in 2010 and twice in 2011).

After his visa applications had been rejected, and partly to increase the chances for Eugene's residence permit in the Netherlands to be approved, they decided to marry in 2012 in Cameroon. Family and friends, from both Cameroon and the Netherlands, were present at this celebration in Eugene's place of origin. The married couple went to Tanzania directly after the ceremony, not for their honeymoon but because Caroline had managed to organize another medical internship in this East African country for a couple of months. Thus, in this third country, they realized their dream of living together, but again this lasted only for a limited period of time. After her internship in a Tanzanian hospital, Caroline decided to move back to the Netherlands to follow the last part of her curriculum. Eugene had to move back to Cameroon as he had no travel documents enabling him to accompany Caroline to the Netherlands. Their separation was again another emotional moment of saying goodbye, without being sure when they would see each other again.

After their Tanzanian experience, they started Eugene's application for a Dutch residence permit. To obtain this permit, the applicant is, among several other requirements, obliged to pass a 'Dutch integration exam'. In this stage of their reunification process, this exam could only be undertaken at a Dutch embassy. The fact that the Dutch embassy in Cameroon closed in 2011 made it more complicated for Eugene to actually take the test. Now, he had to travel to the Dutch embassy in Cotonou, in the Republic of Benin, for the test. For this trip, he first had to obtain the right travel papers, book a flight and find a place to stay. In total, this travel to Benin cost around 1,000 euros. During his stay in Cotonou, lasting from June to August 2013, he took the test four times, all unsuccessfully. Because he had little linguistic education in his youth, he had many difficulties with the Dutch language. Passing this institutional threshold of an integration test turned out to be a very expensive undertaking, as Caroline estimated the costs of a single test to be around 350 euros.[8] They partly financed this process with the financial support of Caroline's parents. Such experiences explain where the observation regarding 'embassy as business', by the Gambian men in front of the gym in Serekunda, comes from (see also Piot 2010). One day, when I visited Caroline at her home, she showed me the 'paperwork' that was involved in this entire procedure. In this labyrinth of letters and files, she showed me one of the first rejections of the embassy that came in the summer of 2011. With a bitter cynicism, she looked at the standard letter indicating only with one single tick mark that Eugene was not eligible to live with her in the Netherlands. She stated: 'This is one of such heights in terms of replies'. The reason why the embassy rejected Eugene was not at all clear from the letter.

After his series of integration tests failed due to Eugene's limited linguistic skills, the couple found themselves in a state of disillusion. There was, however, one employee at the embassy who noticed Eugene's struggle with the language, and she advised the couple 'off the record' to apply for a tourist visa first, so that Eugene could become more familiarized with the Dutch language. Caroline was sceptical about her advice, as they had applied for the tourist visa before but found it rejected on the basis of *vestigingsgevaar* (literally *danger* of settlement) – i.e. a very Dutch policy formulation for saying that there is a risk that the applicant overstays his visa since he might wish to settle. Her reply to the embassy employee was: 'This is a nice idea, but we already tried this way'. Yet this particular embassy employee was willing to help. She called one of her colleagues at the Belgian embassy in Cameroon (to make things more complex, applications for tourist visas for the Netherlands are regularly processed by the Belgian embassy in Cameroon). Through this phone call, she made a case for Eugene by presenting herself as 'the guarantor' when a tourist visa would be granted to this Cameroonian man. This personal communication between employees of two different embassies was a major breakthrough in this trajectory. Eugene received his first tourist visa at the end of 2013 and travelled to the Netherlands. He complied with the European regulations and returned to Cameroon before his visa would expire. Once back in Cameroon, Eugene travelled again to the embassy in Benin to take the integration test once again, but again he failed. In total, he went to Cotonou three times. It was again the helpful embassy employee who suggested that Eugene might get dispensation for specific parts of the language test (reading and writing skills). For this, Caroline hired a Dutch migration lawyer. The lawyer suggested, however, that she had a weak case and advised Caroline to start a second tourist visa application that would allow Eugene to come to the Netherlands for the second time. The logic of the lawyer was that the couple should really convince the Dutch immigration authorities that they really had done their outmost to get Eugene through the regular procedures. Once more, the employee at the Dutch embassy assisted the couple during the application of the visa at the Belgian embassy. Again, a single phone call of this woman was crucial to get the visa. This visa allowed Eugene to stay in the Netherlands again for ninety days in the summer of 2014. In this period of time, the couple started the juridical procedure for the dispensation of the writing parts of the language tests. In this process, Caroline wrote to the employee of the Dutch embassy an e-mail to ask for her support. This employee had moved away from Benin to start a new position elsewhere, but this did not stop her from writing a powerful letter that substantiated the juridical claim of the couple. Caroline phrased this letter of the embassy employee as 'a fantastic story', realizing that without her help the procedures would probably have been even lengthier and more complex than was the case now – if not in vain after all.

From the time they began their relationship until the moment Eugene received his first residence permit, Caroline travelled seven times to Cameroon to spend as much time together with Eugene as possible. On his turn, Eugene travelled three times to Benin, where he tried six times to pass the integration test. He also travelled twice to the Netherlands. During the five-year period, the couple estimated the travel and procedure costs at 16,000 euros (excluding their stay in Tanzania). It was only in early 2015 that Caroline received the good news that Eugene had finally received a residence permit for the Netherlands. Eugene got the news a day later, as telephone lines within Cameroon had been down for some time.

Eugene and Caroline followed the strict rules of the Dutch immigration authorities. The two have in fact been very cautious not to violate any regulations as they believed this would reduce the chances of Eugene obtaining a residence permit in the Netherlands. Interestingly, Caroline once stated that they regretted the marriage with hindsight for all the legal requirements that are attached to it. The marriage needed to be officially legalized by the Cameroon authorities – which was a bureaucratic hustle in itself. After all the signatures and stamps were in the right place of the right documents, Caroline had to go – with a pile of papers, the wedding photo album and copies of birth certificates and passports – through similar procedures in the Netherlands to register their marriage. The immigration authority in the Netherlands frames this as the 'legalization of official documents from foreign countries' (IND 2018: 4, my translation). This process is installed to let the authorities of the third country (in this case Cameroon) confirm that the documents they have granted to the applicant are authentic. Subsequently, the authenticity is controlled by a Dutch consulate or embassy by checking the signature on the authenticity confirmation of the authorities. In this double legalization process, Caroline met with a particular IND representative who actually made clear to her that their marriage had made things far more complicated for Eugene's travel opportunities than necessary. This official probably did not notice the Kafkaesque implication of his statement that the migratory pathway of Eugene would have been a lot easier when they were just known as lovers not as spouses.

Marriage is one of the very few legal pathways for an average African to enter the EU, and this is still a process with tremendous thresholds that requires zigzag tactics, brokering services and a dose of luck for the aspiring movers in question (e.g. Neveu Kringelbach 2016). Even in this legal context, multiple attempts and multiple departures can be seen as the rule rather than the exception. The visa system thus produces multiple preparatory mobilities that may involve border crossings, as in the case of Eugene and Caroline. To collect their visas for the Netherlands, Gambians need to travel to Dakar, and Cameroonians need to travel to Benin. As we have seen, these travels come with their own investments, and they are not free from turbulence. This argument particularly stands for the many young women and men who have invested heavily in their mobility potential, and who have all experienced some intense waiting period. It is of crucial importance to realize that the experiences of Caroline and Eugene in the end resulted in a breakthrough moment. Most would-be movers who take similar preparatory steps actually become stranded along the way – they are confronted with new periods of involuntary immobility (Carling 2002) and have to 'sit' again and regain energy to find new ways towards a next departure. Others have successfully reached Europe, but face repatriation by one of Europe's deportation regimes.

Departures after Deportation

From the viewpoint of EU policymakers, one of the major bottlenecks of EU's migration policy is the return of unsuccessful asylum applicants. Their rationale is that one may only guarantee protection mechanisms to the people in need of protection – the refugees – if one is able to push out the other movers – those 'failed asylum seekers' who have exhausted all legal instruments to claim the right to asylum. The European Commission, and individual EU member states, have drafted return and readmission policies that aim to close the asylum cycle. However, these policies appear to be very difficult to put in practice for a variety of reasons. Among others, African 'partner countries' are said to be reluctant to cooperate according to bilateral and multilateral readmission agreements, especially when the evidence is lacking that it concerns their citizens. In addition, the people to be deported may disappear from the radar and depart to unknown destinations before the 'repatriation services' can knock at their doors. The latter is directly or indirectly facilitated by member states themselves by providing expulsion orders to individuals and families just before they turn into irregular migrants.[9] Policymakers put a lot of effort into inventing more efficient and effective instruments of return in order to close the asylum cycle. One of the practices of EU member states in this regard is to build a cosy relationship with civil society organizations that promote 'voluntary' returns. In the Dutch context, Kalir and Wissink (2016) speak of a 'deportation continuum' by which the practices of state agents and NGO workers converge.

The assumption behind this quest for more effective return instruments is, of course, that the return is 'sustainable'. The policy notion of a 'sustainable return' expects that the mover is there to stay in the place where one 'belongs' – the place of origin (and if this place of origin is not safe enough, then the return is directed to a nearby place that is considered safe enough). Behind this regressive migration policy lies a sedentarist policy ideal of how people should organize their livelihoods.[10] This notion – or what Malkki (1992) calls 'sedentarist metaphysics' – territorializes people's being to a single place and consequently denormalizes movement. This policy approach is particularly problematic for the West African region with its multiple cultures of mobility (e.g. De Bruijn, Van Dijk and Foeken 2001; Pelckmans 2012). In this region, sedentary lifestyles are strongly related to mobility (Gaibazzi 2015). It follows that in this context 'sustainable returns' are difficult to achieve. As Kleist (2018) rightly emphasizes in her study on Ghanaian returnees, mobility regimes may circumscribe migration, but they do not necessarily terminate people's mobility trajectories. Forced returns may easily turn into another departure.

In some cases, the direction of one's departure might change considerably after a forced return. An insightful illustration comes from Destiny – a Nigerian man whom I know from my Ph.D. fieldwork in Istanbul (Turkey) in 2008 and with whom I have stayed in contact ever since, allowing me to revisit him in the Greek city of Heraklion and later in Naples. On different occasions, he told me that Europe was not in his mind when he left Nigeria in 2002. His first move was directed to South Africa. However, since he did not hold the right travel documents, the South African immigration authorities deported him directly to Nigeria. Back in his country of birth, he was convinced by the pastor of his Pentecostal church in Lagos to try his luck northwards. Through a migration broker, he arranged a ticket and a visa for Turkey, from where he reached the Greek island of Samos in the summer of 2008. Since then he has stayed – for different periods of time – in various European countries, including, Greece, Italy, Switzerland and Austria.

In other instances, the aspiration to reach Europe has appeared to be rather persistent and indeed resistant to return migration programmes. The most powerful illustrations regarding this persistency to reach Europe comes from a Senegalese man, for the purpose of this book called Ibrahim.[11] I first met him in front of one his favourite bars in Barcelona. Symbolically, it was a casino bar – where gambling is the main principle of doing business. The gambling attitude is also reflected in his travel story.

Before Europe appeared as a desirable destination, he had travelled as a young man to different places, including Morocco where he took up the idea to move to Europe for the first time in 2005. In 2007, Ibrahim travelled through Turkey with Europe in his mind. Once he reached Greece by boat, he declared himself of Somali origin, which allowed him to easily enter asylum procedures. From Greece, he reached Italy, on a French passport he had bought in the Greek mobility industry. For years, he stayed irregularly in the city of Genoa. He worked at a restaurant, and with the money earned he travelled to France to spend his holidays there. The fact that he lacked the travel papers to cross EU borders did not restrict this leisure-related mobility. At some points, however, this created some trouble – for instance when he was caught at the border in 2008. During a four-hour examination, the French authorities fingerprinted him and took away his French passport. What is more, the authorities found in his belongings a recent ticket of a Western Union transfer with his real name and passport number on it. Ibrahim was now in 'the system' (see Chapter 4). He did not contest that this ticket was his – something that he later regretted. After having spent half a day at the police station, Ibrahim was taken to the Italian border. Here, a short discussion between the French and Italian authorities followed, but to his own surprise he was released with the order to move back to Genoa. This was his first encounter with a forced return, but certainly not his last.

In the subsequent two years, Ibrahim continued to occasionally move between Italy and France without too much trouble. This changed, however, when he travelled to France to attend a music concert in 2010. Somewhere between Turin (Italy) and Lyons (France), he was caught at the border for the second time by an unexpected control in Schengen space. The fact that he now carried his Senegalese passport, in combination with the information the authorities had collected from him during the previous border intervention, made it rather easy for the French authorities to start the deportation procedure. Ibrahim knew he was in big trouble. Besides the repatriation, he feared that the authorities would keep the savings that he had carried with him and that were taken from him during the control. Initially, he did not resist his repatriation. He in fact asked the authorities to return him quickly, since he did not want to waste his time in detention. On the day of the actual removal from France, he was happy to see his money returned to him. He was also relieved to know that one of his contacts was able to collect his belongings in Italy and bring it over to France so he could take these with him back to Senegal. However, he was outrageous about the fact that he was handcuffed at the moment two men took him to the Boeing 747 that departed to Senegal. He insulted the two men who handcuffed him, and he assured them that he had no fear[12] and that they could expect him to be back in Europe after only one month. Despite his resistance, Ibrahim found himself in an airplane heading to Senegal some three years and one month after his departure from Senegal to Turkey.

Ibrahim, however, kept his word. He left again for Europe after having spent only fifteen days in his country of origin. With his savings, he managed to change his passport and identity in Dakar (Senegal), through a hustling tactic that I would prefer not to reveal here. With his new passport he bought a ticket to Morocco, a country that Senegalese can travel to without any visa obligations. He was en route again. He knew Morocco from his previous travels to Casablanca and Tangier in 2005. His first attempt to reach Europe by boat failed. This, in combination with a series of interventions by the Moroccan authorities, considerably prolonged his stay in Morocco. He spent roughly a year in Morocco, living in Oujda, Rabat and Fez. In 2011, he finally reached the southern shore of Spain by embarking a 'Zodiac' (a rubber boat) and was directed to a reception camp in Andalusia. Since the Spanish and Senegalese have signed a readmission agreement on a bilateral basis, Ibrahim did not reveal his real nationality and said that he originated from Guinea. This was the fourth nationality that he performed along his trajectory, after having absorbed a Somali identity in Greece, a French identity between Greece and Italy and a Senegalese identity at the time of his deportation from France. But Ibrahim's story becomes even more complex, since he was deported from the reception camp by the Spanish authorities within forty days (after this period passes, the authorities are obliged to free the detainees). They brought him neither to Senegal (his actual country of origin) nor to Guinea (his self-declared country of origin), but to Mali. In October 2011, Ibrahim ended up empty-handed in an African country he had never been to before in his life. He was only given an expulsion paper, and an envelope with fifty euros. Perhaps the Spanish authorities believed that a return of a broke *clandestino* was the most 'sustainable'.

With the help of the Senegalese embassy, Ibrahim could finally return to Senegal, after having spent a week in Mali. He was mentally exhausted and completely disillusioned about being back in Senegal. It took him eight to nine months to reboost his energy as well as to refuel his financial capital to hit the road again. This time he moved overland through Mauritania and Morocco. He again moved to Spain by rubber boat, and this time he was caught by what he called a 'hunting Zodiac' – a rubber boat of the Moroccan authorities. The border police tied the boats together in order to bring Ibrahim and the other travellers back to Morocco. He was brought (again) to Oujda, and escaped that place soon after. In a different Moroccan city, he worked as a cook in a restaurant. He also engaged in the trading of hammam soap between Morocco and Senegal – a lucrative transnational business. He travelled up and down between Senegal and Morocco once more, and he forgot about Europe for a while. This changed, however, when rumours reached him about a possible strike amongst the Moroccan police and navy. This was his 'grand motivation' to try his luck once more. This time he reached Tarifa in Spain, and from there he found his way to the place I actually first met him: the city of Barcelona. In this city, he feels comfortable, and he invests heavily in progressing his career as a cook.

Concluding Notes: Mobility, Ruptures and Autonomy

This chapter started from the notion of worlding and argued that West African mobility cannot simply be explained by the notion of the root causes of migration. The multiple departures that I encountered are embedded in larger social and historical scripts across the West African region (e.g. Pelckmans 2012; Gaibazzi 2015) and they must also be positioned in a wider palette of im/mobile livelihoods.

Although many interlocutors emphasized the displeasures of sitting, mobility by itself cannot be regarded as a clear-cut road to social promotion. Ibrahim's erratic travel experiences are most telling in this respect. A rough calculation of his trajectory indicates that he has crossed over 29,000 km to reach and reground in Europe. This is a distance that equals three quarters of the total circumference of our globe. Just by way of comparison, a single flight from his place of origin (Dakar) to the place I met him (Barcelona) covers a distance of 3,500 km. The legal deportation from France to Senegal, the illegal deportation from Spain to Mali, the border interventions between Morocco and Spain and the border intervention between Italy and France, could not pin him down. All these efforts to sedentarize his life in Dakar simply failed. Such stories of persistency, zigzagging, detouring, changing identities and all the dynamics related to them, indeed suggest that there is a profound level of autonomy in cross-border mobility. Ibrahim's mobility is profoundly hampered by all sorts of powers, but it is at the same time characterized by a continuous reconfiguration that exceeds the control of states and supra-states (Casas-Cortes, Cobarrubias and Pickles 2015: 900–1; see also Papadopoulos, Stephenson and Tsianos 2008).

Ibrahim's story is on the one hand extraordinary and based on his individual capacity of not giving up. At the same time, there are numerous stories like his that travel across different regions of West Africa. These stories fuel the general notion that one may face enormous barriers on one's way to Europe, but with the right ethos one will be able to find ways – which is the main subject of the following two chapters.

NOTES

1. The Jammeh regime is an illustrative case to make one question whether African governments are indeed aiming for development since it is the 'development *effort*' that keeps them in power (see Ellis 2012: 40–41). To make this point, Stephen Ellis builds on the legacy of the Nigerian political scientist Claude Ake.
2. Hultin et al. (2017) portray President Jammeh as the typical African 'strongman' who embraced the title of dictator and who played ethnic groups against one another. While ethnic tensions have existed for a longer time, he particularly scapegoated and threatened Mandinkas (the largest ethnic group in the Gambia). He once stated in public to kill Mandinkas one by one and place them 'where even a fly cannot see them' (Hultin et al. 2017: 324). Interestingly, Hultin et al. picture migration as one of the societal phenomena that contributed to Jammeh's unexpected loss in the Gambia's 2016 elections. As they write, 'While migrant success stories were once a source of pride, many voters recognized that only Jammeh's departure could stem the exodus' (ibid.: 325–26).
3. Ghetto youth in the Gambian context refers to small groups of young men that gather regularly in daily life. Gaibazzi (2015: 118) describes them as 'places of "global" imagination and laboratories of transnational youth cultures'. Although these ghettos do appear in rural spaces, there is a strong urban connotation to Lamin's expression. Besides this, it is important to note that ghettos have been important sites of state repression under Jammeh's regime.
4. In her ethnography on the 'cosmologies of destinations' of Eritrean refugees, Belloni (2016a) argues that these dimensions of social norms, desires and mobility need to be taken into account in any in-depth understanding of forced migration – which is of course something different than saying that Eritreans escaping from this inhuman political regime do not deserve protection by the Refugee Convention.
5. What I did not know then is that my two 'guides' – Alagie and Lamin – actually knew each other from the time they both went to college (Alagie was Lamin's 'senior', meaning he was an older generation of students). Only after I showed some pictures on my mobile phone of my stay in the Gambia to Lamin when he visited me in the Netherlands, did he tell me how he knew Alagie. The amusing thing is that Lamin and Alagie briefly spoke to each other during my navigation of the Serekunda Market, and at that time they had no clue to whom they were actually speaking. As soon as we found out this connection, a longer telephone call followed, connecting Lamin with Alagie. This is not just an example of how this research on mobility comes with surprising social encounters, it rather underlines the central role of social connectivity in the context of informal spaces and mobility (Simone 2004).

6. In the urban context of Pikine (Senegal), Prothmann (2018) refers to the local Wolof term *toog*, which means 'to sit/to wait', in order to capture the everyday impacts of social stagnation and inferiority related to situations of involuntary immobility (Carling 2002). Considering a similar culture of mobility, yet in a less urban environment, Gaibazzi (2015) rightly notes that sitting does not always hold a negative connotation in the Gambian context. He argues that *taxuu* (sitting/staying put in Soninke language) should not be regarded as an absolute condition, but rather as a positioning of oneself in a field of im/mobility that may also lead to social successes. He defines the negative connotation of sitting, like it is displayed here, as 'just sitting'.
7. Wagner and Yamba (1986: 201–2) argued that in the 1960s Scandinavian charter tourism to the Gambia promoted emigration to Europe as a viable livelihood option for the Gambian youth. As a result, 'Large numbers of youth ... gravitated towards them [the tourists] in the hope of "friendship", economic benefits, and/or the possibility of having a good time in these modern and exciting surroundings ... What is important to note here is the fact that one of the benefits hoped for as a result of these relationships was an opportunity to go to Scandinavia, and most often to Sweden'.
8. The actual price of the *inburgeringsexamen* (integration exam) is 150 euros. Probably, Caroline added the costs of exercise material as well as the costs of the Dutch language teacher who lived in Benin.
9. In the Netherlands, for instance, there is the infamous notion of the 'twenty-eighth day' after a rejected asylum claim. When a judge has confirmed the rejection of an asylum claim, the asylum seeker has a period of twenty-eight days to leave the country on a voluntary basis. If s/he is not acting according to this rule, s/he is likely to be detained and to be forcedly removed from the country. In practice, this often means that people go underground in the Netherlands or move to another EU country beforehand (Bernardt 2016).
10. The same sedentarist logic is central to development policy, which has become increasingly integrated with migration policy. As Oliver Bakewell (2007) argues, development initiatives are predominantly designed to 'keep people in their place'. EU's attempts to fight root causes of migration through development aid is the best illustration of the sedentarist metaphysics (Malkki 1992) behind development policy. In Senegal and the Gambia, various projects to fight irregular migration are based on returning to 'the land' and agriculture (e.g. Gaibazzi 2015).
11. An elaborative story of this Senegalese man is incorporated in the insightful master's thesis of one of my former students – who also brought me into contact with him (Van Ooijen 2016).
12. To highlight the lack of fear, Idrissa used the expression 'Je n'ai pas froid aux yeux', which is a French expression of fearlessness that literally translates to 'I do not have cold eyes'.

CHAPTER
2

Moving through Affective Circuits

The previous chapter highlighted how so-called 'migration journeys' are not easily distinguished from presumed pre-migratory and post-migratory mobility. Moreover, it illustrated that wayfinding, or wayfaring in the 'Ingoldian sense' (Ingold 2007, 2011), is more of a continuous practice than a migratory act from a place of origin to a place of destination. This chapter dives further into 'the ways' African movers 'find ways'. In so doing, I rely to a great extent on the work of Henrik Vigh who has gradually developed his notion of 'social navigation'. Initially he coined this concept in the context of conflict in Guinea Bissau (2006), to later apply it to the context of migration trajectories of West Africans in Lisbon (2009). In the light of mobility processes, the concept of social navigation is particularly insightful as it refers to the ways people move through social and institutional environments as well as to the effects this navigation has on 'possible positions and trajectories' (ibid.: 425). It is a concept that concentrates on people's processual practices in a context of uncertainty, and is therefore about motion within motion. This uncertainty relates to a general instability of 'social environments' in which new spaces of possibility may emerge unexpectedly, but may also disappear rapidly.[1] This implies that while people may be 'on the move', so are the environments they are moving through – i.e. the rules, institutions, networks, borders, communities. With this 'squared motion', Vigh entangles aspired distant futures with instant decision-making, as he writes: 'Navigation is constantly attuned to the way we move in the here and now as well as to the way we move in relation to social goals and prospective positions' (ibid.).

In this and the following two chapters, I relate the notion of social navigation to different relational force fields (Ingold 2011) that profoundly affect the mobility processes of my informants. Such a relational understanding implicates that action or agency is not seen as an individualistic form of autonomous power. Im/mobility trajectories, in other words, are not the outcome of individual decision-making as they strongly depend on the networked relational logic of how rules, encounters, information, capitals and peoples come together in a certain place, at a certain time. Movers, however, may develop skills that help them to navigate uncertain terrains (e.g. Moret 2017).

Before I focus on webs of actors that facilitate and/or hinder mobility (Chapters 3 and 4), I first dive into the affective circuits of my informants, which are constructed by the myriad exchanges of goods, people, money, emotions and ideas across borders (Cole and Groes 2016b). By navigating these circuits, movers negotiate individual aspirations and social expectations synchronically. The same circuits help them to create new openings and new directions in their mobility processes.

Navigating Affective Circuits

Migration studies show a long-standing fascination with the role of social networks in people's relocation processes. Particularly since the seminal work of Granovetter (1973) and Bourdieu (1986), a diverse set of scholars have focused on the ways migrants' social networks lead to social capital that lowers the risks or costs related to their movements. From this starting point, social networks are important mesostructures in migration systems as they bind together countries of origin and countries of destination (e.g. Boyd 1989). Studies on social networks have been welcomed in migration theories since they move away from atomistic explanations of migration and they inherently overcome one of the main epistemological rigidities of modernism – that of the container-like approaches to space (Massey 2005). Recent criticism, however, points to the fact that a rather static conceptualization of social networks – as grid-like entities of stronger and weaker ties – fails to consider the efforts and energies that are needed to capitalize social capital from social networks (Pathirage and Collyer 2011; Schapendonk 2015). In this respect, it is telling that migration scholars have been fixated by Bourdieu's (1986: 51) definition of social capital, as 'the aggregate of the actual or potential resources which are linked to possession of a durable network of more or less institutionalized relationships of mutual acquaintance or recognition'. Seldom have they paid attention to the sentence that comes right after this frequently cited definition, which is: 'These relationships may exist only in the practical state, in material and/or symbolic exchanges which help to maintain them' (ibid.). While the first sentence indeed hints at a semi-structural dimension of networks as it emphasizes the significance of 'durable relations', the second includes the notion that social ties need to be actively maintained in order for them to work (see also Schapendonk 2015). The omission of the efforts and energies attached to maintaining social networks – or what Pathirage and Collyer (2011) have coined 'network work'[2] – has led to the uncritical notion that social capital automatically derives from social networks. This idea has been empirically reinforced by studies that have only been sensitive to the ethnic ties, kinship solidarities and friendships that have actually helped migrants to get ahead, thereby ignoring the numerous network failures, social isolations and strategic investments that are generally part of the same processes. Based on some of my previous arguments (Schapendonk 2015, 2018a), I consider social networks as social accomplishments that are inherently unstable. In other words, social networks are maintained, made and remade and the associated expectations are confirmed as well as contested. As a result, social networks are not to be seen as a social given that are there to help people to move, rather, they are one of the uncertain terrains that are constantly navigated by actors (Vigh 2006, 2009).

In this context, I favour the term 'affective circuits' as introduced by Jennifer Cole and Christian Groes (2016b) over the social network terminology. As they state (2016b: 7), the notion of circuits does not only highlight movements of all kinds (information, people, goods, money, emotions) that transgress bounded notions of community, it also explicitly incorporates the social efforts and frictions involved: 'The circuit metaphor captures the potential for disconnection and conflict: it implies that the social networks through which objects, ideas, and people move are subject to regulation, slow downs, and blockage'.

The attempts to regulate circuits certainly do not only come from state policies and powerful migration apparatuses (Feldman 2012), these attempts also come from friends, lovers, sisters and brothers, older and younger generations. Through these affective circuits, trust may turn into a very fragile asset, expected support may not capitalize in reality, and roles and solidarities may change along the way, often through transforming rituals such as marriage (e.g. Krissman 2005). With this lens of affective circuits, we now further dive into the worlding mobility of my informants.

Dawda and Yahya

Dawda is my main 'connection man' for this research project. I met many of my Gambian informants directly or indirectly through his social contacts. This also includes his younger brother Yahya whom I first met in Italy in April 2014. Over the last ten years, my friendship with Dawda has grown, but it also includes considerable periods in which we did not see each other. During our countless meetings in and around the city of Nijmegen (the Netherlands), he explained to me with powerful descriptions all the ins and outs of his 'trans-world' (Ernste, Van Houtum and Zoomers 2009). I also practised his trans-world by, for instance, helping him with loading some of the containers he shipped from the Netherlands to the Gambia in the last five years. While he put most of the goods in the container, there was often space left for family members and friends to send their stuff as well. This process was based on a detailed administration that took careful note of who was sending what goods to the Gambia, and who was entitled to collect what stuff once the container had arrived there. For Dawda, loading the container was not merely an altruistic undertaking. For each box that his relatives or friends wanted to ship to their country of origin, he charged six euros. With a smile, he stated: 'It is business, so in business there are no brothers and sisters'. In this 'business', his friend Alagie had a special role as the local counterpart in the Gambia. He was responsible for offloading the container and the subsequent distribution of goods.

Dawda is a Wolof man from the North Bank Region of the Gambia. Through his role in the tourism industry, as a security guard and guide, he easily 'connected' to European tourists. He worked in different hotels in Bakau and Serekunda. It did not take long before he established a love connection with a Dutch woman. He travelled to the Netherlands by airplane for the first time in December 2007 to visit his Dutch girlfriend. In accordance with Dutch immigration regulations, he returned to the Gambia after his three-month stay in the Netherlands, and from there the couple started the process of obtaining a long-term visa for the Netherlands at the Dutch embassy in Senegal. Dawda finally got this visa and moved to the Netherlands for the second time in September 2008. The first year of his long stay in Europe was rather difficult for him, but he gradually moved up the socio-economic ladder. After a few years, his Dutch girlfriend gave birth to their son. However, the love affair did not last. Despite the relationship breaking up, in about five years he managed to establish a relatively strong and stable position in the Netherlands. This position included a full-time job, Dutch citizenship and, above all, a rich social life. During one of his recent visits to the Gambia, he married a Gambian woman, named Binta. Binta originates from the same village of origin in the North Bank Region. She joined Dawda in the Netherlands after having followed the procedure of family reunification.

Over the years, Dawda's family members and good friends in the Gambia started to notice his successful migration project. During my stay in the Gambia, I saw his 'line house' (a series of houses under one roof) that accommodates six villagers. This initially included his father, an old and well-respected villager. Sadly enough, the old man passed away a few years after the completion of the house. Dawda had also invested in the retail businesses of younger brothers, including Yahya's retail shop in the centre of the ground floor of the indoor Serekunda Market. When I visited Yahya's former shop, some four years after I first met him in Italy, I remembered how Yahya had told me that he found it difficult to sustain a living out of selling clothes from this particular place. Hence, from his time at the Serekunda Market, he had been searching for an additional income by buying clothes and other products in Senegal to sell to retailers in and around the marketplace. One day, he made some extra money in Senegal, and rather spontaneously decided not to return to the Gambia and to leave for the 'backway' without informing his mother and older brother in the Netherlands. Yahya left in relative secrecy, not informing his family about his plans. Undoubtedly, he had the success story of his older brother Dawda in mind as a source of inspiration.

Dawda only learned about Yahya's departure when his younger brother got in trouble in Agadez (Niger) – an important hub in West African mobility. Due to the numerous roadblocks where state officials and border guards informally seek for extra income, as well as due to the conventional transport costs involved, Yahya had totally run out of money once he reached the city of Agadez. He called his older brother for help. Although reluctantly (as Dawda initially got angry with his younger brother for embarking on this life-threatening journey), Dawda sent his younger sibling about 300 euros through a money transfer agency. This money enabled Yahya to pay the transport to Libya. When I spoke to Yahya about the fact that his brother initially refused to send money, he started to chuckle a bit, probably out of discomfort.

With the money sent by Dawda, Yahya was able to continue on his way to Libya. He spent almost two weeks in the desert, regaining energy in important stop-over places like Dirkou (Niger), Murzuq and Sabha (Libya). In the meantime, his brother in the Netherlands feared that Yahya would get in trouble again once he reached Libya. For that reason, Dawda started a process that puts hustling or 'débrouillardise' in a context of worlding connections (see also Schapendonk 2018a). Dawda bought a second-hand Mercedes Benz in the city of Nijmegen and shipped this car to the Gambia. The car was offloaded by his close friend Alagie, who handed over the Mercedes Benz to the wife of a particular Gambian man. This Gambian man – whom Dawda knew from the time they both were active in the Gambia's tourism sector – worked in Tripoli as a 'connection man', recruiting candidates for the boat passage to Italy. The latter indicates that migrants themselves may become important actors in the mobility industry (Lucht 2012). In the end, the second-hand car that was shipped to the Gambia functioned as the payment for Yahya's 'connection' between Libya and Lampedusa (Italy). On that day in September 2013, Yahya had his 'boat ticket' guaranteed by his brother's friend, and with this ticket he embarked the same boat as Lamin, Saihou, Omar, Amat and Shakur (of whom the latter will be introduced in Chapter 3).

The case of Yahya illustrates that the facilitation of these trans-Saharan journeys relies heavily on the fluid geographies of affective circuits (Cole and Groes 2016a) – the communications, social ties, money transfers and trading of goods that are such inherent aspects of our interconnected world. If there is one reason why the EU's attempts to close its borders and reduce unwanted migration fail, it is because these mobilities are so interwoven with these affective circuits. These circuits are not only vital in establishing trans-worlds between countries of origin and destination, as is usually discussed in transnational migration literature (e.g. Grillo and Mazzucato 2008), they are also central to the wayfinding missions of individual movers. The case of Yahya does not stand on its own. Almost every trajectory that I have come across is positioned in similar worlding circuits. Omar told me how he made use of his Facebook friends in order to find the right connection in Agadez. Alagie had to invest in a love relationship with a Dutch woman to enter the Dutch visa lottery once again. Lamin relied heavily on his Swiss connection during the trans-Saharan pathway. Indeed, as Belloni (2016b) underlines, we need to find ways to relate people's social connectivity to the practices of smugglers and other mobility facilitators working for profit. The role of connection men is crucial in this context. They regularly contact the migrants' family members in the countries of origin. As Omar once explained: 'This connection man make contact with your family in Banjul. So, when the family pays money to the brother of the connection man, this brother makes the phone call to the connection man and then he writes down your name and gives you a ticket for the ... boat'. In these circuits, there often exist thin lines between facilitation and exploitation, altruism and profit, and the migration industry and social networks (Cranston, Schapendonk and Spaan 2018).

Thus navigation has little to do with finding ways through physical landscapes by using maps or GPS devices. Navigation here rather relates to finding ways through these affective circuits in such a way that it enables people to cross borders. In this context, affective circuits are not only less stable than is often suggested in literature on social networks, they are also much more scattered than Vigh's (2009) notion of social environment suggests. These circuits are in no way bounded by localities, cities or nation states. In this respect, the 'bidirectional movement' that is highlighted in the concept of circuits (Cole and Groes 2016: 7) is somewhat misleading for its implication that there are only two poles that matter in transnational lifeworlds – the 'here and there', and the 'home and away'. In the case of Dawda and Yahya, connections were established between Serekunda, Nijmegen, Tripoli and Agadez. The connection man that facilitated Yahya's journey made use of his trustworthy relationships with migrants and their family members to continue his own trajectory – not towards Italy or the Netherlands, but to China instead.

When I visited Yahya for the very first time in April 2014 he had just recently been transferred, together with Omar and Shakur, from the area of Naples to a coastal town in Liguria. In their 'Napoli period' – when the three young men lived together with the other people who had arrived with the same boat from Libya – Yahya was known as 'the barber'. He shaved and cut, among many others, Lamin, Omar, Shakur, Amat and Saihou. After the transfer, the three young men entered a typical waiting stage – they found themselves 'out of time' (Griffiths 2014; Anderson 2014; Fontanari 2017) as well as out of place in Italy's asylum spaces (see Chapter 5). After the three young men had come to fetch me from the train station, they tried to find our way back to the asylum reception centre run by the aid organization Caritas. Everything in the city was still quite new to them. Hence, the young men always tried out different routes through the city. Also, this time, when we headed back to the asylum centre, they chose a different path than on their way to the station. We got lost. Getting lost, however, was not a waste of time or an unproductive disorientation. It was actually *the* way to become familiar with this particular cityscape. The three young men jokingly blamed each other for losing direction, without any further irritation. They jointly tried to find their way back again by searching the modest skyline of the city. Only a glimpse of some red and white cranes sufficed to get en route again. After more than an hour walking, we managed to reach the entrance of the Caritas reception centre. Yahya asked the gatekeeper to let us in. He opened the door and the three men entered, but I was stopped at the gate. Apparently, we had to find a different place to continue our conversation. One year later, Omar recalled this particular moment very well and he had great fun with it. 'It is the border for you', he said while laughing out loud and continued: 'You cannot enter. This is what Europe does for us'. However, that day in April 2014, the fact that his guest could not enter his living space frustrated Yahya intensively. He told me he had informed the Caritas staff about my visit and they had said they were fine with it. He therefore could not understand this blockage. As a typically subjectified asylum seeker, he stated: 'I told them about you, I told them, I don't understand why. I don't understand. But it is *their law*. It is their law, so they decide'.

Network Work in Affective Circuits

In September 2018, Alagie accompanied me to 'the village' of Dawda and Yahya in the Gambia. As a friend of the family and a frequent visitor of the village, he soon directed me to the house of Yahya's mother.[3] Once inside her home, I immediately saw a picture of Yahya on the wall. On this picture, the portrait of a much younger Yahya was photoshopped to a background that showed a large TV screen, a swimming pool, and a chandelier hanging on a white-painted ceiling. This background of extravagance and richness formed a sharp contrast with the sober living space of Yahya's mother. With a sense of melancholy, Yahya's mother talked about the time Yahya was still around. Outside, she showed me the agricultural tools with which he used to work. To me, the rusty tools seemed to be the material leftovers of a forgotten livelihood. They were the relics of a career path that Yahya decided to leave behind a long time ago. When I asked his mother what Yahya was like as a young boy, her reply was translated by Alagie in the following words: 'He was a very active young man, he always moved out. He helped on the lands as a young boy, but later he always moved out. He spent most of the time in Serekunda'. Somehow, this outgoing character that Yahya's mother emphasized was difficult to reconcile with my personal experiences with Yahya. I got to know him as a docile and relatively shy young man. His brother Dawda sometimes even imitated him by remaining silent during conversations and by turning his head from ongoing interactions.

Yahya's mother stated that she missed her son intensively. Besides, she did not seem to understand why it took so long before she could really profit from Yahya's move to the EU. Unlike Dawda, Yahya had so far not significantly contributed to the development of the village. She had definitely hoped for more support – in particular for a better mobile phone so she could actually receive pictures of her son. All in all, she had expected more phone calls, more communication, more support – just *more*. This reflection of the social pressure that many of my informants experience reminded me of the moment Dawda advised his younger brother not to send any money soon after his arrival in Italy. He warned Yahya that a quick first flow of remittances would create higher hopes among the family members back home and would heighten the moral obligation for Yahya of 'doing something' for the village. This advice to delay monetary transfers hints at the fact that movers may find ways to actively 'massage' the social relations and expectations that exist in affective circuits.

On his turn, however, Yahya had also hoped for more support from his older brother living in the Netherlands. During my second stay with Yahya, in May 2015, we had a conversation in which he shared his frustrations regarding the lack of support from Dawda in the period after his arrival in Italy:

> He is making money money money. But Dawda, Dawda, for me he is sleeping too much. I call him, but he does not pick up the phone. I flash him, but he is not calling ... Why is he going to London to his friends there, and not to Italy? For me, I cannot travel to Holland, but for him, it is very easy to come here. Like you! You come here. But my brother is not coming here. Why?! I don't understand. I don't understand. He can come with Mohammed [Dawda's son], and we have a good time, I bring him here [to the beach side], but no ... Also, my brother in Malta, he is asking for his help. Italy is better than Malta, there he has no job, nothing. They keep you on the island, you cannot escape. But, Dawda, he does not come to Malta, he does not come to Italy. He must help, but Dawda is sleeping.

Yahya's frustration illustrates that affective circuits indeed come with isolations, disconnections, useless efforts and severe misunderstandings. In a time when Yahya had a precarious socio-economic and legal position in Italy, he saw his brother enjoying Europe by looking at his Facebook posts and pictures of his visit to his friends in London. At the same time, Yahya felt the moral demands coming from his mother and his spouse in the Gambia to bring prosperity 'back home'. Thus, as is so often stressed in the literature, social networks are of crucial importance for understanding how movers find ways. At the same time, social networks do not automatically work in favour of the ones on the move. They may be a main source of stress and involve considerable emotional labour. Social connections may in fact confront individuals with their own relatively deprived position regarding mobility – which touches upon discussions of the politics of mobility (Adey 2006; Cresswell 2010). On another occasion, Omar underlined this when he explained to me how his previous attempts to leave the Gambia had failed:

> Because the time I came back from Mauritania [after a failed exit to the Canary Islands by boat], I was working on the [Albert] market, together with my friend there. This is my brother who is living in Valencia now, I talked about him. In 2009 he told me he was about to travel with the boat, he asked me to travel with him. So, we sat in the market together, we did business, and he told me he wanted to travel, he asked me to come with him. I said: 'Let me just wait before I got my money ready'. I needed something like 100 or 150 euros to pay. Even if I got 100 euros, I would talk to the connection man and he would understand my situation so I could come in the same boat. But one day, I was in the market, this boy did not come. After two days I went to his house, I asked: 'Where is this boy?' They did not know, and from that moment I knew that this boy had travelled. After nine days I saw a phone call from

Spain. It was him, he said: 'I am in Spain now'. After nine days! Ooooh! I was so happy for him!! But inside I was crying, because I told myself: '*Why, why,* did I not travel with this guy. *Why?!* For only 100, 150 euros?'

In addition, some formerly favourable connections may turn out to be rather unhelpful in the context of mobility processes. They may even turn into a burden. The latter was heavily felt by Dawda, once he had established a good position in the Netherlands. Next to Yahya, he assisted two other brothers with their journeys to Europe in the same period of time (2013-14). One entered Malta by embarking a boat in Libya. His Mediterranean journey was facilitated by the same connection man in Tripoli to whom Yahya had formerly connected. The other brother moved to Europe by the lookalike strategy – but in order to let this work, Dawda had to bribe some authority agents at Banjul airport, which involved a considerable sum of money. He repeatedly stated how he got sick and tired of all the requests he received through Facebook and through the numerous telephone calls from the Gambia. One day, out of frustration, he resolved to 'stop all projects', meaning that he would no longer give financial support to any family member or social contact aiming to reach Europe. Later it appeared that there were at least two exceptions to his statement: in 2015 he financed and arranged the journey of his Gambian wife and in 2017 he did the same for his good friend Alagie.

The navigation of affective circuits in mobility processes is a delicate issue. If one massages one's relations too firmly or aggressively, a sudden disconnection might follow. However, if one does not invest in social connectivity, one is unlikely to profit from it. And, as in the case of Dawda, if one is too supportive to other people, connectivity may turn into a heavy burden for considerable periods of time. People's availability and willingness to assist others have probably always been noticeable through cross-border communications. However, through the working of WhatsApp and Viber groups and Facebook pages, transnational communities are nowadays more easily forged and maintained. Many movers are active members of WhatsApp groups that connect people all over the world, for the simple reason that they are linked to the same place of origin. Relying on older and newer platforms of communication, the network work of individuals is on constant collective display. This makes the guesthouse of Doudou in Milan an important anchor point for mobility processes of newer generations, as we saw in the vignette introducing Part I of this book. This also means that the gains and losses of someone in Europe soon become known by other people beyond the close family and friends. One way of dealing with this ever-present community gaze is by dissociating oneself from it. In this light, Omar was definitely one of the Gambian men who stressed the individual character of his project – which he seemed to cleverly combine with a very social attitude towards others, including Oslo (the man from Central Asia who lived in Oslo). Yahya's mobility also had a somewhat individualistic character since he left in secrecy, not informing his brother in the Netherlands, nor his mother in the Gambia, about taking the backway. Another illustration of individuality that I will now further unpack comes from Franck, a 41-year-old man from the anglophone part of Cameroon.

Franck first tried to reach Europe with a female friend, already in the late 1990s. His friend brought two other female friends, and the four started the journey northwards, to Kano (Nigeria), Zinder and Agadez (Niger). The journey stranded there since one of the women appeared to be pregnant from the moment they had started their adventure. She was taken back home by a Cameroonian man who was on his way from Algeria back to Cameroon. Franck continued, but did not get very far since the transporters abandoned his group of travellers in the Algerian desert. After an erratic time – in which he had walked through the desert and was lucky enough to find a military camp – he was brought back to Agadez, from where he finally returned to Cameroon. In about ten years, he regained sufficient funds to hit the road again, but this time he definitely preferred to travel alone:

> I had a lot of money now, and I decided to go alone. I took nobody, I want to be free and independent, I don't want to have responsibility any more for somebody except from myself. I even told my brothers, I have one brother in London, one brother in America, I told them: 'I don't need your help. This is my project, my individual project. I don't need your money. Don't worry, I know the road'. So with my experience of the first time, I moved fast, I know the tricks, I told them [the transporters and authorities]: 'I know your acts'. In two weeks I reached Oujda [Morocco].

Thus, network work may indeed imply the articulation of an individual endeavour. This is relevant for mobility-driven studies, and migration studies in particular, since pre-existing social networks are often taken for granted as *the* decisive component of migration processes. On their trans-Saharan journeys, and also during their navigation of Eurospace, the establishment of new ties, as well as the abolition of older and unsatisfying connections, is often of crucial importance to the wayfinding of African movers.

Affective Circuits: Views from Eurospace

The networking dynamics displayed above are central to the ways West African movers continue to navigate Eurospace once they arrive there.

Information is shared and contested through cross-border communications. Regularly, my informants stated that they wanted 'to see with their own eyes' whether the information they received about a particular place was actually correct. The cross-border movements also involve many questions about the whereabouts of co-movers. Lamin, Yahya, Omar, Amat, Shakur and Saihou were all more or less kept up to date about the movements of one another. Lamin and Saihou told me how they belonged to a larger 'team' of 23 to 25 people (Lamin counted 23 people, while Saihou referred to a group of 25). The term 'team' referred to the collective of West Africans that arrived in Lampedusa with the same boat and got transferred as a group via Rome to the asylum centre in Naples soon after. The majority of the team came from the Gambia, others from Senegal or Guinea. The group slowly dispersed because of asylum transfers. The six friends that I followed through time–space knew well who of the collective obtained the first Italian residence paper, who was better off in terms of weekly or monthly pocket money from the Italian reception centre, who managed to get some paid job, and who managed or failed in their border crossings. During one of my visits to Saihou in Switzerland (March 2017), I asked him how many of the team members had stayed in Italy ever since their arrival in Italy in September 2013. He started counting and recounting. The final outcome was seven. I shared my surprise about this low number with Saihou, and thereupon he started to laugh and confirmed:

> Only seven, mister Joe. But with this seven people there is Lamin, and he comes and goes. Some other people of the team do it like Lamin, they are now in Italy, but they have moved out before. Only Demba has never left, Shakur he has never left, and one boy who got a paper, he never left. For the rest all of them have moved out.

Intra-EU mobility was for this group thus certainly not exceptional, as suggested by some quantitative studies (Toma and Castagnone 2015).[4] The dispersal of West African movers creates a massive and flexible social infrastructure that stimulates further mobility. Through the mobility of social connections, individual Eurospaces almost automatically expand, producing a high potential for new mobilities. At the time Lamin visited me in the Netherlands, for instance, he looked ahead and talked about the desire to visit new destinations, thereby stressing the important role of social connectivity. He wanted to visit Spain, but he felt that this would be rather difficult since he had no connection there. According to him a better option was Sweden since he had a friend living there.

Interestingly, the movements of my informants were often too rapid to keep track of. Occasionally, I thought I was up to date regarding somebody's whereabouts, but then I heard from a co-mover that this particular person had already left that place. It also happened that some of my informants thought a friend was still in Italy or had returned to the Gambia, while I met this person the same day in the Netherlands. In many of the cases when we talked about a mutual contact, my informants and myself had to deal with contrasting information. For example, one informant told me that our mutual contact had moved to 'a camp' in Germany, while the person involved told me he actually lived outside any asylum centre. Thus, in the light of mobility dynamics, networking is crucial, but it is being complicated by the mobility dynamics at the same time.

Not all friendships that are constructed in Europe along the way are productive as a support structure. During my several visits to Saihou in Switzerland, I always wondered why he lived in an asylum centre that was located a twenty-minute train ride away from the place where he liked to hang out. He actually rented a room from an Eritrean man who was granted this 'Asylheim' on the basis of his asylum application. Saihou called his residence a place for hiding, and the hiding place was not without risks. Saihou paid this man a monthly rent of 450 Swiss francs – almost 400 euros. However, the financial burden was not the only price he paid. Saihou lived there under the constant threat of a sudden control by the Swiss authorities. This particular place of residence surprised me since Saihou had proven he had built some good friendships in several Swiss cities, alongside other Mandinka men from the Gambia. But none of these social contacts seemed to be helpful in getting a proper living space. When I asked Saihou about this, he stated that 'everybody is with somebody' and that there 'is no place' for him, to add later: 'These boys [his friends], most of them, they don't have papers, and they live in somebody else's house, so they cannot arrange this for me'. Thus, social capital comes with severe limitations.

Some Practical Concerns

The dynamic character of mobility processes and social connections also brings practical concerns for the movers. How to store relevant connections? How to keep track of your friends when they regularly cross borders and therefore change SIM cards? Some informants referred to Facebook as an important source for connectivity. However, partly due to the norms transmitted through transnational affective circuits, I have seen quite a number of active Facebook accounts change into inactive ones. Occasionally, this occurred in parallel with a change of telephone number after someone had crossed a border. Social disconnections may be part of mobility processes as well. Some interlocutors carried special booklets to store the most important telephone numbers, others referred to the important role of connections to relatives in the countries of origin. Contact details of wives, uncles and other family members were shared among befriended movers as a kind of 'local foothold' in dynamic mobility processes (Dahinden 2010b). If one really needed to talk to a co-mover but had no idea where to find or how to contact this person, the option remained to call those relatives in the countries of origin who were likely to be continuously up to date about the person's mobility. Occasionally, however, even these local footholds also lacked the latest information about people's movements, leading to a shared concern about somebody's well-being.

Another practical concern related to mobility is the coordination of travels. Some informants needed to be present at a specific place and time to ensure that their residence permits were renewed. Others were in a constant state of preparedness to move to the agricultural site where their labour was needed. They communicated continuously with co-workers or their employers to anticipate their next movements. Such coordination may also involve the attempts to bundle different travel rhythms. In July 2017, for instance, I met a Senegalese man who had just arrived in Lleida (Spain) for the very first time. He had spent two nights in a public park, and so far, he had not succeeded in finding a job through the official channels. In the park, he told me how he maintained a mobile livelihood by circulating between Andalusia (southern Spain) and the city of Lisbon (Portugal). During his seasonal work in Andalusia in 2014, he met his Polish girlfriend. Like him, she had moved to southern Spain to pick strawberries. Since the moment they first met, they both moved to the same place in Andalusia to see each other and to work side by side in the strawberry sector – which required significant coordination. When the season closed, both lovers followed their own mobility rhythms only to meet again a year after for another period of approximately four months. This coordination has also been a main challenge for me, the ethnographer who attempts to follow mobility dynamics – as illustrated in the following section.

The Expanding Eurospace of a JJC

Mamadou is a flamboyant young man from the Gambia. Unlike most of the other men I met in Italy and Spain, he has a Fula background – one of the largest ethnic groups in the Sahel region, but a minority in the Gambia. The Fula people are commonly known for their nomadic and pastoralist identity. I knew him because he often socialized with Yahya, Omar and Shakur during my second stay with them in 2015. He was one of my informants who encountered the cruelty of the Jammeh regime as he was put in prison for about two weeks. Being a trained electrician, he was accused of sabotage after an accident at the construction site of one of the president's houses. After detention, he left the Gambia via Casamance (Senegal) and made his way to Mali. There he worked as an electrician for some months before heading further north. In great detail, he shared with me the ins and outs of his turbulent trajectory through Libya, from where he left for Italy on one of the last days of Ramadan 2014. Being saved by 'the navy' after two days at sea, he was brought to Sicilia. From there he was soon transferred to the asylum centre in Liguria. There, as he told me, he was well received by the previous asylum seekers from the same region of origin. He was especially helped by his contact with Yahya in his first period of time in Italy. As he stated in May 2015:

> Mamadou: Yahya showed us so many places. When we just arrived, he really helped. We did not take a bus, but he showed us by walking. He said: 'By walking you know the city better'. So he showed me the good places, and the places not good for us. I thank him. Without him I would stay JJC for too long.
> I: What is a JJC?
> Mamadou: That is an expression they use in UK for newcomers. When you are a newcomer, you don't know the rules of the city. So people have to teach you … JJC, it means Journey Just Come!

Mamadou and I had stayed in contact since our first encounter, and he kept me up to date with his Italian asylum procedure through WhatsApp and Facebook. In the summer of 2016, he was granted a humanitarian status for two years. From this specific point in time, his Eurospace expanded, as illustrated by the following series of communications:

> [Text message, December 2016: Leaving Italy]
> Mamadou: Brother am about to go out Italy. Am going on the XX dis month. My time is up bro.
> [Telephone call, January 2017: In Spain]
> Mamadou: Really, in the summer we meet in Holland. I want to come in Holland in the summer.
> I: I want to come to Valencia before, so maybe I come to Spain.
> Mamadou: OK! You want to come to Spain?
> I: Yes, I want to meet you there.
> Mamadou [laughs]: But I am moving man, I want to leave Spain, I want to go to Germany brother.
> I: Germany!? So, you stay only briefly in Spain?
> Mamadou: Yes, I know I said before that I will look, but now I want to go there.
> I: So, you did not find anything there in Spain?
> Mamadou: Yea, in Spain there is nothing nothing nothing in here.

At the end of January, he indeed went to Germany, where he stayed at his sister's place. In that period, he started a relationship with a German woman whom he had met in a club. As this German woman lived in Dortmund, he also went there and stayed for about two months in this particular German city. In April, he was in contact with the employer he worked for during his time in Liguria. He checked with 'his boss' to see if the tourism season was open already, which would mean he could start his work again. To my surprise, he decided otherwise and did not return to Italy in the summer. Instead he moved by one of EU's coach services to Marseille (France) to do some raba raba work in the informal circuits of this Mediterranean city. From there he wanted to return to Germany, and in this context, he asked me to give him Omar's contact details. This was the start of some social frictions.

I gave Omar's number to Mamadou, but Omar did not respond to his messages. Mamadou came back to me since he thought Omar had changed his telephone number. He also tried the Facebook name that I had for Omar, but neither did he receive a reaction from him there. I was a bit in doubt as to what to do. I knew that Omar had a more individualistic attitude than other Gambians I had met. He had himself articulated this several times by saying that 'he lived only for himself'. Considering his character, I felt that there had to be a reason for him for not reacting to Mamadou's messages and contact requests. I decided to leave it up to Omar, and I sent him a message with Mamadou's contact details. However, the next day Mamadou confessed to me that he had accidentally sent me his old username, and he urged me to ask Omar again now with the right details. I did, but I feared a negative reaction from Omar. That reaction indeed came. Omar told me 'to forget Mamadou' and that 'I didn't know what was going on'. I apologized to Omar and emphasized that I would not try to connect them again. As a response to that apology, Omar told me that Mamadou did not have the capacity to trick him since they 'were not family'. He articulated the social distance between them, saying: 'We don't know each other, we just know each other in Italy. I don't care about that'.

Thus, the problem between the two men appeared to be deeper and really not of my business. One of the things that upset Omar was that Mamadou gave him two different telephone numbers. According to him, this was a sign that Mamadou could not be trusted. However, soon this negative atmosphere vanished. I was happy to receive a message from Omar that same night: 'I was talking to him right now. He said he made a mistake, that's why. That number was not his number. Now I get his right number'. Social connections can be brittle in Eurospace, but trust may also suddenly reappear.

Connectivity beyond Ethnicity

The case of the Senegalese/Polish couple illustrates that it is of vital importance to not only focus on ethnicity or nationality when affective relations are discussed. In fact, through the dynamic practice of relations, notions of kinship and family stretch and change over time. This is particularly visible in times when institutional settings and regulations shift. In his ethnography of citizenship and kinship in the Bijlmer – the migrant neighbourhood of Amsterdam – Andrikopoulos (2017) paints a highly dynamic picture of mutual relationships within and beyond West African communities. Whereas civic inequality between those with and those without proper documents initially led to document lending and marriages within African communities, these kinship relations slowly transcended ethnic boundaries. They first moved towards transatlantic kinship (with Surinamese and other Afro-Caribbean migrants marrying and lending documents to Africans). Later they evolved towards kinship relations between Africans and migrants from eastern and southern Europe, who have become increasingly present in this Amsterdam district. As Andrikopoulos (2017) describes in great detail, these changes in kinship relations are tightly linked to changes in Dutch and European policymaking. First, in the early 2000s, identity loans based on the lookalike strategy within African communities basically disappeared due to the administrative fines levied upon those who employed unauthorized migrants. The reduction of the transatlantic kinship relations, which were particularly based on marriages of West Africans and Afro-Caribbeans with Dutch citizenship and which helped to regularize a considerable number of Ghanaians and Nigerians in the 1990s, was related to the implementation of higher barriers to family reunification. The emergence of new affective alliances between Africans and eastern and southern Europeans in the Netherlands can be explained by the introduction of a more inclusive form of citizenship at the level of the EU. Based on EU Directive 2004/38 the right of free movement of EU citizens automatically extended to the family members of EU nationals who exercised this right. The European Court of Justice decided that EU member states cannot impose additional conditions, such as previous legal residence. As a consequence, unauthorized migrants become regularized when they marry EU citizens who have left their countries of origin to reside in another EU member state (Andrikopoulos 2017: 140–42). A crux emerges, however, when an unauthorized migrant falls in love with an EU citizen who still lives in his/her country of origin. In this case, the relationship of the unauthorized migrant and EU citizen falls under the national law of that specific EU member state. On this basis the unauthorized migrant cannot start a regularization procedure under the EU Directive. The solution then is to move as a couple to a neighbouring country. For this reason, I have seen some Dutch/African couples in the Netherlands move to Germany or Belgium with – in the end – positive results. This illustrates that illegality is never really an absolute category in life (e.g. Kubal 2013). Others – such as Alagie, the friend of Dawda – were actively looking for a love relationship to increase the chances for either a long stay in Eurospace or the start of a regularization procedure. Hustling tactics of connectivity can again be quite central in this respect, but the network work – the efforts and energies that are put into finding new ties – certainly does not always pay out.

On a sunny winter day, I sat down on a bench in a public park in Germany with Omar and his Gambian friend from the camp, Camara. Camara had a long history in the tourism sector of the Gambia. He combined his role as a tourist guide with the 'bumster' tactics of beach boys, using sexual services for socio-economic gains (Ceesay 2016). Suddenly Camara stood up from the bench, and walked away. He approached a woman who was playing with her child in a small playground, and they talked for some five minutes. He came back, and after a few minutes he again approached somebody out of the blue. Later, when we wandered through the historic centre of this particular place in southern Germany, we were approached in English by a young woman. She asked whether we could take a picture of her at a tourist site. She gave her cell phone to Omar and he made the picture. He returned the phone without any hints or advancements. Soon Camara took over and started a social talk with the woman. Omar and I chuckled a bit and walked away. 'Let's wait over there', Omar said, and we looked from a distance how Camara used his remarkably overacted British accent to gain a level of trust. But all the efforts were of no avail. The woman did not hand over a telephone number, and somewhat disappointed Camara joined us again. Omar could not stop laughing – and cried out loud, 'You bumsteeeer!' This event was an inexhaustible source for joy and laughter in the days that followed. This illustration is not meant to portray Camara as a pure womanizer. It is also not meant to underline that Gambian young men are in pursuit of some enjoyment in a context of boredom and waiting. With this everyday example, I would rather like to stress the continuous efforts and investments that are made in social connectivity – day in, day out. It is a tiring, and often confronting, undertaking, particularly because one is likely to encounter multiple social and racialized boundaries. However, as with the hustling tactics of connectivity in the Gambia, these connectivity efforts are continuously fed by the permanent possibility that one connection does actually work out, which could change the prospects of a regular status tremendously.

Repairing Passages through Social Connectivity

Navigating Eurospace through social connectivity does not only create new openings in the legal sense, it may also be crucial in mobility processes to unknown destinations. Here again, we may draw a parallel between the mobility of Favell's Eurostars and the mobility of African movers who are central to this study. As Favell (2008: 94) framed it: 'Many of the migration stories ... seem to suggest that the moves were a "shot in the dark", adventurous, speculative, "see what happens" types of move'. Based on the hustling and gambling attitudes discussed in the previous chapter, many African movers just try their luck with their movements to new places. This implies that they do not necessarily move to places where they actually know people. These movements thus deviate from the main claim of migration network theorists that social networks form important mesostructures that profoundly affect migrants' destinations (see also Collyer 2005). To illustrate this 'see what happens' kind of movements, I return to the trajectory of Franck – the cheerful Cameroonian man whom I first met in Germany.

After having spent some months in Morocco, Franck entered Spain by embarking a rubber boat heading to Tarifa (Spain). He was caught by border guards and brought to a detention centre in Barcelona. He spent a couple of weeks there, and then moved down south to Murcia (still Spain). The role of social contacts is important here, as he actually moved to one of his female co-travellers with whom he had travelled overland through Africa in the late 1990s. From there, he continued his wayfinding, as he told me so vividly:

> One of the ladies of my first journey succeeded to enter Spain from that first journey. I visited her, she even had a residence paper there. You see!? She was very successful! She married a Spanish man, and she is stable now. So I spent some days with the family and after that I went back to Barcelona. There I did not stay long. I bought a ticket for a bus to Germany. I wanted to reach Germany. Why? Only God knows. I don't know anybody in Germany, I heard very good stories about Holland, but me I wanted to reach Germany. It was my feeling. I did not want to reach London, where my brother is, no, this was my own way. You see? It is me who decided with the will of God. I give this person who bought the ticket online for 10 euros, because this person uses his passport for that. I took the ticket, and entered the bus. I had no papers, you understand, so you don't sit in the bus comfortably. You are afraid of controls. But the only control was the control of the ticket. So I thought I would enter Germany, but the bus stopped in Paris. The driver said, 'Go out, everybody go out'. So, I thought, there must be a transfer. So I searched the bus for Germany, but the driver said, 'This is not a good ticket'. So what could I do? In this city of Paris, the *big* city. I did not know anybody there! My pocket was empty, I did not even have 5 euros. So it was already evening, and I approached this Mali guy, I told him my problem, and he said: 'OK, you can stay in my place for two days, but two days only. After two days, when you don't have the money I kick you out'. So after two days, man, how can I find

money in a new city in two days? It is impossible. After two days ended, the man said, 'I am sorry, I kick you out'. I asked him for one week. And he said, 'OK. One week'. I thought about my situation, and the only chance I had was this. When I was in Barcelona I spent my money, my very last money on *good* clothes. Like a costume, like nice shoes. And I knew, when I am in trouble, I can always use this to sell. That was my only chance. So I went to the market [in Paris], I show my clothes to the market people, and they gave me like 50 euros. This was enough for the ticket. So I asked the man to use his passport for 10 euros, and he bought the good ticket. This bus I took ended up in Dortmund. Dortmund! What can I do in Dortmund?

Franck's arrival in Paris exemplifies that improvisations form an important dimension of the navigation of Eurospace. Like so many of my informants, Franck was confronted with a sudden rupture in his movements and, in order to repair his passage to Germany, had to invest in a new and rather spontaneous connection (the Malian man in Paris) and acts that were closely related to 'débrouillardise' (in Barcelona he invested in a costume to eventually sell it later in Paris). Thus, speculative and open-ended mobilities do come with unfamiliarity and they require specific connectivity tactics that do not fit the strong tie/weak tie logic of migration network theories (Schapendonk 2015). Many movers find a helping hand from friendly people (as for my informants in many cases Africans, but not necessarily from people with the same ethnic or national background) they have never met before. In analysing how social networks function in mobility processes, it is therefore insightful to move beyond the notion of a social network as a *sustained* net of *pre-known* people (Somerville 2015). The next section expands on this argument by highlighting how movers get rid of hindering social ties.

Escape I

Since the emergence of social network theory in migration studies, there have always been critical views on the functioning and significance of social ties in migratory processes. One is the much-debated argument of Alejandro Portes (1998) regarding the negative aspects of sociability (e.g. Collyer 2005). Portes argues that social network membership may imply excessive claims on group members and lead to significant restrictions to individual freedoms of group members. Andrikopoulos (2017) extends this argument to kinship as a mutual form of being. He argues that we should move beyond normative discourses that usually approach kinship relations only in a positive light. In fact, seemingly affective relations can be rather suffocating for the ones experiencing these. Thus, if affective and social bonds are performed and regulated on an everyday basis, then they may also be something to be undone in particular situations (e.g. Schapendonk 2015; Andrikopoulos 2017). Some of my informants have sought different ways to undo earlier established solidarities. In one of these situations, I had a rather proactive role.

On a Friday night, February 2016, I received an urgent telephone call from Saihou. Basically, he asked me to help out a Gambian friend in trouble:

> Mr Joe, I really need your help now now. One of my 'brothers', he is in Holland now, I don't know where, maybe in Amsterdam, but he is in really bad condition. He wants to move to Germany, but he has nothing, nothing. So I want to give him your number, so he can tell the story to you, and maybe you can help him.

Over the years, I received several requests to help informants, as well as family members of informants, in case they found themselves in precarious situations. In the early days of my academic career, I was particularly concerned how my acts of social support would potentially 'harm' the information I collected from the person involved or how it could affect my relationship with other informants. Gradually, however, this concern disappeared. Now I am convinced that there is nothing wrong in supporting people you care about. This is particularly true when one starts to realize that the informants actually help me with my quest for detailed insights into mobility dynamics. In fact, especially in the context of this research in which I got to know many of my informants over longer periods of time, they have become part of my own affective circuits, as I also have slowly but surely become part of theirs. Especially in the context of migration studies, static and one-sided views on guest–host relations – seeing migrants/refugees only as typical guests – seem to easily overflow in research practices as it is sometimes forgotten that not only are refugees/migrants/movers in need of some helping hand, but so too are the ethnographer, geographer and anthropologist in their daily work (see also Aparna and Schapendonk 2018). Warranting this reality, I paid bills and fines for a Congolese friend in the Netherlands who had struggled for years to get his status regularized. I sent considerable amounts of money to Greece and France to a dispersed Cameroonian family with a newborn child. Similarly, I regularly sent money to the wife of one informant whose situation in Spain downgraded. I gave gifts to several informants as a sign of appreciation that they again reserved time to host me. I helped a Nigerian woman in the Netherlands with her job application in the UK, and there are several other examples of financial and social support I gave.

However, Saihou's telephone call made me hesitate. I am not unwilling to help a friend of a friend, but I did not know this man at all. My main concern was: what if I am expected to bring him across the border to Belgium or Germany in an unauthorized way? This telephone call, thus, was a sudden confrontation with the personal question of how far my affective relation with Saihou could push me in solidarity acts towards unknown others, with the possibility of breaking the law. I decided to take this request step by step and that same Friday night I started a WhatsApp conversation with Saihou's 'brother' Malik.[5] Through this first contact I learned very little about the situation he was in. This changed during our first telephone call the next morning. Already from the first second I spoke to him, he stressed the urgency of his situation. He asked me to pick him up in a village, located some 100 km away from the city of Nijmegen. His sudden escape had to do with a relationship crisis as he stated that 'his wife wants him to go'. It also became clear to me that he wanted to move to Germany. Through this desperate call, I realized that I had become an important actor in the social navigation of his next step for the simple fact that I belonged to Saihou's social network. On this occasion, the telephone was handed over (or taken over) by his partner, and in Dutch she explained to me that she did not want him to move 'from place to place', that she did not want to give 'the burden to anyone', and that she only needed some weeks of rest to reflect on the entire situation. What this entire situation was, was still unclear to me at that moment. Thereupon, Malik took over the telephone again and informed me in a rush that he would call me back in ten minutes. This gave me the time to call Saihou once more to see if he had more information for me. He told me that Malik had just recently arrived in the Netherlands, but that his girlfriend wanted him to return to the Gambia again because she thought their relationship would not work out. Saihou even stated that she had everything set to facilitate the return – she even booked the flight. While I was still puzzled about the situation, Malik called me back as promised. He again stressed the urgency and again asked me to pick him up. After a brief discussion with Joëlle (my spouse) about what to do, I stepped in my car, and drove westwards. Malik and I agreed to meet each other at the church of the village he was living. It was roughly a one-hour drive.

Once I arrived at the church, I did not find Malik and started to wander around. After thirty minutes of waiting, I tried to call Malik again. With a gasping voice he said he was on his way and that he would arrive there in ten minutes. Another thirty minutes passed by, and there was still no sign of Malik. To keep myself warm on this cold Saturday, I again walked in circles around the church. After another thirty minutes, I called him again. He was now 'at the bridge', and he asked me with a strong sense of urgency to come there and pick him up. I told him I had no idea which bridge he was talking about, whereupon he referred to a bridge that gave access to the highways. I still had no clue. I insisted and told him it was better if he would just come to me. He said 'OK', and he told me that he would call me in ten minutes 'to direct me'. Another thirty minutes passed by. I decided to get in my car again and drive around while waiting for the call. In the meantime, I tried to reach him again, but his phone was switched off. Around two o'clock, after I had spent about two hours of waiting for Malik, I decided to call Saihou to ask his opinion about what to do, and he said: 'OK, you can go home now, you drove from far, now I don't know why his phone is off'. Just when I reached the highway on my way back home, I received a telephone call from Malik, but to my surprise, a Dutchman started talking to me, asking me about my whereabouts. I told him I was still very close to place A (the village of Malik). The man seemed to be astonished when he stated in Dutch: 'But ohhh, he is in place X' – which was a village some 15 km away from the place we were supposed to meet.

Some twenty minutes later, I met Malik empty-handed and I saw that the lower parts of his jeans were totally drowned in mud. The first, and rather awkward, question I had for him was: 'Where is your suitcase?' I assumed that he had prepared his move, and hence I thought he had taken (some) luggage. He told me he had to leave all his belongings behind, he had to 'escape with nothing'. Contrary to our agreement, Malik had decided not to go to the centre of the village since this was the place his girlfriend would probably look for him. Instead, he had run around the village, crossed agricultural fields and jumped over ditches and, finally, he had ended up getting lost in place X. Desperately, he had asked a passer-by for help. It took me some time before I understood the extraordinary circumstances this Gambian man was in – but an escape it was.

More than ten years ago, Malik and a Dutch woman whom he had met in the Gambia began a relationship. A few years later, they applied for Malik's residence in the Netherlands at the Dutch embassy in Senegal. As in the cases of Eugene and Caroline (the Cameroonian/Dutch couple) and Dawda, Malik had visited his girlfriend in the Netherlands before on a tourist visa and returned to the Gambia later so as not violate the visa conditions. Once he had received the green light for a residence permit from the embassy, after having passed the Dutch integration exam (that took place in Dakar, Senegal), he prepared for his second trip to the Netherlands. He imagined his second journey to the Netherlands as his migratory relocation to a new place of residence. Somehow, just before his departure from the Gambia, however, Malik's girlfriend panicked. As Malik told me:

> On the day of my departure she called me, she said: 'Ohh I am confused now, I think it is better you don't come now, I cancel the ticket'. I said: 'What?! You cancel the ticket?!' At that moment, I already reached the airport, it was even time for me to enter the plane, so I said:

> 'Let me just try'. So the people there they had a list with names on a paper, and I asked: 'Is my name on the list?' They said: 'No', but they said, 'let me check in the computer'. And there my name was there, so I could enter. God helped me with this!

The fact that his girlfriend had intended to cancel the ticket hurt Malik heavily. It is one of the clearest examples that affective circuits are regulated by the actors involved. Her attempt to block his move created immense confusion for Malik. In his attempts to recapture his own situation, he emphasized that they had had a relationship for about ten years already, he told me how they had constructed a love song together that underscored their strong bond, and he stressed how he had waited for years to move over to the Netherlands and how he had sold most of his belongings to co-finance his departure. With 'the help of God', he found a way to continue his journey that was not only filled with hope, but also with feelings of betrayal and frustration (Kleist and Thorsen 2017). Malik had a transit stop in Casablanca (Morocco) to reach the Netherlands the next day. Despite her attempt to cancel the ticket, Malik's girlfriend came to get him at the airport. The fact that Malik had managed to arrive in the Netherlands encouraged the couple to once more try their luck. Malik stayed for about one month with his Dutch girlfriend, but apparently it did not work out. Malik continued to recapture his story:

> I told her, 'Let us just try now I am here'. You know what, because when she came to the Gambia we play love like everything! I always stayed with her, you see, some boys try different ladies, but me I stayed with her all this ten years. I waited for her! ... And then the first day I arrived in Holland this time, her parents come to talk to me. They look at me and they tell me: 'You cannot stay, it is better for you to go back, we want our daughter to be happy, you understand?' I told the father: 'I respect you very much, but this is between me and her, not between you and me. We planned this for a long time now. I come here on tourist visa before, I go to Senegal many times to make the test for the visa, I give up everything at home for her now. So you tell me to go back? I cannot go back, because then I have to sleep on the street!' This was the *first day*, my brother. So, she *invites* me, and then she *cancels* everything. How is this possible?

According to Malik, his girlfriend kept his Dutch residence permit for a while in the hope that Malik would opt for a 'voluntary return' to the Gambia. But a return was certainly not an option for him as he had already invested heavily in this move. Malik saw no other way than to escape and find his own way without this affective relation. Since he was so 'fresh' in the Netherlands, he barely knew anyone beyond the family of his girlfriend. This changed when Saihou gave him my contact details. To my surprise, however, Malik did actually not know my Gambian friend personally. He explained:

> To be honest, no, I do not know this boy. I never spoke to him like face to face. Only now in this situation, I told my brother [a friend] in Switzerland I was in bad condition, and this brother, he is a friend of Saihou, and Saihou could *feel* my story. And he spoke to me, and he said he had a good brother here in Holland. So he connected me to you.

Thus, just as I helped an unknown man, Saihou also assisted someone he had never met before. Earlier established affection is thus not a necessary precondition for social support.

To understand Malik's escape, it is important to note that the Dutch immigration authority (IND) works with a sponsor system, making the partner of the newcomer to the Netherlands to a large part responsible during and after the application procedure of a residence permit. This implies that the partner (in this case Malik's girlfriend) is required to notify any significant changes in the relationship – i.e. the partner is obliged to inform the authorities in case the relationship breaks up and in case the foreign partner is not living any more at the same address. The partner of the newcomer only loses the status of sponsor once a residence permit is withdrawn or once a residence permit of a definite period of time has changed into a residence permit of an indefinite period of time. Not acting according to the obligations of a sponsor (e.g. hiding information or providing misinformation), may have far-reaching, yet different, consequences for both persons in question. The newcomer may lose his/her legal status, the sponsor risks considerable fines and, ultimately, legal prosecution. Furthermore, in cases of violations of the legal requirements, the IND possibly makes the sponsor partly accountable for the costs made in eventual deportation processes (IND 2018). It follows that with these regulations, the state's role in governing mobility enters the private realm of lovers and married couples. This produces 'conjugal regimes' (Groes 2016: 180) that place migrants and European citizens on different levels of hierarchy, especially in relation to legal support and citizenship. Thus, with the breakup of the relationship in this particular case, Malik was likely to lose his legal stay in the Netherlands as soon as the authorities took note of it. Migration apparatuses (Feldman 2012), thus, become tightly hooked up with affective circuits, turning an ex-lover into some kind of immigration authority deciding on someone's legal position. This explains why so many sub-Saharan Africans in Europe experience a sense of physical *and* existential immobility. The former points to the ways in which their whereabouts are heavily controlled in private spheres. The latter is related to the notion of being stalled and not getting ahead in the quest of achieving personhood (Groes 2016). This also explains to a large extent why Malik's relatively smooth entry turned into a rather erratic escape. Finally, it also clarifies why Malik felt heavily surveilled during his act of escape.

After roughly ten minutes I reached the highway again, now with Malik as my passenger. He started to nervously look at the road signs and asked: 'Is this the way to Rotterdam?' When I told him that I lived in a city in the opposite direction, he felt relieved. I reminded him that I also told his ex-girlfriend that I lived in Nijmegen, but Malik was not too worried about that: 'Yes, but she does not know that place. Maybe she can look for me in the station. We have to be careful'. The feeling that he was under surveillance made him not only suspicious about the social environment around us, but also made him think about communication technologies and social media. This was actually the reason why he had switched off his phone while I waited for him at the church – he was afraid that his girlfriend was able to track the location of the telephone once it was turned on again. At the time we arrived at my house, the first thing he wanted to arrange was a new SIM card. The second thing he did was changing his password of Facebook (as his girlfriend had access to the same account). Later I learned that the woman in question was indeed able to locate Malik during his escape by checking the IP address that related to the last time Malik logged in to his Facebook account.

At my home, I introduced Malik to Joëlle and my two-year-old son. While Malik took a shower and washed his jeans, Joëlle prepared some food. I gave him some fresh clothes and Malik called Saihou to ask for his advice what to do next. Saihou thought that Malik was travelling in an irregular way. Therefore, Saihou's advice was to travel without his Gambian passport, and in case of a control, he should apply for asylum. Saihou later texted Malik the number of his contact in Bremen – who appeared to be his sibling, whom I first met some months after this hectic event. Malik, however, had taken his passport with his MVV sticker[6] with him, securing his border passage to Bremen. Thus, my initial concern – and that of Saihou – that Malik's escape involved an unauthorized border crossing was unfounded. The same day I brought Malik to the Nijmegen train station and bought him a train ticket to Bremen. In this German city, he was again assisted by somebody he did not know before – Hamza, the brother of Saihou (sharing the same father).[7]

When I went to visit Hamza in Bremen, he could only spend one day with me since he was preparing his own travels to Norway, the country in which he had lived for over three years.[8] I asked him how he perceived the arrival of Malik and his reply reminded me of my own surprise that Malik had travelled without any luggage:

> The day I come here to pick him up, he passed me by like this [uses his hands to indicate a move of a passer-by]. I thought this is not the man, because he had nothing in his hands you know. I expected him to have a bag like this [points at a bag pack], but he had nothing! I asked him: 'Are you the one who I pick up now? How come? Where is your bag [starts to laugh]?'

The day after his arrival, Hamza brought Malik to a place where he could apply for asylum. Malik asked him to take care of his papers. In order to make an effective asylum claim he had to wipe out all traces of his stay in the Netherlands. From that moment, I did not hear from Malik for about one month, until he sent me a text message from a large asylum shelter in the south-west of Germany. He did not stay long in German asylum spaces though. To both Hamza's and my surprise, he had decided to return to the Netherlands to live again with his girlfriend. Apparently, the couple who had fought in the early stage of their reunification, had found a way to make amends between them.

In June 2016, I revisited Malik in the same village in the Netherlands where I was supposed to pick him up four months previously. Some few months later I also met his girlfriend in person – which was one of the most awkward encounters I have experienced in my academic career. With their reunification, Malik's situation had completely changed compared to the day I first met him. He now held a five-year residence permit, had found a job, and was back in the house he escaped from. However, the fact that his girlfriend had tried to 'block' him and his subsequent sudden escape had left some deeper scars underneath the surface. As we discussed over a beer:

> Now to be honest with you, I don't trust her any more. When I kiss her, I don't kiss her like before, when I hold here, I never hold her like before. So, something has really changed, really. To be honest, I don't know if I leave her. For now, I need to take care of myself first. Then I can maybe leave.

When I revisited Malik nearly two years later, he told me the relationship still lasted – as did the mistrust between the two of them. He commented: 'I know she is checking me. One day I was so angry with her, because she does not trust me at all, if I go to work, then she thinks I am leaving the place, if I work extra hours, she thinks I have run again'.

This act of surveillance in an affective relation reflects a severe power imbalance in intercultural relations (Groes 2016; Cole 2016). Some of my informants ended up as unauthorized migrants after their ex-partners decided to break up. This dimension also produces social scars (for both actors involved) that remain underneath the surface until the moment the sponsor role of the Dutch citizen in the relation is over. Some of my informants felt themselves to be 'free' only after they obtained a residence permit with an indefinite length, or a passport. Early 2018, Malik was in the process of a new round of language and integration tests – if he passed these thresholds, he would be eligible to get a Dutch passport. With the new Dutch passport, his mobility potential would expand considerably in the legal sense. According to the so-called global passport ranking – a list that ranks the power of passports according to the number of countries they give access to – he would move up from place 123 (the Gambia) to place 13 (the Netherlands).[9]

Mobility and Family Life

At first sight, Malik's case above is illustrative for this book, which is somewhat biased towards the mobility processes of young men whose lives in Eurospace seem to be rather untouched by identities and responsibilities related to parenthood. This interpretation, however, is misleading. Malik has three children in the Gambia, two sons and one daughter. He openly struggled with his fatherhood at a distance, especially because he did not want to be like his own father – a Senegalese man who had not paid any attention to Malik, who was raised by his Gambian mother and her relatives. Malik was never part of his father's extended family, and he was not involved in any heritage arrangements. He had actually never seen his father in real life until the sudden moment, a few years ago, when his father was 'looking for him' without any further announcement. What particularly hurt Malik at that time was that his own son saw Malik's father (and thus his grandfather) before Malik actually met him. Malik's disturbed relation with his father was the main reason why Malik chose not to use the name that related to his father's family. This family history was also why it was so painful for him to be so physically far away from his children – according to Malik there was nothing more important in the world than his kids. Two of the three children were born out of a Gambian marriage that still existed. However, he was in doubt as to whether his third child was actually his, as a different woman claimed. During my visit to Malik and his Dutch girlfriend in February 2017, the three of us openly discussed Malik's complicated family situation. Malik expressed a strong wish to move to Senegambia as soon as possible, as he suffered from homesickness. He actually went to see his children the same year. He travelled alone – his girlfriend had work obligations – and spent about one week in Senegal and one week in the Gambia. It was a brief stay, but it meant a lot to him.

Rebalancing Family Life

Spatially scattered family lives in transnational circuits that bind together Africa and Europe are an emerging topic in migration studies (e.g. Mazzucato et al. 2015). In this context of here–there transnationalism (Africa–Europe), it is notable that the physical separation of families and the circulation of children among different (extended) family members is socially accepted (e.g. Poeze and Mazzucato 2014; Neveu Kringelbach 2016). In some instances, it is pointed out that family reunification procedures are actually not favoured by West Africans living in Europe for social and economic reasons (Riccio 2008) – an issue that I also found among some of my informants. However, the fact that physically separated family lives in West Africa are generally accepted, as well as the fact that sometimes a transnational circuit is preferred over a relationship based on co-presence, does not mean that there are no emotional burdens involved in these transnational affective bonds. These burdens are not only related to moral claims by spouses and children, which many of my informants experienced, but also to emotions of homesickness, missing and the quest of being a 'good parent'.

During my visit to the Gambia in 2017, I was able to talk to the wives, brothers, uncles and other relatives and friends of some of my informants in Europe. I spent several days in different compounds, located in different villages, that were partly constructed with the money earned by the movers in Europe. Through these visits I could sense a bit better how people's movements are embedded in different social settings and family aspirations. I talked to Moustapha's spouse (I will introduce Moustapha in Part II of the book) about her wish to have more children, but how due to his lack of papers in Spain her husband was not able to travel to the Gambia. In another village, I was hosted by the wife and uncle of one of my most important interlocutors in Lleida, Pape. Pape's uncle stated that he had always supported Pape's move to Europe, but he also saw the deficit of Pape only being able to marry late. I also discussed with his wife how Pape was missed by her and their children (who spent most of the time in the town of Brikama). The three of us also discussed how the family was concerned about Pape's well-being when he was imprisoned in France. His spouse explained to me that they had not heard from him for a long time during this episode and that they were only informed about his 'problem' by a father of one of Pape's friends who originated from a nearby village and lived in Europe. All these conversations pointed to the different ways transnational connectivity could only partly compensate for the social lacunae that people's movements produce in family settings.

Such a focus on transnational lives between Africa and Europe – that is also represented by the literature – somehow obscures that similar processes take place within Eurospace. In different settings, I noticed how the relational politics of im/mobility unfolded within family spheres (Adey 2006). An interesting case in this respect comes from a Nigerian family living in the Catalan city of Lleida, Nelson and Mandy. This Nigerian couple has two children. Nelson is a church leader in the African community and runs an African shop together with Mandy. Closely related to their shop, over the years Mandy has established an agency in transnational suitcase trade. On her journeys to Nigeria, she transports all kinds of in-kind remittances and brings these products to a small distribution office. From there, her staff transports it to the intended address. Whereas travellers are usually entitled to bring two suitcases, Mandy has a special deal with Air Maroc that allows her to bring three to four suitcases on her travels. Her customers pay 5 euros per kg to get their 'stuff' transported from Europe to Nigeria. In reverse direction, 1 kg of cargo costs 6 euros. Many customers, including owners of African shops, ask her to bring specific ingredients, herbs, textile or cosmetics from Africa to Europe. In this way, Mandy's activities form an important infrastructure for transnational affective circuits to materialize.

During my visits to Lleida I hardly had any chance to speak with Mandy, as she was almost always on her way to Nigeria when I made my way to their African shop. In the light of her highly mobile life between Africa and Europe, Nelson functioned as the stable ground that enabled his wife to be continuously on the move. He once stated: 'If she is around I would be a little bit more mobile'. This indicates that the mobility of some immobilizes others (Adey 2006). This also emphasizes that the restrictions to one's mobility as a result of family life are certainly not only a female phenomenon. As the Cameroonian man Franck also highlighted after his daughter was born: 'Well, I can't go out of Germany with the baby for now, but I like movement. So getting a baby can hold somebody'.

Interestingly, when I talked to Nelson and his daughter about their future plans, they stated that Mandy had started to explore the possibility of moving to the UK, which would of course have severe consequences for the rest of the family. Such a move requires a lot of negotiation of family relations, which may indeed creates frictions. To illustrate this, I will further discuss the case of July – the talented and mobile Nigerian woman whom I assisted in her job application process to one of the U.K'.s universities. Once one of her applications in the UK appeared to be successful, July started to feel both excited and nervous about her future move. As stated before, her several moves to London helped her to mentally prepare for her new life in this metropolis. During various conversations spread over three years, she emphasized that she had to carefully negotiate her move to the UK with her Dutch husband, who preferred to stay in the Netherlands: 'It is not an individual decision because it also has consequences for Paul and for my son. It is a lot of balancing, you understand. Ohh you cannot know the many hours we were discussing this issue. For hours and hours we have been discussing it. Fighting even [laughs]! Ohh, we have been fighting too much'.

Initially the married couple decided to let their son stay in the Netherlands, as he grew up in Dutch society and it would be an especially rupturing experience for him when he had to adopt to the social and institutional environment in London (a concern that was particularly related to schooling). With regard to this, several informants with children in Europe emphasized that having children indeed reduced their flexibility and mobility potential. Later though, the couple decided it was best for the nine-year-old boy to move with his mother to London. This, however, caused multiple practical concerns for July. According to her, it particularly complicated her search for suitable housing since potential landlords 'started to freeze' once she mentioned to them that she was bringing her child. When she had finally found a – shared – apartment, she still had to move out again because of her child. Her flat-mate – a Romanian woman – continuously complained about the actions of a playful nine-year-old boy. Due to this stressful situation, July decided to leave. In this hectic time of finding a replacement, the 'balancing' between her and her husband – as July phrased it – was definitely not over, as she reflected after a stay of seven months in London:

> You have to find a way to deal with it, in a way that does not harm your family. I think for Paul it is also quite difficult, you know. He tells me yesterday, while we were talking that – my family – that is not how I wanted it to be, I just feel that he felt alone and he felt like the family is scattered. And I said, 'Look, that is also new, with a lot of questions', and so on. And it just makes you *wonder*, 'Is it all worth like that?' Yes! And then, yea ... There is of course a lot of travelling you know ... It is quite [hesitates] difficult ... That is why I am asking myself all the time ... '*Am I doing the right thing*? Is there a way to go back there, and do what I can?' ... Sometimes I just don't want to think about it because it is just that I don't have the answers.

During this part of our conversation I felt her doubts and uncertainties. I responded that one only knows in the end whether the result was worth all effort. Thereupon July particularly stressed that she doubted whether her move to London would also benefit her son. In this context, mobility becomes a way to rebalance a scattered family life, but at the same time this harms the process of regrounding, as July continued:

> What we try to do, at least what we have done until now, is to use the chance when Chris [her child] has a holiday. For me, until now, I have this job here, which is quite flexible, I can work at home ... three days I can ... When Chris has a holiday then we can go, in other words, we have done until now. Well, the last time I just thought, 'We are not *here* [in London] and we are not *there* [in the Netherlands], especially for *him* [their son Chris]'. In the holidays, when you have time, then you can get to know the place [London], and you can get to know the people, but then we are *gone!* We are then gone for maybe ten days, because then, when we are in X [a middle-sized city of the Netherlands], then it is the time also to connect with people. So, for ourselves, we think like: 'Look we cannot do this every holiday, that we come over'. So, I told him [her spouse Paul] the next holiday: 'We at least stay here and see what we can do!' And, Paul can only come of course when he has holidays ... He has his job and he has his gigs [as a musician]. So he has to be able to move at a time when he has a break ... That is the difficulty we have all the time. And so, this holiday, I say: 'No, I am not going anywhere, let us just stay here'. He can't come, so.

After this reflection, she remained silent for a few seconds. I commented: 'Wow, that is intense July'. After another silence, she continued:

> Yes, it is not easy sometimes. But, like I said, it is an ongoing story in my mind. But for Paul, a lot of moving to the UK – and I understand that very well! – is quite difficult. Having moved myself I know how it is when you put it that way, even practically, he has his job, he has his pension, you know. So it is also quite difficult. He thinks it can be easy, since I just came over there, but where to start from? I know how it is.

July's illustrations remind us that social ties – particularly when these concern love relationships and children – are in the first place factors that keep people in their places (Faist 2000). An eventual move in Eurospace has far-reaching consequences for the ways affective relations evolve over time. It is indeed about motion within motion (Vigh 2009) – a continuous process of unfolding emotions.

Lost Europe I

There are different graduations of loss in affective circuits. One may lose a social bond because people dissociate from each other, or one simply lost the other's contact details. Some lost contacts are repairable by means of network work and social massaging, others are considered permanent losses. Evidently, the most definite losses are related to decease. Over the years, I have seen intense emotions related to lives lost. It is a rather bitter fact that the politics of mobility (Hyndmann 1997) is oftentimes best articulated in those times of mourning. This was for instance the case for the Gambian brothers Dawda and Yahya when their father passed away in their Gambian village in October 2015. Dawda needed to arrange some practical issues related to work in the Netherlands, but he could easily and instantly travel to the Gambia to be present at the series of funeral ceremonies. Yahya – who at that time had been in Italy for two years – did not have the same right to travel back to his country of origin, and he expressed a feeling of inferiority for not being able to honour his father at this crucial family occasion. Decease, thus, is for many movers indeed related to their less privileged position regarding societal incorporation and its related mobility opportunities (Bird 2018). The unequal distribution of travel rights is an important reason why in many parts of West Africa funerals have increasingly become transnationalized. Mazzucato, Kabki and Smith (2006), for instance, have documented how funerals in Ghana have turned into multi-sited occasions involving not only considerable financial flows across borders, but also simultaneous services in different nation states. This enables people who are not able to travel to the 'real' ceremony in Africa to still be present at the funeral of their beloved ones.[10]

This combination of deep grievance and the politics of mobility may raise existential questions for the people experiencing it. To understand this, we turn to the story of André[11] – a Cameroonian man whom I first met in Morocco ten years ago. In his orange winter jacket, André approached me to give me a strong hug. I noticed how he had visibly aged, and I remembered how he had laughed about me having aged when he saw me during our first Skype video call, roughly seven years after we met each other in Oujda. In Oujda, he had lived in the forest around the university campus for months, waiting for his chance to reach Europe. It was not his time, however. His several attempts to make the 'final jump' failed, and he decided to go back to Cameroon instead. There, he reconnected to the urban economy of Yaoundé, got married and became a father. After some years, however, his European dream seduced him once more to leave his country. He travelled to Turkey together with a female friend – Michelle – with whom he had grown up. Before they embarked the plane to Istanbul in 2015, they dressed up nicely since it was a day of celebration for them. André said about this moment: 'Taking an airplane is like glory [for us]. And for you, taking an airplane is like taking a bicycle'. By emphasizing the glory for him and the normality of travelling by plane for people like me, André just gave me one of the most illustrative quotes pointing at the polarization of mobility potential across the globe, produced and warranted by global mobility regimes (Glick Schiller and Salazar 2013).

Once André had arrived in Istanbul, he started working long hours in the city's textile industry, while also following a biblical education programme to live up to his aspiration to become a pastor one day. In October 2015, after a few months in Istanbul, André's wife gave birth to their second child in Cameroon. When the news reached him, André was euphoric – but he was caught in this euphoric moment in solitude since he was unable to travel to his family to celebrate this moment with them. Moreover, with the birth of his second child and its related positive emotions, the pressure on his shoulders to make something out of this adventurous project soon became heavier. In spring 2016, he once referred to the affective pressures as *chamboulement* (discombobulated) – a reference to the disordering or upsetting dimension of this relation. The transnational relationship between André and his wife deteriorated, and finally collapsed some five months after the birth of their son. André felt disorientated. The divorce, however, was not the only affective hardship he had to endure. A few months after he had reached Greece in the summer of 2016 by means of an unauthorized border crossing, some more bad news reached him from Cameroon.

I had not seen the Facebook message of André informing his contacts about the terrible loss of his son. The young baby had passed away somewhere on the way to a Yaoundé hospital. The few telephone calls we had in this period of time were filled with tears, mourning and silences. André felt humiliated for not being able to be present at his son's funeral. It was an unbearable pain. For weeks, André did not go out. The mourning caused a terrible and permanent headache and he simply could not bear daylight anymore. For his painkillers and tranquilizers, he relied on the people of a small office of Médicins Sans Frontières, housed on the third floor of a rather anonymous apartment in Athens. This was one of the few places where he could speak French – which was incredibly important for him in this devastating period of time.

André is a religious man, and before this devastating news reached him, he had taken up the role of spreading the word of God as a pastor through his weekly biblical seminars in Athens. He now turned to God to find explanations for his unbearable loss: what had he done wrong in life? Why did he deserve this? At times, he related the loss of his son to his European project. His departure from Cameroon, his suffering, was meant to actually benefit the family. He was the one who was supposed to suffer in order to reduce the suffering of his family. He had made his way to Europe – although he openly questioned whether Greece was part of the 'real Europe' for its deep economic and humanitarian crises, an observation that is shared among other migrants (e.g. Cabot 2014). At least he had fought his way in so far, however, once he had reached European territory, he saw it all go wrong. Once there, he heard that the reasons for his departure – becoming a respectful husband and father – had suddenly vanished in thin air. He did not only feel lost in Europe, he had actually lost Europe as the entire foundation of his being there collapsed.

Concluding Notes: 'Connections behind Borders'

This chapter has emphasized the importance of social connectivity in the intra-EU mobility processes under study. Without the support that runs through affective circuits, many movers would not have been able to reach the places where they now live. In addition, affective circuits produce and shape expectations, imaginaries and, hence, itineraries and destinations. As such, finding ways is an endeavour whereby the spatial dimension cannot be separated from the social dimension of movement.

This central role of connectivity in mobility processes was tellingly stressed by Lamin when we discussed potential titles for this book. His suggestion was to entitle it *Connecting Gambians behind the Border*. This proposed title is not only a great illustration of the connectivity/mobility tango that I have highlighted in this chapter. Even more so, the carefully chosen 'behind' hints at the ways in which connections destabilize and circumvent borders, thereby creating new avenues for mobility. The guest house of Doudou, described in the opening vignette to this part of the book, illustrates this point. It is part of an invisible and flexible social infrastructure that consists of intergenerational relations in the countries of origin, diasporic communities in major European cities and travelling collectives (such as Lamin's 'team') that find their ways in different directions.

However, connections do not automatically work out how one prefers. Apart from support, affective circuits also involve efforts, investments, control, boundaries and power inequalities. That is the main reason why I started this chapter with Vigh's notions of social navigation. Movers need to massage relations, downgrade expectations, disconnect from hindering contacts and, at times, deal with unforeseen losses. These endeavours are all understood as navigational practices through which people try to find ways by means of their social connections. As Vigh (2009) underlines, these dynamic practices are hard to reconcile with any concrete geographical terminology. His use of the word 'terrain' is therefore somewhat infelicitous.[12] For all their movement, (dis)connections, care, blockages and frictions, such circuits are neither stable networks nor grounded terrains with clear nodes, stable lines and fixed locations. These circuits fare to a large extent on a 'floating topography' (Simone 2019) that – as we will see in the following two chapters – intersects with other webs of relations that facilitate and/or hinder movement.

NOTES

1. Vigh argues that the instability of social environments is articulated in, but not unique to, West African societies (in his case Guinea Bissau). As he (2009: 430) states: 'All social environments are in perpetual motion, yet some move at a slower pace than others, so that people have time to internalize and routinize change'.
2. Likewise, some scholars have found ways to reframe conventional notions of kin and refer to the energies and frictions or 'kin-work' involved in this mutuality of being (e.g. Andrikopoulos 2017; Neveu Kringelbach 2016).
3. Yahya and Dawda shared the same father but had different mothers. Polygamy is common in the Gambia (see also Kea 2013).
4. Based on the MAFE survey – resulting in a quantitative database on African migration to Europe – it has been concluded that roughly 10 per cent of Senegalese migrants in Europe relocate across borders inside the EU (Toma and Castagnone 2015). This concerns residential relocations, and does not include more mundane movements that are also included in this book. Thus, the study of Toma and Castagnone is about onward migration, and not about mobility. Some other studies suggest that this estimation of the MAFE survey is rather low. In the case of Malta, for instance, it is estimated that only 30 per cent of the 18,000 migrants who arrived between 2002 and 2013 have remained on the island (Skov 2016).
5. This empirical illustration also appeared in Schapendonk (2018b).
6. MVV stands for Machtiging Voorlopig Verblijf, which means 'authorization for a temporary stay'. Technically speaking this is not a residence permit, but an obligatory preparatory phase. Malik actually entered the Netherlands with an MVV sticker in his passport (with both the date of entry and the date of expiration). This grants access to the Schengen zone for ninety days. In the first weeks after his entry in the Netherlands he was eligible to collect his residence permit, being valid for a maximum of five years. This is a separate pass, however, and this pass was kept by Malik's girlfriend.
7. The fact that Saihou and Hamza have the same father does not necessarily mean that they were raised in the same environment. Hamza actually spent most of the time in the Casamance region of Senegal, while Saihou was raised in the urban outskirts of Serekunda.
8. Hamza himself had also a dynamic mobility history in Europe. He entered Europe on the basis of a business visa, which he had obtained by paying a broker in the Gambia. He arrived in Spain, and within three weeks he moved to Norway. There he applied for asylum. He never received long-term residence rights there, but they gave him 'a small paper' that allowed him to work. He worked for a ship company for roughly three years. Then he started to realize that his situation in Norway did not allow him to legally travel to other countries, including the Gambia. His contacts in Spain informed him that regularization procedures in Spain were rather relaxed, and thereupon he 'left everything behind in Norway' and moved southwards. He paid 450 euros to a man who said he could arrange an identity loan (see Andrikopoulos 2017), meaning he would lend him someone else's papers. The

documents he received were fake. The man 'ran away with the money', and once the Spanish authorities found out Hamza held fraudulent documents, they put him in detention (in 2013). This was the same time his little brother arrived in Italy. Due to his detention, however, he was unable to communicate with him. After his release, he actually managed to find work through a similar process of identity loan. He aimed, however, for a more stable legal position and decided to move to Germany and apply for asylum there, mid 2015.

9. According to this passport index a Dutch passport provides visa-free access to 123 different countries, whereas a Gambian passport only provides visa-free access to 45 countries (retrieved 13 October 2018 from http://www.passportindex.org).
10. Likewise, a Ghanaian pastor I befriended in the Bijlmer area of Amsterdam stressed a sense of transnational community when we discussed the issue of simultaneous funeral ceremonies in Ghana and the Netherlands. He thereby also stressed that this has broadened the financial opportunities related to funeral services.
11. Because I was unhappy with the pseudonym I gave him in my Ph.D. dissertation, I decided to give him a different pseudonym in this book.
12. Vigh (2009: 435–36) articulates that the notions of 'environment' and 'terrain' must not be interpreted as 'earthbound' and 'static'. He in fact only uses these words in dynamic terms. Nevertheless, in my reading, the terrain metaphor is difficult to disconnect from a solid geography of the earth's surface.

CHAPTER
3

Navigating Webs of Facilitation/Control

The second force field that requires careful navigation by the movers in question is formed by intermediating actors who facilitate or hinder mobility processes. While realms of facilitation and control are usually strictly separated from each other in discussions on cross-border mobility, I start from the opaque boundaries; the shifting roles of actors that characterize this relational force field (see also Gammeltoft-Hansen and Nyberg Sørenson 2013; Cranston, Schapendonk and Spaan 2018). As so vividly portrayed in Ruben Andersson's (2014) book *Illegality, Inc: Clandestine Migration and the Business of Bordering Europe*, the so-called 'migration industry' is not a homogeneous field of actors sharing the same goal, but rather a networked entity in which state actors and mobility facilitators constantly blend into each other through their practices in ritualized border games. It is a force field that binds together commercialization, humanitarianism and securitization (Nyberg Sørenson 2012), smugglers and border guards (Andersson 2014), migration brokers and aspiring movers (Alpes 2011). At times, these webs of facilitation/control are deeply entangled with movers' affective circuits (e.g. Belloni 2016b).

This chapter thus approaches the African–European web of facilitation/control as one fuzzy mobility regime that facilitates some mobilities while hindering others (Glick Schiller and Salazar 2013). Starting from this notion, the following question emerges: how do movers make sense out of this blurry landscape of multiple actors, suspicion, dubious roles and vague responsibilities? How do they navigate mobility regimes? To answer these questions, I take into account mobility processes on the African as well as European continent. This chapter does not aim to highlight the 'enormous geographic scope' of mobility regimes (Feldman 2012: 79) per se, but rather it seeks to illustrate how this relational force field affects wayfinding practices and experiences. In so doing, it articulates how movers *are turned into* migrants through intermediating practices of mobility controllers and mobility facilitators.

Webs of Facilitation/Control

Starting from a de-migranticized notion of African mobility (see Introduction) makes one sensitive to the ways 'migrants' are actually artefacts. One does not start from the natural difference of migrancy (Dahinden 2016), but is able to identify and unpack the situations and practices that migranticize individuals. Migranticization is then a practice that articulates otherness and outsiderness, and in Eurospace it oftentimes expresses the moral obligation of belonging and assimilation. The migrant is an archetype, and the im-migrant is the nation state's ideal type (Favell 2008). These archetypes and ideal types are actively reproduced through policy discourses and practices. In the framework of Europe's migration apparatus, Feldman (2012: 14) writes: 'Policy officials abstract an ideal "migrant" out of these flows and then codify it in policy writing, establish it as normal and reassess its value in relation to changes in the processes to be managed'. Similarly, Andersson (2014: 100–7) describes how border guards search for typical migrant attributes (e.g. rucksacks) and appearances in African–European borderlands in order to identify candidates for the clandestine passage. In the context of the latter, Malik – the Gambian man who escaped from his affective relationship in the Netherlands – felt highly uncomfortable for having no serious baggage at the moment he embarked the train in the Netherlands to reach Germany. Were there any control, they certainly would pick him for his appearances and question the details of his train journey. For Malik, his lack of baggage was a sign of a lack of a proper travel story. This made him more nervous, as this probably made him a better fit for the image of the stereotypical migrant. Similar processes of abstracting and producing specific types of movers are also induced by actors of mobility facilitation. As we will see, webs of facilitation/control shape destinations as well as mobile identities (Cranston, Schapendonk and Spaan 2018). Before we get there, however, I will introduce Shakur, the last of the six young men whom I was able to follow after having met him in Italy in April 2014.

Shakur

In a period of four years, Shakur saw them all leave. He noticed how his friend Saihou moved between Switzerland, Italy, Germany and the Gambia.

He knew perfectly well about Lamin's tactics for living in-between Italy and Switzerland. He also knew that Omar found some work during his asylum procedures in Germany. He even saw himself being bypassed by Mamadou and other JJCs ('Journey Just Come', see Chapter 2) who had managed to obtain humanitarian protection that helped them to cross European borders (Borri 2017). He observed how Yahya and Omar made considerable progress through the same job he once had. Their progress stood in stark contrast with his own situation, that had stagnated from the first day he entered the reception centre in Liguria. Compared to the wider 'team' – the group of roughly twenty-five young African men who stayed in contact with each other since they arrived in Italy – Shakur was definitely the exception. Since their collective transfer from Naples, he had never left the reception centre. He had never seen any progress in terms of legal status. He was instead confronted with a new state of involuntary immobility – a new state of 'sitting' – that he had actually tried to escape from when he left his country of origin.

In April 2014, I wandered together with Yahya, Omar and Shakur through the area around the city port, not far from their 'Caritas camp'. We passed a couple of bars that, according to the three young Gambian men, were not particularly hospitable towards Africans. When we found a better place, we had a long conversation that mainly reflected on their trans-Saharan travels through Senegal, Mali, Burkina Faso, Niger and Libya. Although they did not travel together at this stage of their journeys, their collective memory informed me that they had faced multiple occasions at which state officials, soldiers, drivers or bandits asked for, or simply took, their money. Generally, however, it was very difficult to identify what kind of actor harmed them because, as Shakur told me in detail, the mobility facilitators closely liaised (either wilfully or otherwise) with the custom officers and policemen who stop and control the movers at the countless checkpoints in the region. Transporters frequently turn into robbers along the trans-Saharan pathway, often with the help of soldiers or other authority agents. Out of frustration, Shakur raised his voice during our talk in the Italian bar and stated out loud: 'They are making money from us, they are making money from us! The drivers and the police officers and the soldiers'. The conclusion of the three men regarding the facilitators and controllers of mobility was straightforward: 'They are all the same mafia!' Thereupon, Omar added: 'That is why I call it ... human trafficking. All of them are working together!'

However difficult the situation, Shakur had always seemed able to find ways to escape. Gunned robbers threatening him and violent policemen detaining him had slackened his movements, but they had been unable to block him. His improvisation skills had proven to be a vital asset to avoid extra payments, violence and moments of entrapment. He explained to me, for instance, how his convoy of trucks was once put to a halt in the desert by the truck drivers in order to obtain more money from the travellers. After Shakur and other passengers were offloaded, a heated debate followed between themselves and the migration facilitators/robbers. In this hectic situation, Shakur and some others refused to pay and were set aside. While the group was watched by two gunmen, Shakur found a way to get permission to pray. He bowed down and pretended to pray, and during this performance he saw another truck approaching the scene. The gunmen were distracted by the arriving truck and in this split-second Shakur ran to jump onto the truck and continued his overland journey. He escaped without paying extra money.

Shakur reached Libya during the civil war that followed the collapse of the Ghaddafi regime. Due to the conflict, he could not reach out to his family for a relatively long time as most communication facilities were cut. During this long period of silence, his family was incredibly worried, and some even thought that Shakur had died. It was through a friend, who actually had managed to reach Shakur through telephone from Niamey (Niger), that his family was informed about Shakur's whereabouts. Shakur would never forget the relief in his father's voice the moment he first spoke to him again.

In the Libyan war zone, Shakur was confronted on a daily basis with a high level of threat and insecurity. During the conflict, sub-Saharan Africans ran the risk of being randomly killed since rebels generally believed they were supportive of the Ghaddafi regime.[1] Once, when waiting for Libyans to pick them up for petty jobs alongside a main road – which was a common practice among sub-Saharan Africans in Libya – he saw how a car passed by and, instead of recruiting workers, the Libyans inside the car started to shoot at the group of black men. Two of his colleagues were shot dead, but Shakur survived. Evidently, these traumatic experiences did not leave him untouched. In some way, however, they served to feed his steadfast determination to make something out of his life. With this persistency, and with Lamin, Saihou, Omar, Amat and Yahya, in 2013, he embarked a boat heading to Lampedusa.

Borders, Facilitators and Predators along West African Pathways

For the first legs of the trans-Saharan pathway, Shakur and his co-travellers relied on the conventional transport systems and convivial social infrastructures that make West Africa a mobile region (Bolay 2017; De Bruijn, Van Dijk and Foeken 2001; Choplin and Lombard 2010). It is therefore of crucial importance to approach West Africa not only as a region with diverse cultures of mobility, but also as a region in which mobility is both politically accepted and stimulated. Like the EU, the Economic Community of West African States (ECOWAS) allows for free mobility of people across its internal state borders.[2]

It is telling that the supranational politics of ECOWAS are often ignored in discussions on the EU's interventions to reduce cross-border mobility in this region of the world. It is well documented how the EU border has gradually shifted southwards. Initially this was accomplished through migration deals with the so-called 'transit countries' neighbouring the EU's outer border, such as Morocco and Tunisia. Later, particularly between 2006 and 2008, when West African *aventuriers* started to depart from the Mauritanian, Senegalese and Gambian coasts to reach the Canary Islands, the EU started to intervene with Frontex missions in the Atlantic Ocean. Recently, the Sahelian–Saharan space has been transformed into an important zone for EU's migration management, which is primarily based on two policy nexus: migration–security and migration–development (Feldman 2012; Nyberg Sørensen 2012). The European Council started 'civilian missions' in Mali and Niger in order to combat security threats such as terrorism and organized crime. In May 2015, the 'fight against irregular migration' was added to the list of objectives for the Nigerien mission called EUCAP Sahel Niger (European Council 2015b). Consequently, the city of Agadez, a major mobility hub on the road to Libya, became one of the main targets for such interventions. The installation of an outpost in Agadez and the new goal of combatting irregular migration were probably the most important reasons why, in late 2015, the budget for EUCAP Sahel Niger was doubled from €9.8 million to €18.4 million (European Council 2015a). This renders the defence sector one of the winners of the continuously expanding mobility regime between Africa and Europe (Andersson 2016).

The EU interventions are not only at odds with culturally accepted practices and the commonality of everyday mobility in West Africa, they are also hard to reconcile with ECOWAS regulations that have existed for decades. It is particularly remarkable that the EU considers the Nigerien city of Agadez as the epicentre of its anti-migration interventions. In a way, this city is located at a geological–psychological boundary – as it is the place where tarmacked roads end and change into fluid desert routes – but it is not very close to the end of the free mobility zone of ECOWAS. Thus, an African *aventurier* is likely to be confronted in Agadez with the EU's borders and the anti-smuggling laws that have recently been installed in Niger, while at the same time making use of ECOWAS regulations of free movement. Furthermore, the recent EU interventions have had a devastating effect on the urban economy of Agadez, destroying livelihoods that have directly or indirectly been related to trans-Saharan mobility (Molenaar et al. 2017). It is important to note that this mobility corridor is first and foremost a corridor driven by age-old trade networks, facilitating intercultural exchange between, and circulations of, populations in the Sahel and North Africa (Brachet, Choplin and Pliez 2011). Goods trading between the two sides of the Sahara has always been the main activity, and with these flows of goods has come the transportation of people.

With the recent increasing demand of transport services in Agadez, which was indeed related to circulations of labourers between West Africa and Libya, as well as irregular migration to Europe, *agences de courtage* (brokerage services) were legally created in the mid 1990s. These transport agencies (which were often established by ex-rebels who signed a peace agreement with the Nigerien state) serve as the wayfarers of the desert space. It follows that in this post-conflict period the facilitation of the trans-Saharan mobility of people has not been targeted as an illegal or clandestine practice by the Nigerien state (Brachet 2018). In fact, many state agencies have directly profited from this mobility by, for instance, offering military protection to convoys in exchange for considerable sums of money.[3] Many of these mobility facilitating services have predominantly been based on trust and good track records (Belloni 2016a). Once Omar arrived in the city of Agadez, for instance, one of his Facebook contacts directed him to a particular Nigerien mobility facilitator. According to Omar, this man had been active for more than twenty-five years in the trans-Saharan mobility sector. He entered the 'ghetto' of this facilitator – a place where travellers are grouped together according to their nationality or language and their mode of travel. He then paid 150,000 CFA francs (approximately 200 euros) for his passage and waited until the next Monday, when his four-wheel-drive jeep departed to a desert town in Libya. For Omar, his connecting service was as regular as a conventional bus service with a clear time schedule and, so far, without any further signs of exploitation. However, induced by EU interventions, Nigerien policies have been profoundly transformed. They reframed the trans-Saharan facilitation of mobility from an illicit practice to an illegal practice. Thus, as Brachet (2018) rightly claims, smugglers, like migrants, are oftentimes also artefacts of policymaking. As a result, since 2016, Nigerien authorities have started to arrest mobility facilitators and accuse them of being involved in human smuggling. As a consequence of the EU's intervention in Agadez, movers are likely to become 'more illegal' even in cases when they are physically still very far away from Europe.[4] Due to a productive mélange of social profiling and the EU's induced policy changes, movers become migranticized and turn into candidates for the 'clandestine passage'.

However, many of my informants who passed this road prior to these latest EU interventions in Agadez already described a major change in the Saharan space between Niger and Libya. Any attempt to distinguish actors of facilitation and actors of control in this particular space fails on the basis of the stories they shared with me. As Shakur exclaimed, facilitators and controllers of mobility are just part of 'the same mafia'. Following Shakur's narrative, the most fruitful distinction we could make in this context is that between *predators* and *scavengers*. 'Predators' are those actors who rely on verbal and physical violence to profit from cross-border mobility. Their methods include assault, rape, illegal detention, hostage, beatings and threatening at gunpoint. Whether these predators are state officials, co-movers, employers, rebels, transporters, a bunch of criminals or violent opportunists, is often difficult to identify. The same actor may wear the heads of 'captor' and 'saviour' or 'guide' and 'policeman' at the same time (Triulzi 2012). Consequently, the question as to which type of actor is doing the harm hardly seems to matter to the movers in question. The priority is to escape those practices as soon as possible and to prevent physical and financial damages as best you can. Next to these violent actors, there are less violent 'scavengers' who seek ways to skim funds from the movers. This group may again include policemen and border guards who are present at the innumerable roadblocks, but also hostesses, *coxeurs* (bus boys), employers and traders. These scavengers postulate bribes, execute illegal taxations, change their services, heighten their prices and possibly start acts of misguidance once they have identified candidates for clandestine migration to Europe. But then again, lines are thin in this web of liaisons. A single and rather innocent act of misguidance by a *coxeur* may direct you into the hands of a violent predator. Movers are then urged to seek ways to escape.

Escape II

When Lamin came to visit me in the Netherlands, we once again discussed his experience in the Saharan space. We had these conversations mainly to prepare ourselves for a joint guest lecture at a Dutch high school. We anticipated what to share and what not to share with the pupils of this school, who were around fourteen years old. How much of the reality of violence and predators could they handle? How much was Lamin willing to share?

Lamin crossed Senegal and Mali without considerable problems. However, he had his first period of detention not in Niger or Libya, but in Burkina Faso. At one of the roadblocks on the road to Niger he refused to pay the requested bribe. Together with a group of travellers he was taken to a police station, where different groups were separated according to their nationality – a regular act of migranticization. The authorities jailed them to force them to pay the requested sum of money. The authorities referred to the Gambia's dictator by saying: 'Jammeh told us no one should pass here'. To describe the situation in Niger on the way to Agadez, Lamin repeatedly referred to 'the collaboration' – a term that could appear as a title of a John Grisham book. The collaboration starts when the drivers ask 'double money' for the journey to be able to bribe the police at the checkpoints. But after the numerous checkpoints, the money the travellers had paid appeared to be not enough. The drivers and the police urged individual travellers to pay again and again. According to Lamin, there were protests, but they had little effect. If protests were too loud, you could easily end up being detained again.

In Agadez, movers could connect to different mobility facilitators and several travel options appeared to them. One could opt for a direct journey to Sabha, or a journey with several stopovers. One could choose between a four-by-four Toyota jeep and a less comfortable but cheaper place on a large freight truck. Like so many African movers, Lamin opted for a direct journey to Sabha by four-wheel drive, and before this trip took place he was lodged in a 'ghetto' in Agadez. The time spent in this ghetto was not easy, but he considered it mainly as a waiting time 'for the desert to get calm'. Although the price for his direct journey to Sabha was slightly higher compared to other travel options, he presumed this was a more secure passage. He crossed the path of the Sahara Desert and arrived in Sabha. Once in this Libyan desert city 'the game starts' – as Lamin phrased it. Upon entering this southern Libyan city, he was directed to a place locally known as Ali's Ghetto – a place ran by a Ghanaian man. Lamin described it as a horrible place, and with a serious voice he emphasized: 'Joris, really, it is not only police or Arabs that harm us, it can be migrants too. Sometimes migrants are the real criminals'. After he met the same boys in Ali's Ghetto whom he had met before in Agadez, he sensed that there was a 'direct connection' between the two places. He felt that there was a key role reserved for the taxi driver at the Sabha station – he must have been instructed by one of the drivers to take him directly to Ali's Ghetto. Lamin's description of Ali's Ghetto made me tremble. It was a place of serious physical abuse, where people had to pay unbelievably high prices for food, where travellers were put next to each other like 'firewood', and where people were ransomed through the same affective circuits that I have described above. As Belloni (2016b) argues, relationships between smugglers and migrants are often wrongfully isolated from a wider social context. During this period of imprisonment, Lamin found no other solution than to involve his Swiss foster parent, Pappy. There was, however, a risk involved. If those in charge of 'the ghetto' would find out that Pappy was a 'white man' they would probably charge him with a higher ransom. Lamin made his emotional phone call and managed to hide the real identity of Pappy by telling the 'Sabha people' it was a Gambian brother in Switzerland who transferred the money. This hectic moment of Lamin does not only underline how affective circuits intersect with mobility industries, it also highlights the politics of escape. Those who do not have the right contacts in affective circuits are most likely to get stuck in places like Ali's Ghetto. Lamin met someone who stated to have stayed in Ali's Ghetto for more than a year.

In Libya, confrontations with predators were multifold for Lamin, Shakur and their co-movers. Some reported being kidnapped at gunpoint on regular workdays in Libya, others referred to the moments that they escaped from detention camps. Lamin knew cases in which groups of Africans who were kept inside a ghetto attempted to break down the 'kidnappers hall'. He also referred to 'shoot-outs' where the kidnappers opened fire on runaway migrants and mentioned animal-like sounds made by people that were simply beyond his imagination. These sounds came from co-movers who were obviously tortured. The moment that Lamin left Ali's Ghetto was, unfortunately, not the end of the violence he faced. After he had arrived in Tripoli, one day, he and a Ghanaian 'colleague' faced a checkpoint with military people. One of the soldiers targeted the gun at them and asked them to pay money. Initially, Lamin refused, but when he saw the face of his 'colleague' he realized he was seriously in danger. This incident, and particularly the rapidity with which the danger revealed itself to him, registered a deep impact on Lamin. He once recalled this moment and told me that 'It felt like you can expect death every minute'. Soon after this intense moment of fear, he went to a cybercafé to get in touch with some of his contacts in the Gambia, but he could not type a word since tears were falling on the keyboard.

The Mediterranean Passage

From a trajectory perspective, it is not very insightful to start from a harsh distinction of regular versus irregular movers. Many informants have entered Eurospace in authorized ways, but have had to deal with precarious legal statuses soon afterwards. The ways they have entered varied considerably: some entered through family reunification programmes, others entered as students or came with tourist visa. The other way around is equally true: one may enter Europe through irregular channels, but receive residence after a considerable period of time. With regard to the latter, I came across a variety of unauthorized border crossings with which my informants managed to enter the EU. Some used lookalike strategies and borrowed or bought passports of others to enter Eurospace. Others climbed the fences of Ceuta or Melilla in order to reach Spanish territory. Even in terms of the boat passages across the Mediterranean Sea, one can identify a wide variety of travel modes. Some reached the Canary Islands after drifting in *pirogues* (wooden fisher boats) across the Atlantic Ocean for more than a week. Others embarked Zodiac boats on the northern coast of Morocco in order to arrive at Spanish southern shores. Some informants reached Greece by 'balloon boats' from Turkey. From Libya, informants embarked generally larger rubber boats carrying eighty to a hundred people. As for the facilitation of these boat passages, there were different degrees of freedom involved as well as different risks, different prices, different insurance mechanisms and different intermediating actors. I have heard stories about movers who arranged their Mediterranean passage by themselves and I have heard stories about actors who to a large extent relied on violence and force to facilitate the crossing, particularly in Libya (e.g. McMahon and Sigona 2018). I have heard testimonies of people who lost considerable sums of money due to acts of betrayal or after a failed crossing as well as of people who made use of a guaranteed crossing, meaning that one pays the facilitators only the full price after actually reaching European grounds. And in many cases, I have heard how individual movers tried different means of entry and how their navigation of the mobility industry was a process of learning by doing.

Yahya, Lamin, Omar, Saihou, Amat and Shakur all spent different periods of time in Tripoli. Again, the politics of mobility are reflected in the temporal dimension of travel. This is particularly important in the light of the level of exposure to serious threats. Omar and Yahya had rather fast transfer periods of at most a couple of weeks in Tripoli, while Shakur was less lucky and spent more than one year in Libya. Referring to this difference, Omar stated: 'I had a good connection, I did not stay long like Shakur, because my family paid through the connection man, I did not stay long, maybe one week. I was lucky because I could pass faster faster, because the connection man only needed ten more people on the boat'. The young men from Senegambia had not met in the Libyan capital before the moment they found themselves at the Libyan shores, together with some eighty to one hundred other African candidates for the boat passage (their estimates of the number of passengers varied considerably). Around eleven o'clock in the morning, the six young men were picked up from different places and brought to 'the river' – a euphemistic name for the Mediterranean Sea that is commonly used among my informants. Their Mediterranean passage was arranged by a web of middlemen, with two central figures – a Gambian connection man who recruited Yahya, Lamin, Omar, Saihou, Shakur and Amat for the boat passage, and a Libyan man called Hassan, the main person in charge.

The connection man is particularly important to win the trust of the boat candidates. Usually, this role is practiced by a person coming from the same region as the passengers to be recruited. The Gambian man in this particular case accepted the car that was shipped by Dawda from the Netherlands to the Gambia as the payment for the journey of his little brother Yahya (see Chapter 2), and contacted the family of Omar to make their journeys happen, as Omar explained:

> This connection man, this boy, he is Gambian boy, even Dawda he knows this boy. Because if you don't have money there in Tripoli, this connection man makes contact with your family in Banjul, or somewhere in the Gambia. So when the family pays money to the brother of the connection man [in the Gambia], this brother makes the phone call to the connection man, and then he writes down your name, and gives you a ticket for the Hassan boat. This connection man ... He is very, very famous among Gambians and Senegalese in Italy. Everybody knows this man.

Lamin confirmed that this Gambian connection man was an important public figure. He described him as a 'big connection man'. Contrary to 'small connection men' who only connect candidates for a boat crossing on an ad hoc basis and charge only small money, 'big connection men' have a more structural agreement with smugglers and get paid for each passenger they recruit. The latter explains that the recruitment activities of the connection man in question – who later left for China – connected many Senegambian travellers to the facilitation infrastructures of Hassan. According to my informants, Hassan is 'a famous chief' who would be 'as rich as Berlusconi'. When I revisited Omar in Germany in January 2016, he stated that not only were many of the Gambians I had met around the Ligurian asylum space connected to Hassan for their boat passages, but also many of the young men in the German asylum space had 'passed through him'.

When the six young men arrived at 'the river', they were nervously waiting for anything to happen. As Saihou stated, there was 'no movement for three or four hours'. When some Libyan men arrived at the scene, the travellers got further instructions, while they were constantly watched by the Hassan team. Some were asked to inflate the viber boat and later all boat passengers had to carry the boat into the water. Hassan, and his assistants, were there to help push the boat into the sea. Saihou described the embarking process as follows:

> Then we had to take it and carry it ourselves [puts his hands above his head as if he is carrying the boat] ... With many, many people we had to carry because it is a long boat, you have to bring it into the water, and at that time it is night-time, so you don't see anything, and you feel the water. If you are there you cannot believe what you see. Because those people, they give you instructions, and they don't care about you. They have guns, so you must act. They give instructions [starts to raise his

> voice]: 'You here! And you sit here! You sit here! Quiet! Shut up!' ...
> And the only thing you can do is listen to these wicked people. And
> inside the boat, there is only the noise of the water. You can only pray
> to God that you cross the river.

In this nerve-wrecking scene, the eyes of the six Senegambian men must have crossed at some particular point. Once at sea, the fate of these young men were mainly put in the hands of the Senegalese captain. Hassan had probably picked him for his experience as a fisherman (Lucht 2012). Whereas many informants had hardly any information about the role of the 'captain', there was one who had actually been captain some twelve years before the Senegambian men embarked their vessel. This man is Doudou – the owner of the guest house in Milan who was described in the opening vignette of this part of the book (see also below).

The Senegalese captain of Shakur, Saihou, Lamin and their co-travellers initially lost direction and headed towards Malta. He was redirected to Lampedusa by the crew of a Maltese ship. Once the viber boat was in reach of the Italian border authorities, the transfer followed where Lamin took the role of spokesman on behalf of all boat passengers, as outlined in Chapter 1. Subsequently, the Italian authorities brought them to Lampedusa. When I asked Omar about what happened next on the island, his primary reaction was most telling:

> When you come from the sea, you are very, very tired my brother, so
> when you arrive there, you don't know all the things that are happen-
> ing. So what happened is, they put you in the register, they ask small
> things about your country, they take your fingerprint and they give you
> some package with clothes. So you put them on, and you go for sleep.

The Connection Man, the 'Driver' and the Compass

The first time I met Doudou in Milan, I was introduced to him by his good friend Babacar. Babacar was one of my main informants in Lleida and he had moved from this Catalan city to Milan mainly to meet up with his friend Doudou. Before I actually met Doudou, Babacar had given me sufficient hints that his friend had a very interesting story in the light of my research project, and Babacar clearly wanted me to interview him. In fact, he could not understand why I did not use my voice recorder during my first conversation with Doudou.

Doudou has always been a fisherman in the Gambia – and through his fisherman experiences in the Gambia, Senegal and Mauritania he had gradually learned how to master fisher boats in different waters, from rivers to oceans. Many years later, this expertise gave him the special role of 'captain' for the unauthorized boat passage from Libya to Europe. Before he arrived in Italy, however, he had spent a considerable period of time in Morocco in the hope of reaching Spain, and he had circulated between the Gambia and Libya after his return from Morocco to the Gambia.

Doudou reached Lampedusa by boat long before irregular migration became a major political issue in Europe. According to his best knowledge, he was the 'second Gambian man' who reached Italy through this central Mediterranean route via Libya. I could not verify if this was true, but the fact that there were less than a thousand migrants arriving at Lampedusa by boat in his year of arrival (e.g. Cuttitta 2014), indicates that he at least was among the pioneers of this sea passage. A fact that made him visibly proud.

After our first conversations in Milan, I was particularly interested in how he was actually recruited by the network of mobility facilitators in Libya. Through his navigation of Eurospace, we met again some two months after our first encounter when he actually came to the Netherlands to spend some time with his Gambian soon-to-be wife who lived in the city of Leiden (the Netherlands). During this 'more or less holiday' trip we passed time in Leiden and I showed him some highlights of the city of Amsterdam. In these places, he elaborated on his role as 'the driver' of the boat. He vividly told me how he was approached by two men, one Libyan and one Ghanaian (see Lucht 2012 for an elaborative account on the role of Ghanaian fishermen). They told him they knew a 'good crossing'. Doudou showed his interest to both men, but one of them challenged him a bit by saying: 'But you don't know how to drive a boat'. This remark provoked the fisherman in Doudou and he replied: 'Who says that?! I have much experience, I worked as a seaman in Senegal, in Mauritania, in many places, so I know how to do it!' He convinced the two men about his skills as a 'driver'. A few days later, the two men returned and explained to Doudou how to navigate with the compass in the Mediterranean Sea. Doudou allowed me to record his explanation of this process, so I put on my recording device, and he took it in his hand and started to explain how he navigated the dark surrounding. He told me that he moved the boat for three hours up north until the moment he saw three lights. During his narrative, he vividly drew a Mediterranean map on the ground with his finger. He drew the African coastline and pointed subsequently at the places of Tunis, Tripoli and Malta. He explained to me that he had to sail westwards for about two hours when the lights appeared. After these two hours, he needed to steer the boat northwards again. If you turn the boat too late or too softly you risk ending up in Tunis. For him, this was the tricky part of the navigation but after that, 'You are free', as Doudou recalled. It still took Doudou almost a full day to reach Italian territory since he was the driver of a big boat that 'could not run' (move fast).

Since captains do not in general pay any money to the connection men, his role as a captain had some significant financial advantages for Doudou. His first attempt to reach Italy actually failed due to engine problems. Together with a Ghanaian captain, he was responsible for the lives of about a hundred people. Together, the two captains managed to return the boat safely to the Libyan coast. The second crossing was successful. His wooden boat was embarked by a mixture of people – Moroccans, Egyptians, Ghanaians, Malians. In the open waters, Doudou's boat approached a big marine ship. Although they did not visibly intervene, Doudou thought the crew of this marine ship contacted the Italian border guard, since the latter appeared to them a little later. I asked Doudou whether he was ever being accused for facilitating irregular migration at that time. He responded:

> They saw me [driving the boat] and in this time I was very, very young, you know. So they thought we fooled people, like if I could not run the boat, because at that time I was very small, so they did not believe me, they did not believe I was the captain, they thought that the big boys were there [points at a different direction].

And he further summarized his brief stay at the Italian island as follows:

> So the time at Lampedusa, OK, they welcomed us, and they brought us to the camp, they started a camp this time, a 25-day camp. They drop you; they give you a six-month document and you can make your *giro* [the Italian word for 'tour'].

With this short-lived document, Doudou made his way to Rome. From there, his navigation of Eurospace started.

Facilitating Mobility in Eurospace

Eurospace is in general terms a mobile space. Some locations in that space, however, are far from easy to depart from. Greece has become the most notable example. While it is part of the Schengen Agreement – which largely abolished the internal border controls in the EU – Greece has no land borders with any of the other signatories. As a consequence of this geographical location, the harbour of Patras in Greece, with its boat connection to Italy, has served as a main point of passage for a long time. In Greece's pre-crisis period, the ritualized border game between migrants and border guards unfolded here, and it is said that it has been boosted again after the 2015 refugee reception crisis (Tagaris 2018). Next to that, especially under the Turkey–EU deal, the Greek islands have changed from a transit zone to a zone of immobilization and encampment, producing humanitarian crises on Samos and Lesbos (Papataxiarchis 2016). There is an important similarity between Ceuta and Melilla – the Spanish exclaves on Moroccan territory – in the way the EU's mobility regime impacted the Greek islands. As on the Greek island, the EU had put pressure on the national and local authorities in these exclaves to discontinue the common practice of transferring 'undeportable migrants' to the Spanish mainland (e.g. Andersson 2014). Whereas the exclaves and the Greek islands are places that are difficult to leave, some locations in Eurospace are difficult to enter for movers without the right documents. The archetypal consequence that Europe has seen over the past decades has been, of course, the emergence and expulsion of the informal camps near Calais (France) (Calais Writers 2017). It follows that the movers' navigation of the web of facilitation/control does not necessarily stop when one has managed to enter Eurospace. To illustrate this, I first continue to focus on André's trajectory – the Cameroonian man who had lost his son at the time he arrived in Greece (see Chapter 2). Before we discuss the issue of facilitation/control, we need to dive into the institutional situation he found himself in at the time I visited him in Athens in March 2017.

Mobility Facilitation: A View from Athens

In the summer of 2016, André connected to the lively web of mobility facilitators in Istanbul for his unauthorized boat crossing to the Aegean island of Samos. He put on a life jacket and sat down in the rubber boat next to a Syrian family. He thanked God for arriving safely at the Greek island. He shared some pictures with me of the devastating living conditions in the local refugee camp at Samos, one of EU's so-called hotspots (Papageorgopoulous 2018). For him, his reception in Greece was worse than his time in the self-improvised camps in the Moroccan forests in 2008 (where I first met him). For him, Greece seemed to be farther away from Europe than Morocco. While he had registered at the camp, he did not apply for asylum, partly because he knew this would come with restrictions on his wish to reach France or Germany one day. Before his asylum application could enter 'the system', he had escaped the island through a fluid network of African movers and facilitators.[5] He went to Athens and here he soon connected to the Cameroonian community that concentrated around a community place called Le Foyer. Le Foyer was not only a place for communal and religious practices but had also previously served as a shelter for recently arrived Cameroonians – like André. However, just after André's arrival, the landlord complained about the many people who spent the nights there and ended this service. Consequently, André and his co-nationals had to look for a different place to stay overnight.

André slowly adapted to the new urban environment and found ways to establish a daily income through his own hustling techniques. André made himself known as a pastor to the francophone African community in Athens. By distributing flyers, he announced his 'biblical seminars' that he organized in Le Foyer. He firmly believed that these sessions would lead to a better income when people felt inspired by his spirit, consults and explanations of Bible sections. With this hope, he slowly explored new openings in Eurospace. In October 2016, he outlined three itineraries to me during a long Internet conversation. The first itinerary was applying for asylum in Greece. The second was buying a fully arranged marriage package that would allow him to regularize his stay in Greece. The third option was paying a *passeur* (smuggler) who could help him to reach France or Germany. The first itinerary would lead to a long process with considerable costs and very little chances of a breakthrough. He stated that he needed some 350 to 400 euros only to start his asylum procedure with a good lawyer and that he did not even know how much the entire process would cost. Some organizations had already approached him and offered their legal advice for free. However, he distrusted these organizations as well as the pro bono lawyers who liaised with these organizations because they were suspected of working for both asylum seekers and the asylum authorities. André – and many others involved in this research project – firmly believed that it was better to hire lawyers and pay their honoraria because then there is an incentive for the lawyers to better defend someone. Yet, even with a paid lawyer, André was well aware that his chances were still limited as he lacked a convincing asylum narrative. He came from a relatively safe country and, with his role as a pastor in his mind, he did not dare to construct an asylum narrative on the basis of performed homosexuality.

His second option was unfeasible for him due to the high prices involved – between 3,500 and 5,000 euros. The third itinerary also required a substantial investment, but it would yield higher chances of success compared to the first two options as new windows of opportunities were likely to emerge once he reached Germany or France. He estimated the costs of a passage to be around 700 to 800 euros: 100 euros for the plane ticket to Italy, 200 euros for the onward travel to France or Germany and 400 euros for a lookalike passport. He could also opt for an *arriver/payer*, an option that gives one the right to pay only after one has arrived at one's travel destination. However, this right expires after three failed attempts. He inclined to the cheapest option offered by the mobility facilitators.

One day in Athens, André was eager to show me the places where 'the action' was. He took me to an informal restaurant in the basement of an apartment building. There he introduced me to the owner of the place – a Cameroonian woman who had supported André during the most difficult period in his life (the loss of his son) by offering him shelter, food and some money to finance his numerous telephone calls to Africa. The place she ran, however, was not only a restaurant. It was a cinema, a care centre, a hostel, a bar, a market, a brothel and a travel centre at the same time. André explained to me how each of the four doors of this basement led to a different world. The first door – that was left half open – led to his sleeping place, but at this particular moment it was occupied by a passeur and two clients. Through the crack of the door I could see how the passeur, who was dressed like a proper businessperson, showed his two clients something on a tablet, possibly the latest flight ticket prices. Behind the second door was another hostel room where two men were actually sleeping. The third door led to the business centre of the place where all kinds of stuff was marketed. The fourth door was the door to paid sex. The mama of the place now knocked on that door to indicate that the time was up. We also saw some inattentive guests entering this door, a mistake that was followed by great laughter among the other people around.

Before we entered this underground place, André told me that he did not particularly like the atmosphere inside. As he put it: 'It is hot over there', suggesting that many of the things happening there created tensions and troubles. I also noticed this when we left the basement and entered the public streets again. In dusk light, I heard someone yelling 'Pasteur, Pasteur!' André was stopped by a Cameroonian man. Although I did not overhear the entire conversation, it was obvious that this man expected André to soon deliver him 200 euros. When we continued our walk, I asked André what this shady conversation was all about. He explained to me that the man had paid him 200 euros for a particular service to help him escape Samos. In the end, this service did not work out for the man, and now the man wanted his money back. But the money was gone – André had spent it on daily needs. Thereupon I asked him: 'So you are a kind of connection man?' 'Not yet', he said, 'but if I arrive there, I would do a much better job than the people you have just seen'. With this statement he referred to the connection man in the restaurant located in the basement. By revealing this potential career path, I was even more concerned about his position in this European city as he had indebted himself considerably. But according to André, some upward mobility in this mobility sector was the fastest route to secure his future mobility to France or Germany – to the 'real Europe'.

In the period of deep grievances related to the loss of his son, André was supported by three women in Athens. One was a Greek woman working for a charity organization. The second was the 'mama' running the informal restaurant. The third, and most important, woman who supported him was Michelle – his close friend since childhood. While they travelled together to Istanbul, André had first found his way to Greece, Michelle followed some weeks later. After the loss of his son, Michelle arranged the funeral ceremony in Athens, and she supported André, mentally and financially, the best she could. Slowly but surely, their close friendship developed into a love relationship. When I visited André in Athens (March 2017), I noticed this through the music-related hints he gave me. He, for instance, explained to me how one of his favourite songs – *En Secret* (secretly), by the Ivorian singer Teeyah – applied to his own situation. Teeyah sings about a secret love that should not be uncovered. Every time André played that song, he seemed to listen to his internal feelings for Michelle. However, the new love became particularly clear when Michelle took me aside just after André had explained to me that Michelle would soon travel to the 'real Europe'. She grabbed my arm, and gently guided me to the kitchen of the underground restaurant where she worked. She whispered that she did not want to travel alone, that she prayed to be able to travel together with Pasteur. Later, André told me he was aware of Michelle's feeling, but he felt heavy reservations due to his previous marriage, and above all he felt heavily confused in this period of mourning.

After I had returned to the Netherlands, however, I could still observe from a distance how their love relationship strengthened over time. My video calls with André changed into video calls with André and Michelle. During one of such calls, they shared with me that Michelle was pregnant – some good news that was celebrated among the three of us. In the summer of 2017, I only talked with André again, and he stated to have more big news. After noticing my curiosity, he teased me, deliberately slowing the conversation and letting me guess what had happened. He further tested my patience by asking me to call him back the next day since the connection was not strong enough. The next day, he finally shared the big news: Michelle had arrived in France. She managed to reach France by means of André's connections in, and know-how of, the lively mobility industry of Greece. They had combined their savings, which resulted in a 'travel budget' of 500 euros. André arranged a lookalike passport for some 300 euros, and the airplane ticket to Italy cost some 170 euros. The fact that they did not involve a connection man made her travel considerably cheaper than they had anticipated, but it also meant that they had only one shot. If Michelle would be caught at the border, the investment would be of no avail after all. Lucky enough, Michelle embarked the plane without any further problem. Thus, in the end, André was right when he said that his role in the mobility industry was the fastest way to secure a mobility passage to the real Europe.

That very same week I contacted Michelle and she talked about her nerve-racking and courageous journey. Initially, she planned to move by train from Italy to France, but she did not manage to make a seat reservation that day. She had to improvise and decided to go by Flixbus – a relatively new bus service that has been increasingly confronted with EU border policies (Teunissen 2018). At the Franco–Swiss border, there was a heavy control by the French authorities. During a two-hour-long control, they searched everyone's belongings and checked all travel documents. This control almost made Michelle freak out. About this particular moment, she stated: 'J'avais mort!' (I was dead!). When the border guard checked her French passport, they asked if she was living in Paris (the destination of the bus), which she confirmed. They did not pay any further attention to her. Michelle reached Paris. She felt relieved that she had managed to escape Athens. At the same time, she heavily regretted that she had travelled without André. She hardly knew anyone in her new environment. To survive the first days, one of her Congolese contacts in Athens directed her to a Congolese family in France who could host her for a while. But after some weeks, her pregnancy became heavier to carry. At that point in time, she moved into a shelter for undocumented migrants. Soon after, she gave birth to her first child. It was not easy for Michelle to have a baby as an undocumented woman in an unfamiliar environment. She cried many times for André's absence. For André, it was the second time that he became a father of a child who was born in a country where he himself was not present. The pressure for him to reach France was now even higher than before. But the fact that his partner had managed to cross the borders and give birth to his daughter, made him realize that there is hope – and more literally: there is life – after a 'lost Europe'.

Concluding Notes: The Production of Mobility

Actors of mobility facilitation and actors of mobility control are key to understanding the ways in which the trajectories under study unfold. The term 'mobility industry' may at first sight suggest that these actors are external to the movement itself. However, we have seen that movers themselves may turn into mobility facilitators to induce their own movements.

Although this book focuses on intra-EU mobility, in this chapter I have explicitly paid attention to the fuzzy web of facilitators/controllers of mobility along the trans-Saharan route. The previous sections underline that mobility must be studied 'in connection with new ways of confinement and modes of exploitation' (Glick Schiller and Salazar 2013: 190). The testimonies of violence in Libya create an ambiguous statement regarding mobility facilitation in this trans-Saharan context. On the one hand, I follow scholars who put forward a nuanced understanding of the role of facilitators in this cross-border mobility. These practices need to be critically historicized (Brachet 2018) and one indeed needs to acknowledge that many of these practices are based on trust relationships (Belloni 2016a). On the other hand, we should be careful that this nuanced understanding does not result in a form of intellectual ignorance concerning the structural violence against sub-Saharan Africans in Libya as expressed in these stories. This violence, coming from controllers *and* facilitators of mobility, is to a large degree co-produced by EU's externalized border policy, including the latest stipulation to force back boats to the Libyan coasts. Eurospace, in that sense, blends into trans-Saharan spaces through its extraterritorial politics of exclusion. Ironically, this violent reality helps to explain the movers' persistent efforts to find ways through bureaucracies and borders once they have entered European territory, as we will learn in the next chapter.

NOTES

1. Ghadaffi recruited many sub-Saharan African men to become soldiers in this conflict.
2. In 1975, sixteen West African states signed the first ECOWAS treaty; four years later these states adopted the protocol related to the Free Movement of Persons, Residence and Establishment.
3. Trans-Saharan travellers are asked to pay some few thousand CFA francs extra for these dubious military services. A Dutch journalist estimated that about a third of the expenditure of mobility facilitators in Agadez is spent on bribing policemen and convoy protection services provided by the Nigerien military (Vermeulen 2016).
4. This reminds me of the expression used by a representative of Pro Asyl – a German refugee rights advocacy group – who stated: 'The closer you get to Europe, the more illegal you become'.
5. To respect the tactics of people that are caught at the Greek islands, I deliberately do not reveal the exact ways he managed to escape.

CHAPTER
4

'The System'

If one had asked me in the beginning of 2014 who of the six young men from Senegambia who entered Europe with the same boat in 2013 was most likely to get stuck in Eurospace, I certainly would not have pointed to Shakur. When I first met him, he appeared to me as a talkative and energetic young man, with a rapper-style attitude. He has the kind of character that is not likely to be discouraged by rules and regulations. Being inspired by Tupac Shakur, he firmly challenged racialized structures of inequality and other societal injustices. Yes, he had encountered many predators during his navigation of the web of facilitation/control in Africa and this had seriously delayed his travel to Europe, but all their acts of violence had not stopped him from moving. However, there was one force field he had not managed to escape from. Ironically, this force field only appeared to him once he had actually reached Eurospace. This force field is what he called, with an Orwellian sense, 'the system'.

Bureaucracy and Beyond

'The system' is a manifold and almost omnipresent structure. In the descriptions of my informants, the system terminology mostly relates to migration apparatuses (Feldman 2012; Tuckett 2015) consisting of daily rules restricting everyday movements as well as rigid bureaucracies and opaque documentation regimes. As Tuckett (2015: 113) writes about the Italian migration bureaucracy:

> Experiences with the bureaucracy of Italian immigrant law are characterized by long waiting times, mix-ups of information, the issuing of expired permits, endless queues, chasing up 'blocked' applications

and documents being lost … For those lucky enough to have secure legal status, encounters with the regime continue through family and friends.

In the case of Shakur and his friends, the narrow understanding of the system primarily refers to asylum regulations and their related facilities in Italy. Shakur was among the 435,385 individuals who in 2013 asked for asylum in one of the EU member states. Some twenty-six thousand of these applicants were assessed by the Italian system. In that specific year, Gambians were not a very visible group in EU-wide asylum statistics. Only in the first half of 2014, did the Gambian backway become perceptible in the EU's statistics because the 11,300 first asylum applications from Gambians seeking asylum counted for some 2 per cent of the total asylum claims in the EU. A year later, during the infamous European refugee reception crisis, the EU saw the number of first asylum applications of Gambians rise to 12,185, but in relative terms these actually became less significant as they counted for about 1 per cent of total first asylum claims in the EU (my own calculations based on Eurostat data).

While the reference to 'the system' suggests a coordinated and coherent entity of governance, it is of crucial importance to note that there is no such thing as *the* Italian asylum system. From its inception, Italy's reception system has been characterized by decentralization with a major role reserved for local actors. Consequently, as Valeria Ferrari (2018) once stated during a conference presentation, there are at least twenty reception systems in Italy and, as such, there are great discrepancies across Italy's regions regarding asylum procedures, refugee acceptation rates and the conditions of reception (see also Vianelli 2017). In addition, there is another dividing line across the country, caused by two general structures of reception. First there is a national programme of reception known as the SPRAR system (Sistema di Protezione per Richiedenti Asilo e Refugiati/ Protection System for Asylum Seekers and Refugees). SPRAR is a system that is put in place to host asylum centres and to offer legal advice, integration support and social assistance to asylum seekers. The SPRAR system is coordinated on the national level, but on the local level, centres are run by different actors, including NGOs, social enterprises and private actors (Vianelli 2017). Since the SPRAR facilities over the last years have proved to be insufficient for hosting the incoming groups of migrants, the authorities have set up a system of exceptional reception (although we could question the exceptionality of it) that exists parallel to the SPRAR. The main coordinating administrative bodies of the CAS system (Centri Accoglienza Straordinaria/Extraordinary Reception Centres) are the provincial offices (*prefetture*). The focus of this parallel emergency system points to a policy view that the majority of the people who enter Italy by crossing the Mediterranean Sea have no future in Italy since they come from safe countries of origin (McMahon and Sigona 2018).

To further unpack the Italian system, it is important to note that another web of reception facilities exists to facilitate the so-called 'pre-reception phase'. Some infrastructures, like the governmental centres CDA (Centri di Accoglienza/Collective Reception Centres), emerged in the mid 1990s in the context of the Balkan war. Other facilities – like the pre-reception centres CPSA (Centri di Primo Soccorso e Accoglienza/First Aid and Reception Centres), which offer first reception and medical assistance in the case of sea arrivals – emerged in the light of mixed migration across the Mediterranean Sea. Later, induced by the strong wish of the European Commission to create a common European approach to asylum, the so-called 'Hotspot approach' added another institutional layer to this complex system. The crux of this Europeanization and harmonization of migration policy is, however, that it starts from the assumption that European space is a smooth and harmonized space where local contexts hardly matter (Vianelli 2017; Schapendonk 2018c).

The juridical procedure in Italy generally follows two steps. The first asylum application is assessed by an administrative body, the so-called CTRPI (Commissioni Territoriali per il Riconoscimento della Protezione Internazionale/ Territorial Commissions for International Protection). CTRPI operates independently from the immigration department of the Ministry of Interior. In case of a rejection, an asylum applicant may request a juridical review, which implies that a judge assesses the first asylum application through a civil court. In this second phase, the asylum seeker is often accompanied by a lawyer – a crucial actor in the web of facilitation and control.

The system, however, goes beyond migration bureaucracies and asylum regulations. The system, in other words, is not a synonym for Feldman's 'migration apparatus' (2012). My informants have related the system terminology to cultural habits, the healthcare system, tax payments and labour market regulations in Europe in general, or in specific EU member states. The system terminology was mostly used to articulate their surprise regarding how things work in Europe or, seen from their position at the margins, to highlight the discriminatory and oppressing mechanisms of European societies. With regard to the latter, some West Africans – especially those in Spain – defined Europe as a 'Babylon system', a powerful, corrupted, unjust and oppressive society (Joosten 2017). The system is therefore even less tangible than a migration apparatus, but it still invokes bordering, ordering and othering processes (Van Houtum and Van Naerssen 2002). Despite its omnipresence and power, however, the system is seldom seen as a determining force. You may escape it, live with it or invert its logics. The system, put differently, leaves room for navigation.

Deservingness and Its Divergences

In the first period after their arrival in the Ligurian Caritas centre, Omar, Yahya and Shakur danced to the tunes of the system. They accepted the arrangements regarding their daily mobility and had a cooperative attitude towards the Caritas staff and its related facilities. In 2014, when I first met the three men, they were cautious not to be late for lunch and dinner in 'the camp' and made sure that they entered the camp before nine o'clock in the evening. Later on, they, as Omar stated, started to 'know their rights' better. Initially, he had thought he had to stay inside the Ligurian city, but later he learned he was allowed to move around in Italy on the condition he reported his absence to the centre.

With more time spent in the centre, it was Shakur in particular who started to notice the limited progress he made, despite the fact that he had 'accepted' the system. As a consequence, he started to openly question the principles of the system. As he stated after having spent roughly one year in the Caritas centre:

> I went to school, I took language classes, I took geography classes, I took history classes. You know why? Because they say it helps you with the paper. So I follow their advice. But now they give us nothing. I quit school. The exam is supposed to be in June. But two weeks ago I decided to quit, because they don't give us nothing. They don't follow their own system, they decide what they want. They don't follow their own system. You know, even my brothers in Napoli, we were in the same boat, as I told you. These brothers there, they got the paper of five years! They get the five-year paper! And they did *not* go to school, they did *not* have language classes. So what is this system?

This system not only created diverse outcomes and curbed Shakur's mobility, it also turned him from an outgoing young man and fan of rap music into an aghast and disillusioned person who stopped listening to popular music and instead spent hours on listening to Koranic texts. He started to embody a sense of immobility on a daily basis, as he commented in 2015:

> Me I don't seek to come outside. To go outside, to sit. No. When you see me, I am always at home, man. I am always at home, man. I cannot sleep good, I cannot sleep, because you think too much, man. *Thinking always!* Too much thinking is not good for people ... You do nothing, all that is left is thinking.

In contrast to his 'brothers', who all managed to get out of the system by either showing patience or by literally moving away from it, Shakur found himself stuck for more than four years (from the time he entered the asylum Liguria early 2014 to May 2018). This exceptional state of being can hardly be explained in the legal sense. That is to say, Shakur's story of forced migration did not deviate considerably from that of his peers. While some obtained a refugee status and others humanitarian protection, Shakur did not see his legal status improve in any sense. His less privileged situation can best be explained as a matter of deservingness. As Casati (2018: 800-1) so powerfully outlines in the case of Sicily, being an asylum seeker 'spurs a set of expectations regarding the social characteristics and the "right" behaviour'. Shakur was unable and, above all, unwilling to live up to the 'master frame of the "deserving migrant"' (Chauvin and Garcés-Mascareñas 2014: 426) that would probably have led to some form of legalization. The difference between Yahya and Shakur is most telling in this respect.

When I revisited Yahya, Shakur and Omar in the same Ligurian city where I had met them one year previously, I learned that the Caritas staff arranged jobs for a selected group of asylum seekers. They had found part-time jobs for Omar and Shakur at a nearby dockyard. Next to painting, they did the 'heavy work', as Shakur called it. For Yahya, however, the camp had arranged a relatively better position as he worked full days for a family who were building a new bed and breakfast in the nearby hills. His job came with a contract, regular payments and housing. During a visit to a beautiful Ligurian beach – which was an uncommon practice for Shakur – Shakur compared the favourable position of Yahya with his own situation:

> Yahya has a contract job now, he is there for three months, he is making full days of work. Me and Omar, we work only half a day from eight to twelve. We work at a place where they make ships … We help the people who are making the things. We do the heavy work, but also we paint sometime, we do everything they ask us. That is why we say Yahya is the *Tycoon*.[1] He has a paper for one year, he has a contract job, he *is* a guarantee here. So he is the *Tycoon*. We are just camerados, because we don't have any guarantee here. They give us an identity paper, but this identity paper is just to show at the police, it is not a travel paper.

The contract job and the legalized period of one year gave Yahya a better position in the asylum community. When Shakur explained further the social figure of the Tycoon, he stated that it is the status of the 'cool man', someone who can live 'by oneself a good life', someone who 'looks good, thinks good and feels good'. Around six o'clock in the evening, Yahya came to the beachside to join us. When I noticed the presence of this tall

Gambian man, I enthusiastically greeted him with his new social signifier of Tycoon. With his typical shyness and placidity, he kept shaking my hand and emphasized with a big smile that I was the real Tycoon. At the time of our extensive greetings, I was happy to notice he had made some considerable progress. However, the progress turned out to be only relative when I accompanied him to his new work and living place.

A black Chevrolet waited for Yahya and me in front of the local train station. Inside the car was an Italian woman called Daniela. In her best English, she tried to start a conversation with us. She stated she was very surprised that I was a white man, because when Yahya had told her there was a friend visiting him at his living place, she had imagined a black man from Africa, not a white man from the Netherlands. Yahya laughed a bit. While we drove up to the hills, she explained to me how the family, after the *pater familias* had passed away, had been busy transforming their former grape farm into a place of mixed activities. They had now started to combine small-scale agriculture with tourist accommodation. As a result Yahya and his Nigerian co-worker named Paul (coming from the same Caritas centre) had mixed tasks, varying from taking care of the animals to heavy construction work. Being Yahya's boss, Daniela repeatedly stressed that Yahya was a real gentleman. To emphasize this, she had a remarkable and rather uncomfortable illustration: 'He always wears perfume. When he comes to the pigs, even there he wears the perfume. He is a good worker'. Besides his scent, it seemed to me that Yahya's polite and docile character fitted the image of the perfectly submissive labourer for this Italian family.

When we reached the place, I was impressed by the beauty of the landscape. The two guesthouses and the construction site where the third residence was built were surrounded by wooded hills. When I said out loud that the place was really beautiful, Daniela added: 'Yes, Yahya is really lucky to be here'. Yahya seemed to just swallow her words and only nodded his head. However, later, when we sat down together with Paul, the two men actually stressed that this beautiful landscape had its clear downside: boredom and social isolation. Unlike the other workers at the construction site, they also spent their nights at the compound. They shared a small bedroom, in which they spent most of their time in the evening surfing YouTube and trying to connect with their friends and families elsewhere in the world.

That evening our conversations gave me further insights that the alleged progress of Yahya was rather limited. The two men explained to me how the Caritas camp had arranged this job for them, but also how this job came with clear limitations. They consistently referred to a specific 'contract' with Caritas. This contract initially stipulated that the asylum seekers in the centre receive 60 euros a month for pocket money from the camp. However, now with their job, the contract got a clear labour dimension as well. In the first months, the Italian family did not pay Yahya and Paul directly for their hard labour. The payment went through Caritas, and this created severe frictions. Paul told me that the family paid Caritas 800 euros each month for the labour involved. However, the two men only received 500 euros. With an expressive anger that I had not seen before with him, Yahya added:

> The problem is first, it is *Caritas*! Caritas they bring this system! I know that, because we are working here eight hours, and they are paying 800 euros [to Caritas], but they *cut* that money. They take 300 to Caritas, they pay me 500. They look for their interest ... I know it from that lady [of the Caritas centre]. That lady, she gave me the paper ... I have this paper here and it tells me that I am working here for 850 euros. I have the paper here. That lady wrote that paper. But I never saw that money.

Daniela's brother later confirmed that, indeed, Caritas served as a labour brokering service. Fed by such arrangements, there is a widespread frustration among asylum seekers in Italy regarding the notion that reception facilities 'steal funds' from them (Casati 2018). When Yahya received his residence permit, the arrangements of the Caritas camp ended. From that moment the family paid him directly. According to Yahya, however, this direct payment gave him a salary raise of only 100 euros per month.

It follows that the broad and complex interpretation of my informants regarding 'the system' as a regime that is hooked up in migration apparatuses but at the same time goes beyond the spheres of bureaucracy, could not be more accurate. There is an interesting parallel with the business of bordering Europe. As Andersson (2014) so powerfully describes, local NGOs, international development organizations and security companies all liaise with the EU and its member states to curb West African mobility to the north. As a result, this industry is built on a double standard of militarization and humanitarianism. Similarly, the Italian reception facilities where Omar, Shakur and Yahya found themselves are characterized by a mixture of control, humanitarianism, labour brokerage and exploitation. These seemingly opposing moralities are melted into a system that forms an uncertain, if not nasty, environment to be navigated, as we will see below.

It is important to know that the labour arrangements between Caritas and the Italian family not only helped Yahya to reach the social status of Tycoon, it also contributed to the regularization of his stay in Europe. Prior to the so-called European refugee reception crisis in 2015, it was a common practice in Italy that newcomers with subsidiary or humanitarian protection guaranteed their long and regular stay through labour contracts. This is how Yahya gradually climbed up the social ladder in Italy. After 2015, however, this practice was to a large extent replaced by the handing over of expulsion orders to West Africans, creating a 'large undocumented and yet non-deportable population in Italy' (McMahon and Sigona 2018: 504).

In the context of his enhanced situation, Yahya became increasingly concerned about Shakur's lack of progress. As he outlined in May 2016, at his working and living place with the Italian family:

> Yahya: I need Shakur to work here, because this people, they need to help Shakur to have documents. But Shakur did not want the job.
> I: And that is I think the problem with Shakur, there is too much in his mind.
> Yahya: Yes even me, I told Shakur that is the problem. I think Shakur *is* the problem, because that Caritas people want him to work here. Shakur does not like it. He refused. When you don't work here, that people never help you with the documents. So when I came here … Everything went fast. So I advised Shakur: 'Just look at *your* interest, if you can work, you can get the documents, but you need to stay here. I think it is better than sleeping at home [in the camp], without no money, and without a document … Anytime, you can have the document, but you need to stay here'.
> I: Like Omar, he was also working here, and he got the paper.
> Yahya: Yea, he got the paper, and after he was gone. I told Shakur to work, work … If you have documents after, you can go anywhere you like to go.
> I: It is just like playing the game.
> Yahya [nods his head]: But if he stays like this, not working, he has the stress, because of the time [he spends] for this people.

When I spoke to Shakur about this issue, his unpacking of the system was spot on. He started with explaining why he had decided not to work for the Italian family:

> Shakur: This place is not good. I worked there for one month, but the people there they asked me to stay in their place, you see, to sleep there in their place. But me, I say: 'No, let me travel up and down every day'. They did not like it too much.
> I: But why did you not want to stay there?
> Shakur: Because they let you work like their slave! They let you work like their slave, like they own you.

It is probable that in his mind Shakur connected the situation in Italy to the situation of exploitation and forced labour in Libya. The conversation continued:

> I: Is it?! But Yahya speaks good about them, he told me they are treating him like their family.
> Shakur: Yes, they treat you good, but you work like a slave.

I: They treat you good, and they let you work like a slave?
Shakur: Yes! That is what I am saying. They treat you good, but you work like a slave!
I: For me this is interesting, because if they let you work like a slave, it can never be a good treatment.
Shakur: No man, I am telling you, they treat you good, but you work like their slave. Your life is only a cost for them, they don't care about your life, but they see it as their cost.

In Shakur's reading, two extremes that to me seemed impossible to reconcile – good treatment and slavery – were transformed into a cosy consensus through the institutional arrangements between Caritas and a rich Italian family. These arrangements seem only to work out for those characters – like Yahya – who are willing to follow the Italian ethos of the 'deserving migrant' (see also below). 'Deservingness', as Noemi Casati (2018) explains, largely relies on migrants' display of gratitude and victimhood in a context of asylum.[2] During the conversations I had in Italy, some Gambian informants stressed that one needs to be 'patient' regarding the Italian system of reception. Others – like a good friend of Mamadou (the 'JJC') – pushed this role a bit further. This Gambian man whom I met in Naples stated that one needs to be 'obedient'. When I asked what he meant with this, he stated: 'To be obedient is like first they tell, then you follow. You must be obedient, you must respect their rules, so you have to wait for your time'.

Shakur simply, but firmly, refused to play this role of the deserving migrant and took his losses. This was hard for Yahya to understand, as he saw being obedient as a temporal performance from which you could eventually profit. In Yahya's reading, one indeed needs to dance to the tunes of the reception system – but this dance is not everlasting. Thus, while the reception system reproduces the idealized migrant as a docile subject, we at the same time need to do justice to the capacities and tactics of navigation of the individual movers within this system. Yahya expressed this by using the term 'snake way' country to describe the Italian system. For him a snake way country is a country of limitation, corruption and not talking straight. But he emphasized that he was able to navigate this system, as he stated: 'Italy knows how to *make* the snake way, but I also know how to *use* the snake way'.

Asylum and Informal Labour: The Case of the Snowman in Germany

The hooking up of asylum systems with labour systems is certainly not only a feature of southern EU member states. In fact, if one performs the role of deserving migrant in the German asylum system – which at least means going to language classes and starting with other integration activities – the

German asylum procedures may grant working permits. Franck, the cheerful man from the anglophone part of Cameroon, had seen these rules change during his short presence in Germany. Whereas the German system initially granted labour rights to asylum seekers after one year, he heard that they recently started to give these permits after three months. But according to Franck, the procedures were far from easy and highly politicized. After two years in Germany, Franck found a job for six evenings a week as a dishwasher in a restaurant. The 1,060 euro monthly salary put an end to the monthly government allowance of 300 euros. Considering he had to pay the rent of his asylum project related to the local church and had to take care of his newborn daughter and his spouse, he was in search of other possibilities to increase his income.

His *vorläufige Unterbringung* (temporary shelter) was coordinated by Caritas and housed dozens of asylum seekers in an old basilica in a small village of roughly 20,000 inhabitants in southern Germany. When I entered his living space, I first had to pass through a security check, whereupon I was instructed to carry a visitor's badge with a German Red Cross label. I put the badge around my neck, and we entered the beautiful baroque monastery. In Franck's room, which he shared with another Cameroonian man, we had a delightful dinner and spoke extensively about asylum, Africa, borders, family life and Europe. He also showed me pictures of the birth of his daughter. When I pointed at a white woman who appeared in several pictures, Franck explained that he was coupled to her by a church-led buddy system. He said:

> Ohhh, I have a madam here, she is treating me like her own child ... This lady, she helps me so much. Every letter that I receive from the government, for my Asyl or maybe for my daughter, every letter goes straight to her. She takes good care of it, because sometimes I myself do not know what to do, and she knows the system better.

Later, when we went out, we met the woman. She had a conversation with an older man who was also related to the church programme. The woman approached Franck and said this was the man he had to talk to for fresh information regarding a new job opportunity. According to Franck's vocabulary, this was the 'connection man' who could arrange a new job for him. The job was rather remarkable as Franck was asked to clear the snow from parking lanes of private houses very early in the morning. The man showed us a twelve-page handwritten list of addresses where this service was needed. While listening to the old man, Franck nodded and inquired in his best German about the payment. The deal was that he received 10 euros per hour of removing snow. He therefore had to carefully check the weather forecasts and especially the snow expectations.

After the explanation of the job, the man rather unexpectedly asked Franck whether he could join him today for a small tour so he could show him the addresses where he was expected to show up as 'the snowman'. Another man from Eritrea, who had watched the conversation from a distance, was also there to make the tour. Franck, however, hesitated. He was not sure whether this flexible task could be combined with his restaurant job. And, above all, what about his leather shoes? He did not want to waste them. Yet, the woman insisted and put further pressure on her pupil: 'Das geht doch?!' Franck lost his nerves, and said with a slight increase in voice: 'Nein, das geht nicht!' And by pointing to his shoes, he added: 'Das sind gute Schuhe, this is leather!' Whereupon the woman responded: 'OK, then you come to me and we look for new shoes upstairs'. Franck was happy. It seemed that he had pushed his situation somewhat in his favour.

A little later Franck and I embarked a funny looking Fiat Panda together with the old German connection man and a rather silent Eritrean man. I found myself in a clownish situation that was particularly formed by the constant miscommunications between the four of us (which mostly led to repetitions of what had already been said, only louder) and the old man's enduring quest of finding the right addresses for the two workers. On top of this came the poor driving skills of the old man. Later, when Franck and I walked downtown, the old man's driving skills were a source of great joy and laughter for us. Franck repeatedly referred to our erratic ride by saying things like: 'Ohh my God! I rather take a truck through the desert than to drive with this man'.

During our absurd ride, the German connection man repeated endlessly: 'Remember the address, you have to remember the address!' And: 'You must write down your hours when you have worked on the form that I gave you'. The confusion increased when the Eritrean man tried to explain to the old man that he had not given him the intended form. But the old man did not get the point. His enthusiasm and good intentions just overruled any question and any request for more information coming from his two African passengers. He just continued with an insisting tone: 'You must check the weather on the news, when you expect snow, you come to the house at six o'clock, at seven o'clock the snow must be gone!' The Eritrean man tried to digest this new flood of information when we stopped at the first address, being located just a stone's throw away from the basilica. We actually could have walked there. The connection man looked at Franck when we stepped out of the car – 'Do you remember the address?' Franck nodded his head and followed the old man, while giving me sufficient hints that it was better for me to stay in the car. They came back in fifteen minutes, and it all seemed to be clear to Franck now. When he and I were able to speak again in private, he explained to me why this job was convenient for him. He almost excused himself to me for taking this opportunity – probably he sensed my second thoughts about the typical labour arrangements. I felt that I was just witnessing the micropolitics regarding how Europe expects African movers to be the grateful subjects expressing the right mix of readiness, acceptance, adaptation and flexibility regardless of the tasks that are thrown at them.

Before we entered the car again, the old man opened the tailgate of the car, and Franck could catch a glimpse of a crate of beer, upon seeing which he joked: 'Für eine Stunde auch ein Bier?' The old man replied: 'No, there is no beer for you, you are Muslim right? You don't drink'. And he closed the tailgate. Franck – a proud Christian, and a great fan of Guinness beer – looked at me with a thunderstruck and open-eyed gaze. He sighed and got into the car again, without saying a word. Back in the car, the challenge for Franck was to explain to the old man that he had still not received the form to register his hours. This man was not only old but also quite stubborn as he was sure he had given the form to Franck. Franck tried his best German, but he could not convince the man. I tried my best German, and still the man was quite sure that he had given the form to Franck and the Eritrean man. Franck took a deep breath, and asked: 'When did you give it?' The man could not actually recall it and when we arrived at the second address, he checked his papers and found the forms under his list of addresses. Unsurprisingly, Franck decided to quit the job even before it had actually started.

'Business Systems' and Their Funniness

As with so many asylum seekers in Italy, Yahya and Shakur both deeply distrusted the Italian system for its obscurity (e.g. Sanò 2017), but they applied different tactics in dealing with it. Yahya performed the docile and cooperative migrant. He accepted the job offer at the Italian family through the Caritas connection without any form of resistance because he felt it would help him in his asylum process. Shakur, however, refused 'the system'. Like the criticism regarding the visa lottery on the streets in the Gambia (see Chapter 1), Shakur's impression was that the reception system was partly based on a financial incentive. He continuously framed it as a business system. The Italian CAS system – the emergency reception infrastructure that has been put in place next to the national SPRAR facilities – has indeed opened up a network of subcontracts in the context of asylum and refugee reception. The extraordinary status of CAS makes it less prescriptive compared to SPRAR, which creates ample opportunities for commercial actors, even in cases in which they do not have expertise in the field of asylum (Ambrosini 2017).

With his resistance to the system, Shakur also expressed some behaviour that obviously irritated others. I noticed this on the day I accompanied him and a group of 'colleagues' to one of the Ligurian beaches. None of the young men seemed to pay attention to the tourists and Italians around us, except for Shakur. While we walked on the boulevard, he annoyed some Italian women with some sexually tinted comments. Since I was walking next to him, I felt embarrassed and actually asked him to stop it. He refused and stated: 'If they do not respect us, I annoy them!' This seemed to be his general attitude towards European society, and the Italian asylum system in particular.

Shakur's resistant attitude came with a growing suspicion concerning the reception facilities he found himself in. On that same beach day, Shakur warned me – in the context of my research project – about two African men who joined us (one Senegalese dressed with a yellow shirt whom we called 'The Yellow' that day and one long Malian man whom we called 'Le Grand'):

> Everybody in the centre is talking about you, standing in front of our door, looking at us. They all think, 'What is the connection, what is the connection', you see? ... But these guys [The Yellow and Le Grand], do not interview them, because we do not trust them. They have a double role, they are with us, but they talk all the time to the Caritas people, you see? They are double agents! Double agents you can never trust!

With these comments in mind, I indeed felt some tension and distance between the two men and the rest of the group. Although I never had the chance of verifying this information with one of the two suspicious men, I was intrigued by the thought that an eventual presence of double agents well fit the Orwellian notion of the system that resonated in most of Shakur's continuous criticism. Following this reading, the system is deeply entangled with social networks and people's affective circuits.

The friends of Shakur well noted that their 'brother' was caught up in the system that they had managed to escape. Shakur's stagnation in this labyrinth created a mixed sense of incomprehension and compassion among his co-movers. Although some could not understand why Shakur was so stubborn in resisting the system, they all felt that the system was highly unjust and arbitrary. Like the visa system, the asylum system was considered a lottery given how heavily its outcome depends on one's luck. After Shakur's undocumented period had lasted for about two years, Lamin framed the system as something 'funny'. Surprised, I asked him what was funny about the entire situation. He explained:

> I think it is funny because they really don't know what they are doing. So Shakur and me for instance, we come from the same area, we don't differ too much. But his situation is so different. It is funny, because

they create this programme for us, but they don't want us. So they create a system for people to stay, but they don't want us. That is funny man!

The notions of funniness and luck are indeed apparent. If you are lucky you are transferred to a reception centre that gives you more pocket money than other centres, grants you better legal advice than other centres and allows for more everyday freedoms than the other centres. If you have no such luck, you end up in a stringent regime that controls your daily behaviours. Thus whereas the EU strives for a common approach to asylum procedures, and whereas some thinkers plead for a global refugee distribution system (e.g. Hathaway 2018, for a critique see Schapendonk 2018c), there are vast discrepancies to be identified in the system of one of the most important refugee receiving countries in the Global North (Vianelli 2017).

On other occasions, and in other places outside Italy, the system appeared to be 'funny' to my informants. Malik – the Gambian man who escaped from his relationship in the Netherlands – referred to funniness with regard to his asylum assessment in Germany, and in particular to the process of fingerprinting:

> Malik: But like the funny thing is: when I put my finger here, the guy said he saw my finger in Italy. But I have never travelled to Italy even. Haha.
> I: Haha, so they tried to link you to Italy, but you never crossed there!
> Malik: Ya! I don't even know the way to Italy [we laugh]! And then he said, 'Yeah, I saw your finger in Italy!' He said he told me the truth. I said, 'OK' [bursts out laughing again].
> I: So the system said you travel through Italy.
> Malik: Ya [he cannot stop laughing]!
> I: That is *funny!* How comes your fingerprint is in Italy?
> Malik: Really, really, really, it is very, very funny. I say, 'Agh, look at this! The system is lying!'
> I: Sometimes you can only laugh with the system, right?
> Malik: Ya ya ya ya. Maybe the system was confused, because many people put their fingers there, in Italy.
> I: Maybe also they put pressure … So if you say, 'Yes, yes! I was in Italy', then they maybe send you to Italy. I don't know.
> Malik: Yaaa [with a more serious tone now].
> I: They are maybe just lying and then they hope that you just say, 'Yes yes, I come from Italy', and then they send you there.
> Malik: Maybe … They were just talking like that.

This snapshot of our conversation hints at two possible explanations for the remarkable event that Malik described with a combination of disbelief and great joy. First, it is not unthinkable that the system includes administrative mistakes due to the everyday realities that surround this rigid computer-based system. These everyday realities can be highly unstructured, hectic and full of deviations (e.g. Campesi 2015). Secondly, it is well possible that the street-level bureaucrat indeed bluffed in the hope that Malik really moved through Italy. If this second explanation is correct, then it underlines that not only asylum seekers make up stories to craft a legally effective asylum narrative (e.g. Berger 2015; Khosravi 2011), so too does 'the system' in its attempt to differentiate legitimate from illegitimate movers. These dynamics constantly feed each other and reinforce the climate of mutual suspicion between the asylum applicant and 'the system'.[3] The difference is, however, that the asylum applicant is criminalized by receiving societies for this act of misrepresentation (e.g. Berger et al. 2015; Andersson 2014: 220), while the system generally gets away with it. In the same light, we should understand the illegal deportation of Africans, as we have seen in the case of the Senegalese man Ibrahim who was deported to Mali after a deal between the Spanish and Malian authorities. This suggests that fraudulent practices and brokering services do not only facilitate movement from Africa to Europe, but also in its opposite direction.

Systems Compared

When it comes down to 'the system', Eurospace is an unequal landscape. Despite the many efforts to harmonize migration, mobility and asylum policies, there exists 'a sheer heterogeneity of practices and experiences of reception' (Vianelli 2017: 365; see also Campesi 2015). Furthermore, different rules and practices exist among different member states concerning the stimulation of the mobility of non-EU nationals. The policy report on labour mobility of the European Migration Network (2013: 6) underlines this discrepancy by stating: 'Member States, acting legally, can and do limit or encourage such mobility [of non-EU nationals], according to their national policies and priorities, thus creating differences in rules and practices across the Member States'.

Through their cross-border mobility, the African movers have developed a collective capacity to compare systems across the EU. Even if they had not moved to a certain EU member state themselves, there were always many contacts who could provide information about residence conditions, labour rights and reception facilities. Some movers only noticed the differences after a border passage, others actively studied variations in the system in order to navigate their next movements. In their eyes, the three national entry points of this research can be summarized as follows: Italy is not easy as the system there is slow, shadowy and unpredictable, but at least there is always room to manoeuvre in its informal economy. Spain has basically no asylum system for Africans, but there are other ways to get your papers, mainly through labour contracts. The system of the Netherlands is extremely strict in terms of asylum opportunities as well as regularization procedures through family reunification or labour contracts (see also Andrikopoulos 2017).

While relying on experiences and information of co-movers, many African movers navigate different systems consecutively, or at the same time. Omar and Amat entered the asylum procedure in Germany, not to find protection (since they had found protection already in Italy) but to find access to the German labour market. Franck – the Cameroonian man who travelled from Spain to Germany – also navigated this unequal space. To his surprise, when Franck stayed in a migrant reception centre in Barcelona, he was actively discouraged from entering the asylum system. According to the NGO staff he was talking to, there was no use in his applying for asylum since his chances were negligible:

> I even asked the people there: 'Do you have an asylum system or what?' They say, 'No, there is no asylum here for you. You go! Europe is *big!* Spain has nothing for you, so you better move!' They even gave me a *mappa*, a Europe map, and they explained to me all the countries. I was very, very surprised ... In Barcelona there was this NGO who told us to move.

Upon his entrance in Germany, Franck did enter the asylum procedures. When he evaluated the two reception systems, he reinforced the typical image of Germany as having an organized system based on humanitarianism, while the Spanish approach was more laissez-faire and disorganized. However, this does not mean that the German system has no downsides. To my question of whether the German system was actually better compared to that of Spain, Franck replied:

> The system is not so much better because here [in Germany] they don't give you any information. In Spain they say just 'No' [to asylum applications], because they think you can get a permit through working. In Germany you ask Asyl, but you hear nothing. And they sometimes let you wait for five or seven years. If they don't tell you anything for seven years, it becomes your prison, you see.

Interestingly, Franck reflected both directly and indirectly on the European system's level of integration. With phrases like 'Europe is one for the system, but not one for the people' and 'Everywhere in Europe there is the same problem for Africans' he suggested that Africans are likely to face similar institutional barriers to a regular long stay in many different EU member states. After having been in Germany for more than three years without any progress in his legal status, his negative feelings about the German system intensified. At the time of my second visit to him (January 2016), he drew a parallel between his experience in the Mediterranean and his current state of being in the opaque system:

> We are in the middle of the sea, and we are swimming. We are in the middle of the sea and looking for help [his Cameroonian friend sitting next to him nods his head, confirming this narrative]. We are in the middle of a struggle, and we don't know where it ends ... We crossed the sea but we entered another one here in Germany. Because from the last time you come here [refers to my visit in 2015] ... We can say we are still in the same struggle. That is why I call it a sea. This system, agh, this system makes you feel lost. They ask you for this paper, that paper, you enter this process, but then they say the laws have changed! So after the sea, there comes another sea.

Franck's feelings of being lost amidst a sea of procedures and paperwork primarily come from frustration related to the stagnation of his asylum procedures. He had heard basically nothing from the authorities for about two years and had 'just continued with his life'. Continuing with his life involved finding progress in other dimensions of life, a process that was not free from disappointments either. He had found work in a computer company for a trial period of three months, but in the end he was not hired due to his defective German. He started a relationship with a woman from another non-EU country whose asylum was formally rejected by the German authorities. This woman later gave birth to their daughter. But their relationship and newborn child opened up an entire new field of rules and regulations – another 'sea'. The most important intermediator and legal advisor for Franck was not a lawyer but the older German woman whom he had got to know through the church programme.

In the navigation of the system, asylum, labour contracts and family reunifications are important issues. The different regularization opportunities are carefully taken into account when people scan their next possible destinations. One illustration comes from Mo – a Gambian man whom I met in Barcelona. He had just returned from a two-month stay in Sweden where he had found a temporary job. Once he noticed I came from the Netherlands, he waved his hands above his head and cried out: '*Holland*, that is my *host* country!' He considered the Netherlands his host country because his travel history to Europe was anchored to my country of birth. Based on his professional profile as a development worker, a Dutch family living not far from Amsterdam invited him three years in a row – in 2003, 2004 and 2005 – to stay in the Netherlands. None of the visits lasted longer than three months. In 2006, however, he travelled again to the Netherlands, but this time he 'found his own visa', meaning he did not rely on an invitation of the family. In that year, he moved on to Spain. When I asked him why he did not stay in the Netherlands, he hinted at a significant difference in the system: 'You know for some things, Holland is a good country, but for other things, Spain is better. So, if you come in search for papers, Spain is better. So I came here, I worked here, and after I got my residence paper'.

In Spain, Mo managed to 'find a paper through a contract' by working in the agricultural sector around Almeria. He knew well that this regularization through a labour arrangement was impossible in the system of the Netherlands. Mo, in fact, felt himself to have exchanged the strict Dutch system for a looser southern European model of migration management. However, for others, their move from northern to southern Europe actually resulted in long-lasting bureaucratic procedures. One example comes from a Cameroonian woman, Nadine, who entered Germany on a student visa. She renewed her visa various times, extending her stay in Germany up to several years. After this period she moved to Italy, where she enrolled in another study programme in Venice. This move from Germany to Italy brought her a hard time, particularly due to the complex registration procedures of her first child, who was born in Germany. She compared the Italian and the German systems as follows:

> In Germany, it was like totally clear, you just have your *Termin*, your appointment, and when you come, [you are there] for only like five minutes, if you have all your documents that they ask. They just print the visa, and place it in your passport. You are in, you are out! In Italy there is a whole jungle ... My first son stayed like three years without documents ... I could not do nothing, but the whole procedure is so complicated, first of all you go to questura [police station] and then you get like an appointment, and the appointment is not easy. You just go and you think you are back in Africa, because you are getting to one office, and there are thousands of people waiting, fighting, just to get a number. And that number does not guarantee you to get a document. So we went there days and days with my little ones. I had two kids at that time, so it was not that easy to get there. It was really horrible. I think that aspect you can say, uhm, Germany is really like organized. In issuing your visa and stay permit, Italy is really difficult, to have the stay permit. It is not a matter of having the finance, but the procedure is almost impossible. Some people just get stranded in Italy not because they want to be illegal ... but just because you don't even know where to start ... You don't know the reason [for not getting the documents] and you don't even know *who* to go to. Because when you go to the police people, they don't even know the migration law. They don't even know what to tell you. So you have nobody to even try to get a conversation, or to explain your situation. People like my son waited for three years [to get a residence permit].

Nadine grounded for about thirteen years in Italy, married there to an African man with a permanent residence permit and gave birth to two more children. Her family status finally entitled her to change her German residence permit into an Italian permanent residence permit. After her relatively long stay in Italy, which included multiple flexible movements that she described as 'more or less holiday', she divorced her husband after ten years of marriage (something she did not want to elaborate on). Three years later she decided to move back to Germany with her three children. Even with her Italian permanent residence, she felt restricted in Germany, especially when it came down to labour opportunities. As a diversified tactic, and to lower her barriers on the German labour market, she decided to apply for a German residence permit as well:

> Now I have both. Yea, I have both for like three years ... But my children still have to have a document, but they are still here with the *illimitato* [the unlimited residence permit], the one of Italy, because the German system says I must have a job to proof that I am able to ... take care of my children, and I don't want to come to their country just to get access to their social system.

With her different university degrees of different universities in different nation states (bachelor's degree in Germany and a master's degree in Italy), this ambitious woman worked on a temporary contract as a research assistant at one of the northern German universities. Besides her native language, she fluently spoke English, French and Italian. Despite these qualities, she faced severe barriers regarding her career, particularly in academia. With a deep frustration, she stated that one may expect the 'people on that level' to be 'different', but 'they are even worse'. Her bitter experience with academia was a reason to try her luck once more in a different place in Germany. After she had arrived there, she sent me a message to say she had found a better job and that she was 'still migrating'. That last text message was followed by a smiling emoticon with tears.

A Borderless Zone with Borders

The installation of internal border controls during and after Europe's refugee reception crisis has been a delicate political issue. For my informants, these border controls may indeed imply stricter controls, significant delays of their travels and in some cases a severe interruption of their being in Europe. Yet the implementation of internal border controls in Europe is all too often framed as a reintroduction of borders. The point is, however, that borders and barriers have *always* existed for African movers, even in times when the Schengen Area was not questioned by populist tendencies or under the political pressure of a refugee reception crisis. They emerge when people are randomly controlled (with controls that are never really random), they appear during regular public transport rides and they appear in hospitals and at traffic lights and during administrative controls in the workplace. We have also seen above that borders even enter the intimate spheres of love relationships. For people living without the right papers, it means that a small mistake may leave very deep scars.

While my informants were confronted with this mobility regime in their everyday lives, I noticed the omnipresence of borders during my own fieldwork. While meeting up with informants in Barcelona, Bergamo and Rome, police officers more than once questioned our get-togethers. The most telling event happened in Bergamo where I met Charles. When Charles shared parts of his travel history with me whilst we sat down on a sidewalk in Bergamo, he suddenly said: 'Can you stop this?' His hints were strong enough for me to hide my voice recorder. Since I sat with my back to the street side, I could not see the police car that had stopped behind me on the sidewalk. When I turned my head, I saw two policemen with dark sunglasses approaching us. With a rigorous *'Documenti!'* they ordered us to show our identity documents to them. Charles, and his friend sitting next to them, handed over their papers almost guilelessly. One of the police officers took the papers of the two men to the police car and checked them by communicating with a colleague who was probably based at the police office. His colleague standing behind us asked for my documents as well and I explained to him that I had left my passport in my hotel. On that February day in Bergamo, I was the only undocumented person among the three of us. But this was not considered a problem at all. When the policemen had left the scene, an intense discussion among Charles, his friend and me followed on blackness, whiteness and borders. The three of us shared a deep frustration at the unequal treatment that can only be understood through the notion of Europe's racialized mobility regime (Khosravi 2011; Balibar 2004). But my interlocutors seemed to have been confronted with these processes for too many times to get really angry, as Charles commented: 'So that is life for us ... That is the kind of stuff we are talking about'. These unpleasant encounters destabilize the main starting point of this book to de-migranticize discussions on migration and mobility (see Introduction; Dahinden 2016) since they clearly articulate a sense of migrancy through processes of differentiation and structural expressions of incomplete citizenship. For Charles, such confrontations induced the feeling that he just never truly belonged in Europe. In February 2015, he stated that it was most likely that he would return to Nigeria within the next five years. Already in July of that very same year he wrote to me he how he had 'left the streets and returned home'. According to my latest information (July 2018) he has not since returned to Europe.

Over the years the omnipresence of borders has further been intensified by an increasingly virtualized system of 'touchpoints' and 'encounters' between mobile people, objects and data (Johnson et al. 2011). A telling illustration of this comes from one of Lamin's train travels from Italy to Switzerland. That journey he faced two types of controls that quickly followed each other. The first control was at the train station of Brig – a Swiss town located along the Italian–Swiss border. Swiss border authorities entered the train and asked Lamin to hand over his documents. He gave them his Gambian passport and his Italian residence permit. They checked Lamin's documents, and nothing appeared to be wrong. The next stop, however, he was to his surprise approached by police officers. They asked Lamin to disembark the train and to follow them. Lamin recalled this episode as follows:

> So I was going down, and I was like: 'What is the problem?' They were like: 'We are police, so we are doing our job'. I said: 'Look. But what is the problem?' They asked me: 'So you are going to Switzerland?' I said: 'Yes I am going to Switzerland'. 'And what are you going to do in Switzerland?' 'I have a friend that I visit often'. And the police guy was like: 'You are always crossing the border, you know'. I say: 'Yes, because I have a friend that I visit sometimes'.

When Lamin told me this, I wondered how the police knew that Lamin was a frequent border crosser. There are no entry or exit stamps put on any document when you cross the Italian–Swiss border. Since there are no structural border controls, it is also unlikely that border guards or police officers had recognized Lamin as a frequent mover. For Lamin, however, it was clear: according to his interpretation the border police had communicated with their colleagues at the next stop since they actually targeted him directly. Probably, they had asked their colleagues to check Lamin's past travel behaviour – and the key to this was Lamin's Italian train *abbonamento*, a card that digitally stores one's train travels. The police had asked him to hand it over, and they had controlled his past travels. Suddenly, one of the police officers had stared at the computer screen and told Lamin: 'But you overstayed'. The travel details indeed suggested that in one period of time, Lamin had stayed longer than ninety days in Switzerland (the maximum period of time spread over 180 days). However, what the train details did not show was that Lamin had left Switzerland in the meantime and had gone to Germany. For that travel, he had not used his Italian *abbonamento*. Lamin tried to explain his situation, but it did not bother the policemen as they repeated that they were 'just doing their job'. While Lamin was becoming more and more angry, he also had to undergo a drug test. With a cotton swab, they wiped Lamin's neck, and soon after the test appeared to be negative. Furthermore, Lamin got fingerprinted by force – an issue that really touched him. His frustration reminded me of a remarkable comparison that Lamin once made. When I visited him for the first time in Switzerland, he stated that being fingerprinted is like having HIV/Aids. He must have seen my puzzled face at that time, not really knowing what he meant with that statement, so he added: 'The fingerprints bro! Once you give them, it is incurable. Once you give them you have HIV/Aids'. After he got 'infected' by the Swiss system, Lamin's Gambian passport was again thoroughly investigated. After that, he could leave. With a few hours delay, Lamin reached Pappy's house. There he explained what had happened, and he shared his deep frustrations with the words: 'This is really shit. If this is what it takes to come to your country, I will never come again'.

In this episode of Lamin's mobility in Europe, the Swiss border appeared to him as a borderscape where different mechanisms of control intersect. The authorities could not find any traces of bad behaviour on the basis of the documents he carried with him. They needed to find a way to hook up conventional border controls with other methods of mobility surveillance. Thus, border guards may indeed be increasingly present within EU's Schengen space as a result of national security reflexes, but their activities are only a small fraction of bordering practices that are dislocated from the territorial boundaries of a nation state (Johnson et al. 2011).

Destiny

Within a time frame of eight years, I met Destiny in very different places – in bustling Istanbul, in pleasant Heraklion, on the outskirts of Rome and in the city centre of worlding Naples. During this period, I stored at least seven different telephone numbers for Destiny. The impermanence of his reachability helps to explain why he did not think of me when he saw a Dutch telephone number on the display of his mobile phone in Italy. In fact, he thought the call came from his Dutch pro bono lawyer. Destiny got in touch with this lawyer when he was detained by the Dutch border police soon after his plane to Schiphol airport had landed. I only heard this news after he was deported back to Italy. His detention actually explained why we had no contact for months. The news about his detention deeply puzzled me since I was sure that Destiny held a residence permit of Italy that allowed him to travel across Eurospace. As soon as he got his Italian residence permit, he started to travel frequently between Austria and Italy without any noticeable problems. His journey to the Netherlands appeared to be harsher. He was selected by the Dutch border police and a thorough control followed. Initially he thought the border police had made a mistake, but soon after, he realized that he was in serious trouble and that his mobile life in Europe had been stranded due to a problem with his passport. Destiny travelled to the Netherlands with his Italian residence paper and his Nigerian passport. The documents were 'real', but the Dutch authorities found out that the passport had been obtained by what they define as a 'fraudulent' process. For this reason, he was accused of entering the Netherlands illegally. Destiny had indeed 'asked someone' to collect his passport when he lived in Europe without the proper documents. But he assured me that the passport was real and belonged to him. According to his lawyer, however, there was no doubt that the passport was collected with a false identity, and on that basis the Dutch authorities indeed accused him of entering the country in an unauthorized way. In fact, the Dutch prosecutor argued that if the passport was obtained through identity fraud, then there were enough reasons to question the legality of his residence permit in Europe. However, as Destiny's lawyer also told me, the Italian authorities confirmed that the Italian residence permit he was holding was actually his and was obtained by Destiny in the regular way. To sum up, there is a Nigerian man who is a legal resident of Italy who travels to the Netherlands and who is stopped at the border because the way in which he obtained his Nigerian passport is considered fraudulent by the Dutch authorities. Destiny spent two months in a Dutch prison and after that he was transferred to a migrant detention centre in Rotterdam where he was forced to stay another five weeks. From this slightly different prison-like space, the Dutch authorities attempted to deport Destiny: not to Italy, but to Nigeria directly.

Destiny is not a troublemaker – at least, this is not how I got to know him. He is a fairly docile Nigerian man. I remember very well how he was constantly outshouted by one of his Nigerian friends in Istanbul in the period I first met him. Instead of competing with his friend's expressive behaviour, Destiny preferred to avoid severe discussions and stayed in the background. I seldom heard him talking negatively about his social environment, and I seldom heard him articulate his personal drive to reach Europe. His ambition to reach Europe resonated in things that were more subtle – like in his email address that started with 'destiny4Europe'. After having struggled in Greece for roughly three years, he found his way to Italy from where he hustled his way forwards. He spent some time in Switzerland and later returned to Italy. From the time he entered Eurospace, it took approximately seven years before he obtained his first stable residence permit. In those seven years, he made a living in different informal economic circuits – street vending in Greece, informal trading between Italy and Nigeria, and other small hustling practices. When I visited him in April 2014 in his living place in Rome, he mainly expressed his own daily hardships: he was still 'fighting' for the paper and he was still not married – which troubled him deeply since he would soon turn forty. Roughly a year later, I saw him in his new place of residence (Naples) and his life had changed considerably. He had received a message from the Italian authorities that he would get his five-year paper soon, which was a major breakthrough for him. A new horizon had appeared. This time it was not opaque and uncertain, it was clear-cut and written down on paper by the authorities. What is more, he had found a woman in Nigeria whom he really liked and he hoped she would be his wife in the near future. His hopes were also related to the fact that with the small earnings he had made over the years, he had recently bought a plot of land in the Delta region of Nigeria – his region of origin. When I oversaw this gradual, multifaceted process, I complimented him for making 'very good progress'. He replied: 'I feel that way, as you say. I finally can say that I am happy. And it does not matter how you begin. I mean, some people start with very good progress, but they end with a big disaster. Some start with disaster, and then they make really good progress'.

However, the confrontation with the Dutch borders two years later indicated that the uncertainty and insecurity related to lives of undocumented migrants seeps through in the periods of time in which they are regularized. Thus, whereas some scholars have rightly argued that many irregular migrants are not unauthorized in absolute terms because they find themselves in a legal grey zone (Kubal 2013), it may equally be the case that people who are in fact legal residents in Europe also find themselves in semi-legal situations. I do not actually know the details of how the borders of Eurospace intervened during Destiny's travel from one Schengen country (Italy) to the next (the Netherlands). Maybe he just had the wrong gaze when he entered the baggage hall of the airport, maybe he wore the wrong shoes, maybe the authorities had traced him already when he disembarked the plane. In any case, this border event had a major impact on the 'really good progress' he had made over years.

In the period just after his deportation from the Netherlands to Italy, Destiny asked me to contact his Dutch lawyer since there was a chance that he would be financially compensated for the time spent in the migrant detention centre of Rotterdam (not the regular prison). According to Destiny's lawyer, this second phase of detention was unlawful since the Dutch authorities did not act according to the Dublin Regulation, which meant that they should have sent Destiny directly back to Italy based on his Italian residence permit. This would have prevented a long period in migrant detention, with all kinds of human suffering involved. Destiny put this legal crux as follows: 'Nederland, honestly speaking, they are strange huh! They said … my document is OK. But I told them: "You say my document is OK, and the document says you should take me back to Italy." But they could not do that'.

When I spoke to Destiny's lawyer, he was surprised that Destiny had a contact person in the Netherlands. He stated he could have used me as a witness in the legal procedure since it would have helped when someone had identified Destiny as Destiny. Destiny's lawyer was now ready to start another legal procedure to challenge the reason for Destiny's prolonged detention and the emotional costs involved. Moreover, he argued that if Destiny was able to get the same residence permit in Italy on the basis of the same identity details, it would strengthen the case that he had actually been detained on wrong assumptions. After all, the same documents with the same details would help to prove that Destiny is really the Destiny who is represented in the passport. With this 'new' proof, Destiny's case could enter a legal review process. In order to start this procedure, the Dutch lawyer had already contacted Destiny's lawyer in Italy. All things were set. However, while Destiny was of course interested in a form of financial compensation, he also felt that the damage was already done. Although he had experienced deportation before when he had tried to reach South Africa, he now really felt as though he were being treated like 'a real prisoner'. And that hurt. Moreover, it frustrated him heavily that the Dutch authorities took not only his Nigerian passport but also his Italian residence papers. They themselves acknowledged that there was nothing wrong with that paper, so why would they keep it? For Destiny, this was 'wickedness' with significant consequences. He now had to go through the bureaucratic labyrinth once again. I felt sorry for him since this would require again a lot of 'paperwork'. In the end, Destiny decided to forget about his Dutch experience as soon as possible, and to not expend any energy any more on his fights against the Dutch state. He had no plans to revisit the country any time in his life, and even if he had such plans, he still had to await the five-year entry ban that the Dutch state gave him on top. Destiny thus lost his relatively stable position in Eurospace for another period of time. As he stated, he came from zero and now he had to 'fight again'. Cases like this induce the fear among my interlocutors that the authorities take papers for 'no reason'.

Bordering Mobility: A View from a Dutch–German Borderland

Borderlands have archetypical inhabitants – the border people or 'borderlanders'. The borderlanders at each side of the border are often portrayed as one people, sharing a specific identity that blurs the national divide imprinted by the border. Partly for this reason, the European Commission has invested heavily in so-called 'Euregions' for their potential contribution to the further integration of a postnational European space (e.g. Kramsch, Mamadouh and Van der Velde 2004). The relatively small city in the Netherlands I live in – Nijmegen – is located at such borderland. Being located only 7 km from Germany, it is characterized by cross-border circulations of commuters and shoppers that make their ways from nearby German villages to Nijmegen, and many others move in the opposite direction (e.g. Spierings and Van der Velde 2013). Next to the archetypical borderlanders, there are 'other' borderlanders making use of largely uncontrolled mobility as well as the legal and economic differences at each side of the border. The Congolese man Maggis, for instance, moved together with his Dutch girlfriend to the German side of the border. With this move, Maggis hoped to be able to regularize his stay based on EC Directive 204/38 that was discussed in Chapter 2. As such, borderlands are not only laboratories for European integration, they are also typical spaces of mobility and semi-legality (Rytter 2012). Maggis' move to Germany, which spanned a distance of only a dozen kilometres, offered him new windows of opportunities. He framed his move as 'a new step, a new country, a new life'.

Before he relocated to Germany, Maggis' life had reached a deadlock in the Netherlands. After his repeated asylum claims were all declined, he faced a nine-month period of detention. Inside the migrant detention centre he was confronted with different approaches to 'sending him back to Africa'. The Dutch Repatriation and Departure Service (DT&V) particularly put pressure on him to accompany them to his national embassy in Brussels in order to arrange the necessary *laissez passer*. Thus, like the mobility facilitators in Greece, this to-be-arranged mobility required the necessary paperwork. When Maggis refused any cooperation, DT&V started to 'push' him, as Maggis explained:

> The first time he [the DT&V staff member] came, he told me, 'You have to go to the embassy'. And then [the second time] they said, 'If you don't go to the embassy then, we send you by force. You understand?' I said: 'OK! I feel I don't have any power any more, do what you want!' ... And then, one day they came to me and said [starts to talk with a calm and kind voice]: 'Ohhh, the IND wants to see you, people from IND ... They want to talk to you about your problem again!' I said: 'Ah, but, I talk to IND four times, the IND did not give me anything ... So why do they want to see me now?' He said: 'Oh nooo, they will give you a chance [for a new procedure]!'... I said: 'No man, I am not crazy, I am not stupid'. He said: 'Oh no, just try, maybe you get paper, for status'. I said: 'Nooo, I don't want that paper any more. I only want my freedom'. ... He said: 'So you don't want to speak to IND any more?' I said: 'No! I don't want to speak to IND. If IND wants to see me, I am here, in this place! The IND knows that I am here. They can come ... So

> why do they want to take me from here [to the outside world]?' And then, when I spoke to somebody [another detained migrant], he said, 'Aghh, you made something good, if you go ... the IND always brings some people from you government, your embassy'.
> I: To arrange?
> Maggis: Ya! The IND gives them [the embassy staff] money ... If you come there, then the people see you, and say: 'Ah, he is from Congo! Allez!' And then paff!

The soft approach of the DT&V official indicates that harsh systems attempt to build affective relationships with potential deportees. As a response, Maggis performed the unwilling and stubborn man. Interestingly, he himself looked for ways to massage his social relation with the DT&V official, as he stated:

> I was also trying to get him. I was trying to act like being one of his people he like, so I was trying to get him. And you know after the time that I was sent out the prison, this person came to me and he told me: 'You know actually I did not want to send you back, you are a good guy'.

The nine months of detention ended only after a judge prohibited the IND to detain Maggis any longer. Thereupon, the IND gave him an expulsion order – a document that emphasizes he was no longer allowed to be in the Netherlands. This resulted in a legal discord: Maggis was obliged to leave the Netherlands, but the Dublin Regulation forbade him to move to another European country. A two-month period of doubt, exploration and discussion followed that not only affected Maggis, but also his girlfriend. In this process, Maggis was assisted by his lawyer as well as some volunteers from a hospitality organization in Nijmegen. They helped him to understand the subsequent steps of his regularization procedure. Without their legal advice, Maggis would have probably not felt comfortable enough to make the move to Germany. Before the relocation of the couple took place, he visited the German village several times to arrange some practical issues. Also the actual moving of the belongings of the couple to the new house went smoothly.

Just before the couple relocated to Germany, Maggis managed to get an informal job in Nijmegen. Partly based on his contacts with the hospitality organization, he was hired as a janitor for the night shelter that houses undocumented people in the city. Since Maggis had spent many nights in this shelter himself in the time he did not have a secure place of residence, he already knew the rules and regulations and the particular politics that come with the shelter (see Noten 2016). Maggis felt somewhat ambivalent about his new role as janitor since it came with the task of controlling the behaviour of the sojourners that are allowed to stay in the shelter between six at night and ten in the morning. However, it was one of the few opportunities he got to earn some money. For several weeks, he was an undocumented border commuter residing in Germany and working and socializing in the Netherlands.

It is telling that Maggis was confronted with borders not during any of his border crossings, but during an unexpected control in his German place of residence. His unfamiliar face in his new place caught the attention of a police officer, and he asked Maggis for his papers. As he could not hand over the document this man asked for, he was brought to the police station. There, his fingerprints were checked. Being identified as a 'Dublin case', he was returned to the Netherlands and handed over to the border police. A Kafkaesque situation followed when the Dutch police officer told Maggis that he was not allowed to be in the Netherlands. Maggis replied that he was not in the Netherlands at the moment he was caught. In fact, the German police had brought him to the Netherlands. Nevertheless, an official warning followed and the Dutch authorities articulated Maggis' *inreisverbod* (the entry ban) that is related to the expulsion order he received earlier.

This unpleasant border event did, however, not stop Maggis from commuting the border, and there is a cruel logic behind that. For Maggis, as for many other people living in irregular situations, the border is in fact everywhere since he himself *is* the border (Khosravi 2011: 61). Any police control anywhere (be it close to the border or not) would again confront him with migration-related bureaucracies and, possibly, detention. This became clearer once again when he and his girlfriend went to the Dutch authorities to declare Maggis' fatherhood of a soon-to-be-born baby. When the civil servant asked for their papers, Maggis panicked. He had arranged a Congolese passport in the meantime, but he knew that this was insufficient without a Schengen visa or residence permit. The civil servant told him she had to 'check this [Maggis' papers] more thoroughly'. What had started as a happy moment for the couple, soon turned into a border event of control and paperwork. Maggis decided to escape and left the room. After some hours, the civil servant told Maggis' girlfriend – who had stayed behind – that 'The Congolese passport was not fake', and that Maggis' fatherhood was successfully declared. No further questions were asked. Just after his son was born, I accompanied Maggis to the local authorities to declare the birth of his son. When I drove him from his German residence to the Dutch side of the border, he was very nervous that this minor administrative obligation would again create a border event. Maggis, however, is an intelligent man who over the years has learned how to massage bureaucratic relations in the Dutch system. He was helped by the same civil servant as the previous time. This appeared to be an advantage. When she kindly asked for the passports, Maggis only handed over the passport of the mother of the child and nodded his head benevolently. The civil servant understood the message and finalized the subscription without further ado. Back in the car, Maggis felt relieved about the fact that his son now was 'in the system'.

During the entire period that he commuted along the Dutch–German border in irregular ways – a period lasting for roughly one year – Maggis was stopped three times. Every time this confronted him with the risk of another period of detention. This was particularly stressful at the time he had actually become a father. Fed by his precarious situation, Maggis and his girlfriend all the while pushed further their idea to marry – which involved yet another complicated administrative procedure. In the end, their marriage plan worked out and, as they hoped, finally leading to a German residence permit for Maggis. However, this still did not erase all borders for him. Every time he approached the border during his continued commuting practices, he embodied the border. Two months after he had received his residence permit – a pass with the size of a bank card – he stated: 'Sometimes I even forget I have this *pasje* [little pass], then I become stressed when I come close to the border, but then I realize, "Ah! No, I have it!" And sometimes I just think, "This paper is a fake paper. How can this be real? It is so small, it is nothing".'

It was, however, not only him reliving a history that continuously confronted him with borders. Roughly six months after he received his legal status in Germany, he sat on a public bus going from the German side of the border to the city of Nijmegen. The bus was stopped at the border, and Maggis saw two Dutch border guards entering the vehicle. One of them was an older man whom he had before encountered. The other man was younger, and Maggis had never seen him. The latter approached him and asked for his travel papers, which led to the following situation as Maggis described it the day after:

> This young man, he took my paper, he asked: 'Do you speak Dutch?' 'Ya man I speak Nederlands, I lived here several years'. So then he spoke Nederlands with me and he asked: 'OK, do you have a passport, because you can only travel with this paper with your passport'. I told him: 'No man, I know the rules, I can travel with this paper to Nijmegen without any problem, there is no need to take my passport with me. If I work in Nijmegen, yes, then it is different, but me I just travel there'. He asked me again: 'Do you have your passport?' And I told him the same story. But I was not angry, I was very *tranquil* [relaxed], because I know I was right. He told me: 'In that case I need to check your paper'. So he went out of the bus and he made the phone call to the IND ... I think the people of IND gave him all the information, and they told him that he should leave me. But this took a very long time, maybe ten

minutes, fifteen minutes. And this for me was not a problem, but I felt sorry for all the people in the bus, some people started to act a bit nervous you know … So, then the young man came to me, he said: 'Here is your paper, everything is correct'. Then the old man told this young man: 'Say sorry to him, because you let him wait for nothing'. Then this young man said sorry.

Maggis never really made this explicit, but to me it appeared that this small excuse meant more to him than just an excuse of an individual border guard. I felt that it symbolized a personal victory over a stringent mobility regime that had made his life stagnate for about seven years. As if the border guard had spoken with the voice of the regime itself – saying sorry.

Concluding Notes: On Finding Ways

In four chapters, this part of the book – 'Navigations' – has outlined the hustling practices that my informants use to bind together different passages of their trajectories and find escape routes where necessary. Their navigational tactics indicate that the African movers in question are somehow prepared to 'switch gears' (Simone 2001: 18). In times of residence they are at the same time ready to move, change scenes and transcend borders. This preparedness is reflected in many expressions of my six informants from Senegambia, such as 'trying your luck', and 'raba raba'. This cocktail of mobility willingness, readiness and creativity is very hard to control through repressive measures. In fact, the omnipresence of borders and control within Eurospace may be an important explanatory factor in why African movers continuously 'try their luck', as it is also illustrated by Maggis' mobility between Germany and the Netherlands (see also Schapendonk 2018a).

The trajectories discussed furthermore underline that, however harsh the apparatuses of facilitation/control appear to be, specific moments and encounters emerge as openings in 'the system'. These openings allow for social negotiation and many of these negotiations produce their own affective relations. The contrast between Shakur's resistant character and Yahya's specific performativity of the deserving refugee in Italy is telling. They both shared a deep frustration concerning the Italian system – but they have navigated it differently, with different results. Consequently, the openings in the system and the required navigational techniques do not simply lead to an argument that emphasizes individual agency in mobility processes. In fact, it articulates the *relational* dimension of the situations at play. Whether the movers' efforts and negotiations actually help them to get ahead strongly depend on the intentions and efforts of the people they (attempt to) connect with or are confronted with. This relationality is what my informants most probably would call 'luck'. This relationality also blurs the lines between migration apparatuses and social networks, between webs of control and affective circuits, and between autonomy and deportability. The interrelations between the seemingly different components mean that African movers need to find ways through a 'navigational continuum' (Vigh 2006: 48) of uncertainty, opportunities, mobility, rules and borders.

NOTES

1. Lucht (2012) explains that the label of 'Tycoon' is also used among Ghanaians in Italy.
2. See Ramsøy (2014: 52-6) for a discussion on how deservingness and refugeeness affect the social lives of West Africans in Spain who have not been granted with a refugee paper.
3. Khosravi (2011) highlights the nigh impossibility of crafting an effective asylum case in the Eurocentric hearing system. The applicant needs to be able to describe the slightest detail of his/her life before and during his/her flight. In that sense, 'truth telling' is connected with the capacity to remember details. At the same time, however, when one *is* able to present a perfectly consistent and detailed asylum narrative, one is accused of 'fabricating the case' (ibid.: 33-4).

PART II

Re-viewing Europe

Lleida, Spain, April 2016

Moustapha was confused, and so was I. When we walked along the beautiful Segre river, away from his mosque towards the bridge that gives access to the city centre of Lleida, we tried to recapture his mobility pathway since the moment we last spoke to each other. We struggled to get the important events in chronological order, which was not uncommon during the dynamic conversations I had with him. So exactly when did he arrive in Italy? And when was he detained by the French border authorities? Was that before or after he had reached Italy? But if it was really before he had reached Italy, then how come that he just returned from Milan?

I had met Moustapha one year before – April 2015 – in the apartment that he shared with Pape and Babacar. The three Gambian men entered Europe between 1996 and 2001, and since then they all three had bumpy career paths in the Spanish pre-crisis construction and agricultural sectors. Over the years they managed to achieve rather stable legal positions. Moustapha, however, lost his residence rights after his Spanish wife divorced him some years ago. My first impression was that the three men lived rather grounded lives in Lleida. They rented an apartment together, had work and rich social lives. Some five months after our first encounter, however, they had all left their apartment in Lleida. Babacar left for the Gambia where he spent time with his family and started a taxi business. He returned to Spain in February 2016 and, from there, he moved to Milan where he stayed in Doudou's guest house for some months. Pape made a 'European tour' to visit some old friends in Amsterdam and Hamburg. After his tour, he returned to Spain from where he moved to the Gambia to reunite with his family and work on his land – which suggests that mobile pathways are not disconnected from agricultural permanence (Gaibazzi 2015).[1] Finally, Moustapha first moved to a nearby village, some 50 km away from Lleida, and worked there for a horticulturist. When the fruit season ended there, he also made his way to Milan, where he was hosted by his brother.

Although the three Gambian men had initially kept me up to date about their travels, from October that year our communications went down. At that time, I was concerned that I had lost some of my good research connections. During my next field trip to Barcelona and its surroundings, I decided to just give it a try and went to Lleida to look for them. In the surroundings of their apartment building, however, there was no sign at all of the presence of the three men. I learned more when I ran into another Gambian man who recognized me as the man who spent time with Babacar last year. He knew my three interlocutors very well because he had shared the apartment – where he himself still lived – with them. When I asked him about their whereabouts, he stated that according to his last information Pape was still in the Gambia. Subsequently, he made a phone call in order to verify his latest information that Babacar had departed to Italy. And Moustapha? He expected him to return from Italy any moment now.

The next day, after a long period of fieldwork in the agricultural spaces of the region, I returned to Lleida. Meandering the city, I saw an African man staring at me from a bench. It was Pape who had just returned from the Gambia. He stood up and hugged me warmly. After our greetings and first conversations, he called Moustapha. When Moustapha came down to the same square it appeared that he had arrived in Lleida only yesterday. During this period in Lleida, I witnessed how mobility trajectories became disentangled after the agricultural season closed, only to re-entangle again when the season was about to start. Almost everyone seemed to return from somewhere. All around me I saw how African men were busy with their 'network work' (Pathirage and Collyer 2011), trying to update their information about friends who had moved elsewhere, sharing their new telephone numbers with others, asking for new numbers via mutual contacts, et cetera. As Pape commented on this networking practice: 'If you move too much, you change too much'. In this setting of reconnecting, it did not appear extraordinary that an ethnographer came there in search of seemingly lost contacts.

In this period of rebonding I spent several days with Moustapha. The reason for our confusion was that I – despite the insights that I had gained so far in the course of my research project into the diverse mobility dynamics – still had a rather reductionist understanding of his mobility trajectory to Milan. I initially thought he just moved there, got into trouble at the border, and after this trouble, tried once more to reach the city. It appeared, however, that between October 2015 and April 2016, Moustapha had travelled three times to Milan. The first time, he reached Milan without any problem, and upon his arrival he just called his brother who hosted him for a few weeks. Through his brother's connections, Moustapha quickly managed to find a petty job as a dishwasher in a restaurant. The 6 euros per hour payment was at least higher than the 4 euros he had earned per hour in the Spanish agricultural sector. After a telephone call from his lawyer in Spain, Moustapha returned to the area of Lleida for some 'paperwork'. To make some progress with his re-regularization process, he needed to present specific documents to his lawyer and sign others. His intermediate stay in Spain did not last long since he travelled back to Milan in December. However, after the terrorist attacks in Paris in

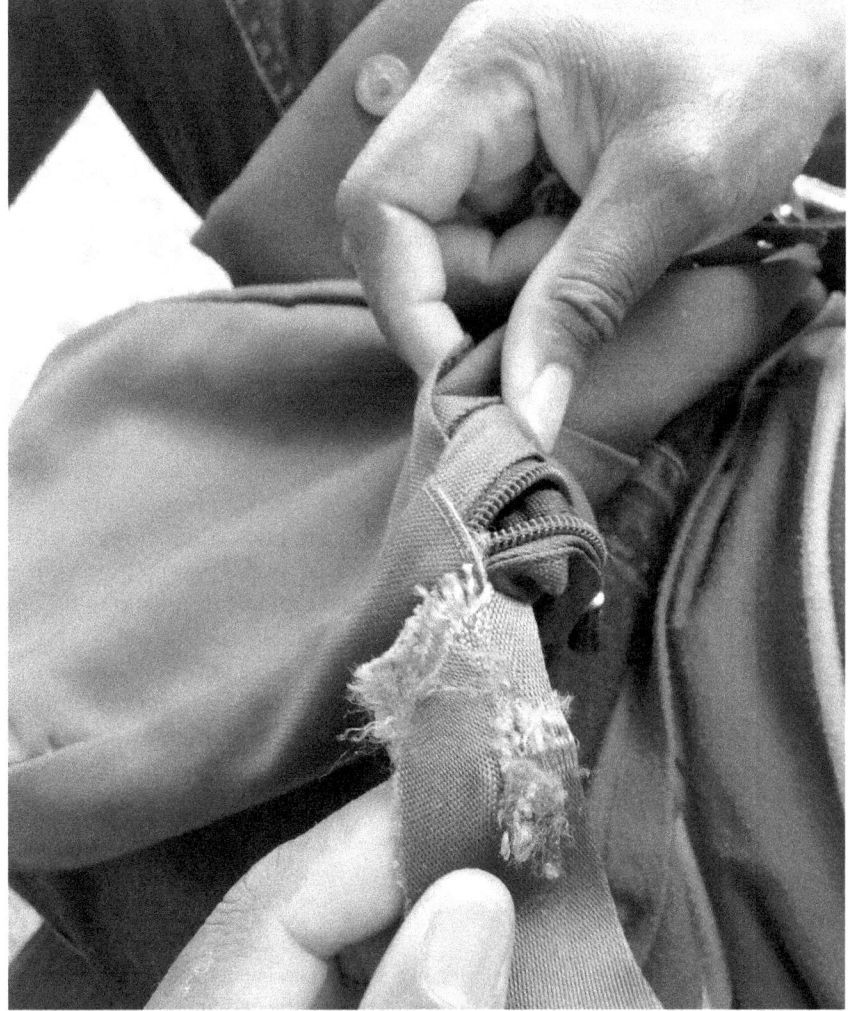

Illustration PII.1 A risk? Photograph by the author.

November 2015, the French government had a securitization reflex that included the intensification of border control. Moustapha was caught. His irregular border crossing, and the small quantity of soft drugs he carried with him, resulted in his imprisonment for several weeks. In this period, Moustapha not only became mentally exhausted, he also suffered from a heavy hernia in his back. Moustapha was clear about this place – to him it was a 'real-life inferno'. It made him rethink Europe as a place where human rights are respected.

During his detention, the French authorities took 'everything from him': his credit card, his 'pre-residence card' (which Moustapha described as the proof that he was in the regularization procedure) and his telephone. All his belongings that he took on his trip were held in custody by the French authorities. He seemed to be most angry about the loss of his phone because this meant he lost most of his valuable contact details. The fact that they took his pre-residence card led to more frustration. It meant another considerable delay in his regularization procedure as he needed to apply for it again. It took him roughly one year to get back to the same point in this juridical labyrinth as when he lost his documents.

After the French authorities released him, he made his way from Spain to Italy once more, this time without any trouble. He stayed there for a few weeks. This was the last time that he had crossed EU's internal borders. In my follow-up meetings with him (September 2016 and July 2017) and numerous communications, he often emphasized how he had given up on travelling inside Europe since the French experience had hard hit him. One day he stated: 'No! For me, I don't take any risk any more, no travel, no ganja. I even stopped smoking'. Travelling and smoking were now framed by Moustapha as two aligned 'bad habits' that had caused him a lot of trouble. Not long after this conversation, I stared at the frayed straps of the little bag he carried with him. It seemed that it would not take long before the bag would become detached from the straps. I touched the bag, and jokingly said: 'You tell me you don't take any risk in life any more, but to me this is risk'. Moustapha's first reaction was that there was no risk involved since there was not too much money in it – only his keys and his documents. 'Your documents?!' I replied. Moustapha burst out laughing and said: 'You are right. It is risk'.

NOTE

1. The three men had their families living in the Gambia, including children. Babacar and Pape regularly visited their families, however the recent irregular status of Moustapha made it impossible for him to do the same.

CHAPTER
5

In Place/Out of Place

Like most mobility research, there is an important risk attached to this study of African movers in Europe. By emphasizing movement, dynamics, fluidity, one may forget about stillness, rest, processes of settlement and people's emotional attachment to places. In the context of this particular study, this risk goes beyond academic discussions of theoretical and methodological biases since it may easily lead to political statements regarding the notion that mobility is a sign of people's failure to 'integrate' into receiving societies. Such a rationale could ultimately lead to more restrictive policies and dangerously sedentarist arguments regarding the alleged non-belonging of mobile groups in contemporary Europe (Mac Laughlin 1999; Sigona 2005).

The mobility lens that is central to this book offers, above all, a relational perspective of im/mobility (e.g. Adey 2006; Schapendonk and Steel 2014). In this respect, many mobility scholars remind us that mobilities are facilitated by, and grounded in, specific localities. It follows that the dynamic trajectories of the African movers under study are not placeless undertakings, but are in fact inherent parts of processual mobility/locality configurations (Dahinden 2010a; Bolay 2017; Gaibazzi 2015). As the geographer Pascual-de-Sans (2004: 350) articulates: 'The study of mobility is ... inseparable from the study of permanence, of settlement and of the relationships individuals and social groups have with places'. This chapter therefore aims to do justice to the struggles, times and efforts my interlocutors have put in processes of grounding somewhere. Even in the most ephemeral conditions – like in the contexts of shifting socialities of asylum (e.g. Parr, Philo and Burns 2003) or self-made camps (e.g. Calais Writers 2017: 111–57) – people have invested in a certain form of local anchorage (Lems 2018). Awful places may turn into homelike places. At the same time, I argue that the mobility disposition of my informants does come with different levels of ambivalence towards processes of emplacement (e.g. Bolay 2017). In other words, place attachments do not necessarily lead to the idealized and integrationist version of a new and single home place where people stay and assimilate.

In understanding these mobility/locality configurations, it is crucial to take into account placemaking capacities that make people feel in place as well as the processes that restrain them from living grounded lives. Regarding the latter, we have already seen various examples of the ugly faces that Europe may present to African movers. Experiences of exclusion, racism and marginalization may explicitly appear to them as a result of, among others, verbal humiliation, xenophobic aggression and physical violence. As discussed in Chapter 4, these experiences may be produced by 'the system' in more or less expected ways, such as discrimination on the labour market, encampment in asylum procedures, ethnic profiling by authorities in public spaces and other expressions of a racialized mobility regime (Schwarz 2018). Even more so, however, they may emerge from the more hidden, everyday and mundane practices of European life: a gaze on a public bus, the blockage by a bouncer from a club, the suspicion felt during an ordinary encounter, the snowball that is thrown from behind. The experiences and emotions attached to these occurrences make many of my informants review – or better re-view – their position in Europe at some point in time.

Placemaking and Its Ambivalences

When I met Lamin for the first time in January 2016, he had already left Italy. My earlier established connections with Omar, Shakur and Saihou helped me to get in touch with him in Switzerland. After our first greeting at the Bern train station, we looked for a place to sit down, drink tea and talk a bit. It appeared, however, that Lamin himself had just arrived in this city since he excused himself for not knowing the place. I suggested to stay close to the train station, but according to Lamin this was an environment that was heavily surveilled by the authorities and therefore not a suitable place to relax. We passed Starbucks, which he described as a 'no-go area'. He had just heard from his 'brothers' it was not safe there and added: 'Switzerland is a control state, a police state. They can ask you for your papers just now, now'. We passed a few other bars and restaurants, but some were too crowded, others were mistrusted by Lamin for their 'whiteness'. Even though his stay in Switzerland was entirely authorized, the cityscape required careful navigation. As seating ourselves in public space came with feelings of uncertainty, we decided to continue wandering the city.

During this first encounter, it struck me that Lamin was generally positive about Italy. His reflection contrasted heavily with the rough and negative stories about Italy that I had heard from his friends. He in fact stressed that 'Life is good in Italy' and that he was happy with his job. Italian life is good – 'when you are outside the system', he quickly added, referring to the suffocating asylum procedures. Lamin furthermore underlined that his stay in Switzerland would be rather brief, he thought of staying there only for three months (which is also the maximum time he could legally spend in a different Schengen country). At the same time, he told me how he invested heavily in learning the German language as this would help him to adapt better to the Swiss environment. The language programme he followed was partly financed by Pappy. Like Alagie's first anticipations of a long stay in the Netherlands (see Chapter 1), Lamin sought ways to ground in Switzerland – which would ease his imagined mobility in the near future. Between 2016 and 2018 he maintained an im/mobile livelihood between the regions of Liguria (Italy) and Bern (Switzerland). One day, he phrased this practice of circulation as follows: 'For me moving to Switzerland is like moving from one house to another house because I have this connection [with Pappy]'. I assured him that this formulation would turn up as a quote in my book.

Lamin indeed stayed in Switzerland for approximately three months. When I met him again in Italy in May 2016 he received me at the train station with the words: 'Welcome to my home!' He seemed to confirm my impression that I had during our in-between telephone conversations about his attachment to Italy. He repeatedly stated that he was 'cool' in Italy, that things were more *'tranquillo'* since he was not subjected to the 'millions of control' he had faced in Switzerland. That same day, however, it appeared that home in this Ligurian city was not really homelike for the social distances and barriers he experienced in his daily life, as he stated:

> You can live here for fifteen years but then still you can have no Italian friends. I tried it even with my former work [in a restaurant], I like those guys there, and we had a good time ... but they never go out with me or come to my place to chop food. Of course, there are some open-minded people, but very, very few.

Lamin, thus, encountered many social barriers in his daily life in Italy. It follows that the distance felt between 'outsiders' on the one hand and 'citizens' on the other is not only a condition that shapes the lives of undocumented people (e.g. Bloch, Sigona and Zetter 2014). One may think to have transgressed a border and reached one's destination, however, new invisible borders may then appear (Khosravi 2011: 75). Lamin concluded in the end: 'It feels like home [in Italy], but in Switzerland I was happier'. The ambivalence in his conclusion is telling – he started to know Italian society very well and appreciated many aspects of it. Yet, there is always the confrontation of being the outsider. For recent arrivals, social isolations are perhaps most felt in the places where one does one's very best to belong. Daily participation and daily investments also mean daily confrontations with othering practices and non-belonging, an issue that has been described by some scholars as the 'integration paradox' (e.g. Van Doorn, Scheepers and Dagevos 2013). As a consequence, 'local footholds' (Dahinden 2010a: 61) of movers remain to a large extent social bubbles since they consist of a clustering of people in similar socio-economic situations – an observation that is shared by Favell (2008) in his study on 'Eurostar' mobility. These bubbles are present in places where movers seek ways to build social capital. For many of my African interlocutors, these are the worksites, public parks and reception centres where they come into contact with other movers. These are the places for social interactions, the sharing of information and the building of friendships.

These lived geographies, however, do emerge with their own borders and boundaries. This became particularly clear to me when, one day, Moustapha drove me around in the agricultural spaces between Huesca and Catalonia. When we entered a town called Alcarràs, I could not notice any significant difference compared to the places we had just passed. For Moustapha, however, we seemed to have entered a significantly different environment, as he stated: 'This is a Fula zone'. In his navigation, the Huesca zone we just came from was the Mandinka and Bambara zone, and further west, around the city of Gerona, the Serahule/Soninke zone began (an observation that is confirmed by survey material, see Gaibazzi 2015 based on Kaplan 1998). Moustapha's map of these Spanish agricultural spaces suggests that ethnicity is an important social glue in the West African placemaking processes in Eurospace. However, there are certainly significant processes of identification that transgress these bubbles of ethnicity (Dahinden 2012). Lamin, for instance, lived in an apartment together with some Egyptians. His close friend Saihou relied heavily on his relationship with an Eritrean man to feel in place in Switzerland, and there are many more examples.

According to Yahya, Saihou and Omar, Lamin is one of the most intelligent persons from the Gambia. It did not then surprise them, nor me, that he was hired by an association of civil and social promotion that seeks to enhance the self-organizing capacities of asylum seekers and refugees in Italy. For Lamin, this meant a welcome additional monthly income of 500 euros, and this job could easily coexist next to the restaurant job he had during the peaks of the Italian tourist season. Lamin offered translation services and personal and legal advice to the people in asylum procedures. He accompanied them to doctors, dentists and all kinds of administration services. Through his work, he removed social barriers and contested legal boundaries. Thus, Lamin managed not only to move out of the Italian (asylum) system, he was now actually fully incorporated by that system and had become an inherent part of it – a fact that created some personal ambivalences for him. When I visited Lamin in his Ligurian anchor place in May 2017, he was not in a very good mood. Recently, Italian life had started to look less bright for him. He had lost his restaurant job as the owner, an Italian man, had sold the place. The latter had decided to uproot himself from Italian society and start his own adventure by relocating to Senegal. Lamin respected the adventure of his former boss, but he was upset to have lost his job. To make matters worse, his contract with the refugee support organization was about to end, and it was very uncertain whether he would get any contract extension. He started to doubt again his emplacement in Italy, as he told me: 'Sometimes I think I need to live here [in Italy], but then again I change my mind. Like now. Now my situation has changed because I lost my job. Now I think again about what to do, because my situation was good, but now I don't know any more'.

Doubt and ambivalence again became dominant emotions in this episode of Lamin's life, confusing the straight-line hypothesis that a long stay automatically leads to stronger place attachment. This is furthermore articulated by the fact that Lamin actually had a very concrete opportunity to live a settled life in Liguria. Pappy offered to buy a house that Lamin could subsequently rent from him. But Lamin disliked this idea and kindly rejected the offer. He preferred to have an open horizon and to not have too many place-related obligations. He literally said that this house would make him feel 'restricted' in terms of his future mobility. He elaborated: 'Because this house means you must stay and live in Italy, but I don't know if I want to know. Maybe I find a job in Germany or Holland, so how can I live in this house?' The expression 'I don't know if I want to know' reflects a general aversion among movers to consider migratory destinations as final. It resonates with Saihou's aversion to 'sitting' that we saw in Chapter 1, but in the particular case of Lamin it took place outside the realm of asylum politics and the waiting they involve. Lamin seemed to be aware that feelings of belonging are likely to shift over time (e.g. Boccagni and Baldassar 2015), an issue that is further discussed below.

Binta

Although I knew she would be present in her hometown in the North Bank Region of the Gambia (the same village from which her husband Dawda and his little brother Yahya originate), it nevertheless somewhat staggered me to hear Binta greeting me in Dutch. Alagie and I approached her, and her two-year-old daughter, and big hugs followed. Binta went to the Gambia together with her daughter to attend the series of ceremonies related to the recent decease of her father – a well-respected man in the village and its surroundings, which was proven by the visitors who came from far to attend the ceremony. Binta was glad to be together with her family for most of the forty-day period of mourning and praying. It was also a good occasion to show her little daughter for the first time to the people she loved and missed the most. Dawda stayed behind in Nijmegen, basically due to work obligations.

Binta guided me around the village. She introduced me to her mother, her 'second mother' by whom she was raised, her older and younger brothers, her family members living in neighbouring compounds and her good friends. In the few days that I spent in the village, I could sense that Binta found herself in a social environment that made her feel 'in place'. The contrast with her situation during our first encounters in Nijmegen could hardly be more evident. Through my multiple visits to Dawda's home, I had been able to notice her struggles related to her feelings of social isolation in the first period after her arrival in the Netherlands. Despite the fact that mobility and circulations are highly gendered in the Gambia (Gaibazzi 2015) and other parts of West Africa (Bolay 2017), Binta was certainly not an inexperienced traveller. As a young woman she had had her vocational training in Serekunda, and for years she had circulated between Serekunda and 'the village' when she worked as an accountant for a non-profit organization that aimed to enhance female entrepreneurship. Her mobility capital (Moret 2017), however, did not help her to ground in the Netherlands. Whereas she could rely on relatives in Serekunda, she had hardly any social contacts in Europe besides her husband and his brothers, who did not live close by. In the meantime, her own brother reached Italy 'through the backway' and later moved to Germany, but for three years they never saw each other in person. Moreover, Binta felt that her husband did not give her much assistance in this first period after arrival, as she once stated with some irritation: 'Dawda is always too busy'. She also openly complained that Dawda did not really show her around in Nijmegen. She hardly knew the Netherlands and never went to see other places in Europe. Her social isolation and limited geographical mobility seemed to reinforce one another.

At the end of my stay in the Gambian village, Alagia, Binta and I sat together. It was one of the rare moments that day in which I had the chance to talk to Binta, since she had been busy arranging the ceremony. I openly reflected on the contrast that I noticed regarding Binta's social position here and in the Netherlands. I shared my impression with them that I could now better understand what she actually must have missed in Dutch society: the social gatherings, the mutual teasing, the laughter, the flexibility and collectivity in caretaking and upbringing. In her village of origin, so it seemed, she never felt lonely. Alagie was the first who reacted to my observation by stating that the first three months in the Netherlands had been very difficult. Quickly, however, Binta overruled him and insisted: 'It was more than three months, it was a whole year. That first year, ohh I wanted to move back home!'

Binta's wish to leave the Netherlands and return to the Gambia gradually disappeared. After a year or so, I saw her transform from a rather silent and docile person into an assertive and powerful woman. She managed to build some valuable social relations in her neighbourhood, in particular with an older Dutch woman. Binta felt supported by this woman who helped her not only with her Dutch language skills and integration exams, but also with taking care of her daughter. Binta's social progress worked in tandem with some economic breakthroughs. She found a job as a cleaner in a popular clothes shop. Moreover, through specific social networking, she managed to set up an informal business as a hairdresser at home. She cut children's hair for 15 euros, and the price for adult haircuts varied between 20 and 40 euros. In an ordinary week, she received one to three clients. With a Muslim feast day approaching, more Senegalese women came to her house for her services. With a Christian feast day approaching, some Ghanaian and Nigerian women visited her to get their hair done. This informal economic activity suited her daily life perfectly, since it could be easily combined with taking care of her children. After the birth of her second child, she had to quit her formal cleaning job, but she continued with her informal practices as a hairdresser. She felt, however, that her clients never became close friends – except for one Ghanaian woman whom she saw more often lately. Although her social life had enriched to some extent, she still missed the warmth of her Gambian friends and family. In that sense, she was well aware that Nijmegen would never be like her life in the North Bank Region of the Gambia.

Binta went through difficult moments, but her future in the Netherlands began to look brighter. From April 2017, after roughly two years in the Netherlands, she even dared to think about further personal development considering she explored opportunities to follow an educational programme to become a midwife. The fact that she had passed all integration exams also made her a good candidate to apply for a Dutch passport. She only had to wait another two and a half years because she would only qualify for a passport after she had lived in the Netherlands for five years. During one of my last visits to her home in Nijmegen (August 2018) she dreamed out loud that she could easily reach Canada with the Dutch passport. A return to the Gambia seemed to have moved to the back of her head, her imagined mobility now being directed to other places.

Structural Eventuality in Eurospace

Disillusions seem to be a significant part of the lifeworlds of African movers in Eurospace. Although I firmly disagree with the caricatural image that African prospective movers see Europe as a paradise where money grows on trees, I have certainly come across deep disappointments regarding the limited socio-economic opportunities that appear to them in Eurospace. As the case of Moustapha in the opening vignette of this part of the book illustrates, this does not only apply to those who have recently arrived in Europe. Just as often, those who have lived in Eurospace for a considerable period of time, but who face once again a legal deadlock, a period of undocumented living or joblessness also become disillusioned. Such severe interruptions point to what I call the 'structural eventuality' of the daily lives of African movers in the margins of Europe. Originally, this term appears in the writing of the French philosopher Françoise Dastur (2000), who argues that time itself brings chance and contingency into this world.[1] Whereas Dastur uses the term as part of her plea for a phenomenological philosophy, I rather use it to point to the movers' unstable position in the margins of Europe. This position is structural for the fact that some people are more likely to be hit by specific precarities (see also Vigh 2009) – in fact, for some movers it translates into a sense of deportability, which intensifies feelings of insecurity and fear (De Genova and Peutz 2010). However, this position is still eventual for the many escape routes that make movers transgress these precarities. Margins, in other words, are not understood as structural conditions with determining power. As we have seen in the previous chapter, margins often leave room – or more accurately, *produce* room – for navigation, gambling and escape.[2] Other precarities do not last as long and change considerably over time. Although migration scholars tend to start from a strict categorization of either documented or undocumented migrants, the precarities movers face are not strictly tied to one specific category of travellers. Some precarities felt by unauthorized travellers blend into situations where people do have the right documents to reside and move in Europe. In Italy, for instance, movers with the right documents risk deportation when they are accused of criminal offences (Della Puppa and Sredanovic 2017: 372). Similarly, unauthorized movers may encounter the same opportunities and relative freedoms as people who do not live in unauthorized situations. They are claimants of rights through acts of citizenship (Isin 2009; Balibar 2004). For these reasons, I consider structural eventuality as a different condition than 'structural precariousness' (e.g. Cross 2013) as the former points to the multiple possibilities of moving in and out of situations of precarity as well as the multiple moments of feeling in place or out of place. It is a position in which neither vulnerability nor stability can be taken for granted.

As a result of this structural eventuality, many, if not most, 'mobility careers' (Martiniello and Rea 2014) of my informants in Eurospace were definitely not steadily improving in terms of the degrees of freedom involved. At times, the structural eventuality made people doubt their place in Eurospace, as in the case of Lamin. Others felt how their stability slipped away from them, like in the case of Destiny (Chapter 4). Moustapha, the man introduced in the opening vignette to this part of the book, always felt very stable in Spain when he was married to a Spanish woman. After he lost the right to residence in Spain, he was initially still rather confident that his legal situation would soon change for the better. However, the border incident on the French–Spanish border and his subsequent imprisonment in France made him lose much of his positivity. As with the spatial im/mobility trajectories of my informants, experiences of success and failure as well as of lived freedoms and borders are likely to alternate each other in incoherent ways (see, for instance, Kleist 2018 and Massa 2018 for more discussion on incoherent trajectories). Holding a legal status does not necessarily mean that one is freed from all precarity and uncertainty, while irregular statuses do at times allow for individual freedoms, new occupational niches and other forms of transgression (e.g. Tsoni 2013). Consequently, people move back and forth between societal, social and individual phases of hope and uncertainty (Drotbohm 2017: 36; Kleist and Thorsen 2017).

Binta's case also illustrates how for many movers the hardest time is the first period after arriving in a new place – especially in settings of undocumentedness (e.g. Bloch, Sigona and Zetter 2014), marginalization and otherness (e.g. Tsoni 2013). Additional examples have already been outlined in this book: Maggis, the border commuter who never really managed to build a socio-economic life on the German side of his borderland; July, the Nigerian woman who struggled heavily during her first period in the Netherlands and experienced a similar process after her move to London; Saihou, the Afrostar who zigzagged through Eurospace and could not ground in the periphery of Germany where his 'Asylheim' was located. In all these cases, place attachments are related to ambivalences.

Opaque Place Attachments

It is particularly telling how place attachments are limited and restricted by the asylum system. Through its architecture of exclusionary enforcement (Mountz 2011), the asylum system is in fact specialized in the isolation and othering of people, whereby movers are basically asked to not ground, to not participate, to not feel welcome, but to wait (Khosravi 2011). My conversations with informants sometimes made them aware of the prolonged time they had been waiting. For instance, in early 2017 I exchanged videos and photos with Franck – the Cameroonian man in Germany. On this occasion, I also showed him a video of my two-year-old son. Thereupon he clearly remembered the time that my spouse was pregnant and said: 'You see how long we stay here. We stay here like a stone. We stay here like a stone, water comes but the stone is not moving, we are like this'. Below, I further elaborate on the limited place attachments in the context of asylum, and the tactics that people develop to live with these.

During my visit to Naples, in April 2015, Saihou (the Afrostar) and Amat (the wrestler type from Senegal) gave me an 'asylum tour'. They brought me to those places that had shaped the first period after their arrival in the Italian mainland. We first went to a place that Saihou always had enjoyed intensively, not only for its astonishing view over the Gulf of Naples, but also for its image of luxury and richness. However, they also showed me places that had affected their being in less happy ways: the isolated environment of the camp, the building where they gave their fingerprints and the beachside where they passed their time waiting. Their daily rhythm during this episode of their trajectories was highly structured. They left the camp in the morning to go to beach. To get there, they took the same bus every day. After a ride of fifteen minutes, they started to hang around at the beachside. After a few hours of 'sitting' they returned to the camp to report themselves again just before dinner. As Bendixsen and Eriksen (2018: 92) write in the context of waiting and irregularity in Norway, their everyday routines were largely 'pursued not as living but as mere survival in so far as they take place in a context devoid of direction and content'. At one specific moment of the asylum tour we negligently watched a football game between two African teams. Watching was a usual practice in this asylum context. At this moment, I asked Saihou whether he had ever felt so discouraged in this place that he wished to be back in the Gambia. His response was illustrative for his waiting time:

> You know when I stayed here for this six months, there was too much stress for me. You are new, just coming from 'the river' [the Mediterranean Sea], and you don't know what to do, or what they do to you. So, you can only wait, and this makes you thinking all day. In this time, I smoked too much. Not cigarettes, but you know, like ganja. We came down here, we looked at the sea, and you just smoked. That's why I say, I cannot even remember if I wanted to go back to my country, I don't really remember. The stress was too much, and when the stress is too much, I smoke too much.

For Saihou, the asylum stress and the ganja created an opaque place attachment and literally a lack of memory.

Similar to Saihou's situation, opaque placemaking processes happen in the asylum centre that is located just a stone's throw away from my home in Nijmegen. This asylum centre is one of the few centres in the Netherlands that is placed in the middle of a lively residential area. The relatively large building that houses some 300 asylum seekers, however, has a very typical role in Dutch colonial history since it once functioned as barracks for Dutch soldiers – the so-called *Koloniale Reserves* (Colonial Reserves) – who were sent to the overseas colonies. Not many people living in my neighbourhood seem to comprehend the irony of this. In this surrounding, I met Tijan one day. As a fisherman, Tijan mastered the West African waters in front of the Senegalese, Gambian and Guinean coastlines. This previous mobility contrasts sharply with the situation in which I found him during our first encounter.

Soon after he reached Schiphol Airport in a disorientated state, not knowing what to do or where to go, he was caught by the asylum procedures. Apart from the asylum relocations, he had never travelled around the country. He did not go to Amsterdam or other places that other people consider highlights of the Netherlands. I met him occasionally – in the supermarket, in the city centre and in the small public playground in front of the asylum space. One could read the asylum void from his face. There was, however, one very special encounter between the two of us. On the day my first son was born, I hurried to the supermarket to do some last-minute grocery shopping. There I ran into Tijan, who was also in a celebratory mood. On the very same day my son was born, he had received the news from the IND that he had been granted a refugee status.

When Tijan visited my home some weeks later to celebrate the two happy events that had coincidentally happened on that same day, he looked back at his asylum time and shared his main frustration with me and Joëlle: 'But you know, the worst thing about all this time, all these asylum years, is that nobody asked me on any single day, "Tijan how are you doing? How do you feel today?" Inside the camp they don't pay attention to your struggle. So that left me so discouraged'.

Tijan waited for the moment that the authorities found a suitable dwelling. Although his wish was to stay in Nijmegen, the authorities directed him to a small city in the centre of the province of Gelderland. He accepted. He considered this new city his 'destination', at least for the time being. Six months after his relocation, I visited him. One of the first things that I noticed was the large poster on the wall of his living room, showing two swimming dolphins. He told me how these dolphins reminded him of his time as a fisherman along the West African coast. Indeed, small things like a poster on a wall may turn an abstract space into a place filled with emotions (Cresswell 2004: 83). Tijan was grateful for this spacious apartment that even included two bedrooms, which allowed him to invite guests to spend a comfortable night there. Lately some of his friends from Nijmegen had come over, and they indeed made use of the hospitality facilities of Tijan's new place. His friends congratulated him on his new accommodation. Tijan, however, still had ambivalent feelings, as he explained:

> My friends, even they think this is a good place, this place is bigger than the places they live in. But I tell them: 'This is not Nijmegen, this is X [the name of his current hometown]'. It is a small town. It is boring, there is not so much to do. And that is why you can have a bigger house for the same money.

Tijan still needed to ground in his new place. As Lems (2016: 317) so tellingly writes about a Somali woman who arrived in Melbourne after she had lived in limbo in Dubai for years: 'Taking in all the strange and unknown features of this new place made her realise how much she had become part and parcel of another place, a place she had left behind'.

With ordinary social engagements (going to the gym, talking to his neighbours), Tijan tried his very best to make his 'destination' his new home. He got along well with one of his neighbours, an older woman who sometimes cooked for him, but he also felt that others distrusted 'the newcomer'. Most tellingly, Tijan compared his new start in this 'small town' with growing up. Adapting to a new home takes time, and it is a process of learning by doing. He compared his new start to his arrival in the city of Nijmegen when he initially had also not known anyone but had managed to gradually build a social infrastructure around him. Nevertheless, he started to think of a plan B. He sought ways to register himself in the city of Amsterdam. He particularly liked the city for its lively African communities, but also for its mobility infrastructure as he indicated: 'Your travel is very, very easy with the airport close by'. He now saw the airport that he once entered in a disorientated state as an opening for an im/mobile future. Grounding, thus, has little to do with localism and sedentary living since it 'provides a solid basis from which to reach outwards' (Pascual-de-Sans 2004: 350).

Place Gymnastics: A View from Coconut Island

Tijan was offered an opening by 'the system' and tried to attach himself to his new residency. But how to overcome the empty space–time of asylum that he had gone through before? How to deal with this system of exclusion on a daily basis? How to fill the days of non-action, non-belonging and waiting? Through Omar and his friend Camara, however, I learned that there are ways to coop with this emptiness. I call these tactics 'place gymnastics'. To understand them, we need to travel to Coconut Island.

Illustration 5.1 Heading to Coconut Island. Photograph by the author.

During one of my visits, Omar and Camara talked extensively about Coconut Island for two days. As self-trained tourist guides, they promoted it as a paradisiacal place. It is definitely the best place in the wider surrounding, they assured me. Having been born at Coconut Island, and with his skills as a self-trained tourist guide and bumster, Camara impatiently waited until the moment he could show me the place. To get there, we needed to leave the main node of connection in this village with some 4,000 inhabitants – the local transport hub with Wi-Fi facilities. A walk of thirty-five minutes. When we reached Coconut Island, I realized that I had passed this 'paradise' already a couple of times without actually noticing it. I had just lacked the sensors. Camara arranged a chair, and I closed my eyes. The heath soon warmed my back. I heard a cacophony of African languages and other languages that I found difficult to identify. Coconut Island is an international place. I opened my eyes and looked left. I saw the snow outside – a reality check. I put off my winter jacket and shawl. With their humour and laughter, Camara and Omar had created a rabbit hole that connected this remote asylum emergency shelter in southern Germany (itself an island-like space for its isolation from the rest of society) directly to the palm beaches of the real Coconut Island in the Gambia. They invited Afghans, Eritreans and two friendly security guards to join their place gymnastics. They welcomed them to the smiling coast of Africa.

Unknowable Spaces of Exclusion

'This is a racist place', Omar assured me while I stared at the closed door of a club that was totally deserted when we passed it during our day trip through the city. The club is located in a small German city that Omar frequently visited to enjoy its nightlife. This place was one of the few possibilities to escape the boredom of life in the German asylum space (where Coconut Island was located). To get there, one needs to walk half an hour from the asylum shelter to the nearest train station to embark on a train journey that may last up to one hour if one takes the slow train. In front of this empty club, I listened to Omar's story of a bouncer who had blocked not only his entrance, but also that of a Nigerian man who was married to a German woman. It was one of the many illustrations he gave of the borders that emerge in German nightlife. In this particular setting, Omar's frustrations were particularly fed by the 'wickedness' that the border guard was not the typical European and white authority agent but a Turkish bouncer who most probably himself had also experienced some racialized dividing lines in European society.

Borders indeed divide urban spaces. They create stratified embodied experiences both during the day and the night. While they remain invisible and unnoticeable for me – the white, male, European 'ordinary citizen' – they appear to be all around me for 'Others'. This existential difference in everyday life has been skilfully described by Tsoni (2013) in her writing about the migrant spaces of Athens. She explains how she moved across the urban environment without too much friction, while her interlocutors tactically manoeuvred the same environment, leading to fragmented and bordered routines filled with detours, sudden stops and U-turns. Tsoni (2013: 162) reflects on this difference as follows:

> Daily movement and survival in interstitial migrant spaces required exhaustive exercising of capacities that the ordinary citizen has atrophied for lack of training. And so I had been tripping its wires and setting off alarms and detonators, staggering through erupting minefields of boundaries through which I went unscathed while others near me risked losing their very lives as they tiptoed around and sidestepped their lines across the city.

Tsoni's observations relate to Khosravi's (2018) question regarding the extent to which I – the ethnographer – am really able to understand the experiences of unauthorized travellers and other African movers. Based on my time spent with Maggis, Saihou, Dawda, Omar, Moustapha and many others, I can only agree that my attempt to capture the experiences of borders and mobility is nothing more than a rough and reductionist sketch as so many aspects get lost in translation and interpretation – an issue that was also articulated in my confusion with Moustapha (see the opening vignette of this part of the book). For other dimensions, I just lacked the right sensors. My accounts of how Omar encountered borders in German nightlife or of how Lamin interpreted Starbucks in Bern as a no-go area are therefore not so much phenomenological representations. These accounts are unable to represent *their* worlds. Instead, they must be seen as modest representations of *my relation* to their worlds (Ingold 2013: 7; my italics). In this framework, Ingold refers to Miyazaki's method of hope when he coins the term 'correspondence' – an argument for a more modest, and perhaps more relational form of knowledge production. Correspondence is a way of opening up our perceptions to what is going on in order to better respond to it (ibid.).[3] In many instances, however, I still found it really difficult to comprehend to what and whom I exactly should relate. How to understand the violence in Libya that Lamin faced? How to truly relate to André's personal losses and Saihou's void after arrival in Italy? Many of such situations I encountered lacked a fertile ground for relatedness and they only appeared to me as unknowable spaces (Cabot 2016). The latter also applies to exclusionary practices related to skin colour.

Lost Europe II

Some of Abdoulah's routines appeared to me as strikingly similar to those of vendors who have regular shops in the same street of Rome. This Wolof man from Senegal has a fixed location to sell his stuff and he opens and closes his 'shop' on the usual hours. His regular customers know when and where to find him. Every morning, just before half past nine, he arrives and starts to prepare his workplace for the day. He first cleans the place by throwing used tissues, old receipts and small plastic bags in the garbage can. He wipes the sidewalk and then checks his merchandise and displays it to potential customers as attractively as possible. He furthermore arranges his storeroom, checking the availability of specific goods. He does not need a key or a password to enter his storeroom, instead he needs to lay down on the sidewalk to grasp a large bag from underneath a random car. His routines further deviate from other retailers when he starts to search for useful stuff out there in the street, like a small wooden crate or pieces of carton, that could possibly make his working day more comfortable. Before his working day really starts, he connects to the Wi-Fi network of the hotel behind him and puts on his headphones. The waiting time for customers is filled by entertainment and news messages from his country of origin. In this way – as in the case of Coconut Island – Adboulah's placemaking acquires a translocal or worlding dimension.

One morning, when I visited Abdoulah in Rome, he had to reinstall his workplace. Someone had placed six waste bags exactly at Abdoulah's spot. When I saw his irritation, he told me that he suspected his 'main enemy' of putting the bags there deliberately. This enemy was an Italian waiter with his own routines of working and publicly assaulting Abdoulah. During my visits to Abdoulah in Rome, I more than once heard the waiter's loud claims 'Mia terra!' (My land!) and 'Questa e l'Europa!' (This is Europe!), and I heard Abdoulah's equally loud replies. With those six waste bags to get rid of, it took Abdoulah extra efforts to start the day. A few hours later, he returned from a short break. He went to the bathroom of the befriended hotel. Upon his return he saw another small plastic bag lying at his workplace. It made him outraged. He walked across the street and put his head close to that of his main enemy – who had a victorious smile on his face. Abdoulah stood there face-to-face with his enemy. Some passers-by stopped, probably to wait for the first hit. Only after Abdoulah returned to his workplace, did I understood that his enemy had gone a step further in his strategy to discourage Abdoulah in his daily activities and to make him feel out of place. Abdoulah looked at me, pointed to the plastic bag and cried out: 'C'est le kaka des gens!' (This is human shit!). This shitty expulsion strategy of the waiter seemed to be effective, at least for the time being: that day Abdoulah moved out of his sight and tried to make some money elsewhere. He returned the next day and cleaned the place again to open his shop.

Several other informants were confronted with human faeces during their presence in Eurospace. I heard stories about xenophobic acts in

Athens, where aggressors made 'bombs' of nylon – sometimes filled with raw eggs, sometimes filled with faeces and urine, but always filled with hate. Others faced physical threats and violence from xenophobic aggressors in this Greek city. Informants who dared to fight back sometimes got in deeper problems when the police arrived at the scene. This became clear from the story of Jude – a young Nigerian man whom I knew from my time in Istanbul in 2008. He moved on to Greece and through the Balkan route he reached Germany in 2014. I visited him there three times. Jude – a seemingly fearless and physically strong man who was raised by the 'rough side of Lagos' – told me vividly how he and his friend one night were attacked 'from nowhere' in the streets of Athens after his friend had sought contact with a Greek young woman. He was punched in the face twice, and blood began to flow from his mouth. Despite being overwhelmed by the surprise attack, the two African men somehow managed to escape. By running away, they thought they would arrive in calmer waters. They were wrong. Apparently, the aggressors had contacted the police and when the two African men reached the metro station nearby, the place was filled with police agents – in Jude's words: 'They managed to bring all the police'. At the police station, they learned that they had been accused of stealing the woman's smartphone and some 150 euros. In Jude's wallet though, there were only 18 euros, and the phone that he carried was a cheap Nokia, not the smartphone the 'victim' described. Nevertheless, Jude spent five days in a Greek cell. For him, there was hardly any difference between racist violence and police work, an observation that is shared by some scholars (Antonopoulos 2006; Cabot 2014). In that sense – as Aparna et al. (2017) argue in a different context – not only migrants may lose direction, but Europe, as the self-appointed leader in security, freedom and justice, may also be helplessly lost. This argument is shared by Moustapha – the Gambian man of the opening vignette of this part of the book. During his process of re-viewing Europe, he noted that Europe had not suffered only from a financial crisis. According to him, there was still another, deeper crisis going on:

> People say there is no crisis any more, because the economic system is better now. But I think, we still live in a time of crisis, it is not an economic crisis, but a humanitarian crisis. We don't know how we can treat each other good, you know. We don't know how to treat the foreigner. We forget about this humanitarian side you know. That is why I say we still live in a crisis. There is humanitarian crisis in Spain, in Greece, in Turkey, in Libya, everywhere.

The humanitarian crisis Moustapha talked about deeply affects the daily lives of individual movers. At times, it creates madness.

Going Mad

The personal struggles with the system and the legal deadlock he had been in for years had severe negative effects on Shakur's health.[4] He suffered from structural headaches and insomnia. His lack of progress made his head spin and co-produced a jaded version of the person I once met in spring 2014. Since Caritas created a hard border for me – I was not allowed to enter the 'camp' – I was never able to catch a glimpse of Shakur's state of waiting inside the centre. For a long time, I assumed that this centre was a typical asylum space, until the moment Shakur told me about the Italians living there: 'They bring sick people to our Caritas place. We live there together with sick people. They give them a room, and we have our room. Every day when we wake up, they are taking their medicines … If you see an Italian person there, you know it is a sick person there. They bring that person to cure!' Shakur continued his outburst of frustrations by pointing at some reflectivity among the African movers of the place. He referred to one Nigerian man who started protesting: 'Even the Nigerians, when they start complaining … One of them said: "I am a mad man!" And then I said to him: "We are all mad men because we are living with mad people! I am a mad man living with mad people, then you are mad too!"'

From Shakur's point of view, the Caritas centre symbolized an overlap between asylum processes and mental disorders. This is, in general, not such an unusual observation as many asylum seekers are confronted with trauma, depression and anxiety in their daily lives. Moreover, the waiting and frustrations that 'the system' produces usually place further mental pressures on the shoulders of people (e.g. Griffiths 2014). They often feel confined in time–space through a process that Andersson (2014: 215) calls 'mortification' – which is a direct reference to Goffman's (1961) work on the asylum spaces for mental illness. In this context, the outburst of Shakur stands out for its aversion to the form of clientization with which so many people in asylum situations are confronted. Shahram Khosravi (2011: 71) writes as follows about his own experience as a refugee in Sweden:

> I was not seen as a 'normal' and 'healthy' individual. Apart from the medical examinations of my body, I was treated according to the most positive interpretation, as a child who did not know what was good or bad for him. The clientization of the refugee began as soon as she or he entered the camp.

At the edge of deportation, stress is likely to intensify, and mental pressures are likely to emerge. This was relived by Maggis, the Congolese border commuter living on the Dutch–German borderland, when he looked back at his nine-month period inside a migrant detention centre in the Netherlands.

He was particularly intimidated by the fact that this detention centre was located at an international airport, as he commented: 'The first day I was there, I did not know there was an airplane there. I was sitting and then Pooooffff! I said: "OK, that is how they are going to send me back to my country!" I said: "Ya ya ya, the airplane is there. The airplane is there".' Out of stress, he wanted to hurt himself, but a fellow detainee found a way to calm him down:

> One time I was thinking that I was breaking my head [pushes his hand against his head] in the wall. Because I felt like, 'Ohh what is this life?! What is this [hits his head again]?!' Agh. Sometime, somebody was behind me, for him it was already his second time [in the detention centre]. And then he said: 'Oh you must be quiet, be quiet, be quiet! ... I know many people who already became crazy in this place. In this place, it is not my first time, it is my second time. I have already experience. Don't think about it, if you feel this, go back to sleep. Or put music, some of your music, maybe, then you forget about it'. I tell you Joris, this was a very difficult time for me.

For Sarah, one of my female interlocutors in the Netherlands, the fear of a rejected asylum application and the related deportability, together with the birth of her second daughter, were simply too much to handle. The authorities had already threatened her and her family with repatriation, which was her reason for going underground. I first met this young woman in an apartment inhabited by Cedric, one of my Nigerian informants whom I had before visited. When Cedric directed me to his living room this time, we walked through the corridor and passed one of his bedrooms, and there he stopped for a moment. He knocked on the door and opened it. I was quite surprised to see an entire African family sitting on two mattresses on the ground. The family included a mother, her two daughters and her granddaughter. They had entered the Netherlands roughly two years before, and their asylum claims had recently been rejected. The oldest daughter was Sarah, the mother of the four-year-old child in the room. At the time of our introduction, she was visibly pregnant. The father of the soon-to-be-born baby was a friend of Cedric – a Cameroonian man. This Cameroonian man had asked Cedric to temporarily make room in his apartment for the family, and so he did. When the pregnancy became heavier, Sarah, her mother and her underage sister decided to make themselves known again to the authorities. They ended up in different asylum locations in the Netherlands.

After the birth of her second child, Sarah's health conditions rapidly deteriorated. When I was about to visit her in an asylum centre, she redirected me to the mental hospital where she had been hospitalized. Besides the Cameroonian man, her mother and her sister, I was one of the few who came to see her in these weeks. She talked about her pain of being separated from her children. She explained to me how she, time and time again, relived the moment that the police took her away from her four-year-old daughter in the asylum centre. She told me how she was desperately waiting for the moment to see her new-born baby again. She assured me that she had not fallen ill, but that she was just very, very tired. She referred to the Dutch repatriation service as the main reason why she ended up there because they had just put too much pressure on her. I realized that these visits were not the moments, nor the setting, for any questions, but for listening and comforting the best I could. I told myself that my visits to Sarah should not be part of my research project. Her situation was – and should remain – an unknowable space (Cabot 2016) for me and the readers of this book. At the same time – and that is why I do write about Sarah – I feel that there is precisely a need to talk and write about these excesses and human losses in asylum procedures. Not in the first place to illustrate the emotions that they give rise to, but to find ways to address the politics that produce them.

When Sarah left the mental hospital, she was transferred to another asylum location. This camp is described by the Dutch authorities as 'a sober location for families with minor children' who have 'no longer a right to reception'. In this camp, the authorities continued the process of her repatriation. The fact that she was sent to this location is a form of institutional violence since it, unsurprisingly, did not help Sarah to recover. Her mental condition again deteriorated and was soon followed by another hospitalization in a different place. After this hospitalization, she was again transferred to yet another asylum location. In total, she stayed in five asylum locations and two mental hospitals. For about three years, Sarah was displaced in both a physical and existential sense. One day, after her first period of hospitalization, we walked outside the asylum location where she then lived. When we reached the gate, we saw two busses of school kids entering the asylum terrain. Probably an enthusiastic teacher had organized an excursion to the asylum centre. An hour later, when we returned at the same gate, we were approached by a journalist and a woman carrying a camera. When the journalist fired his questions at us with the camera running, he referred to a violent incident caused by an asylum seeker living in the asylum centre. Did we not feel unsafe here? What did we think of the incident? We ignored the questions and made it to the gate. Two busses with school kids, an ethnographer visiting you, a camera thrown in your face and a journalist firing questions, I could only wonder what Sarah thought of all this. Seemingly, she hardly paid attention to these events. Possibly, it was her existential void that protected her. Or perhaps these events were just 'normal' in this environment of abnormality.

Groundings

Through the years, I accompanied Moustapha several times to the small village in the Huesca region where he works every year as a seasonal worker. He showed me the fields where he picked uncountable kilos of *melocoton* (peach) and other fruits. The fields were a green oasis of 20 hectacres, located in an environment that he called the 'moonlands' for its emptiness and lack of life. We once visited his village in the preseason period. During this time, Moustapha's workplace was not easy to reach. The bus connections to the village in the foothills of the Pyrenees were limited. During the season, the numerous African workers can rely on a very flexible, and therefore effective, transport system. As Moustapha explained to me, every African man with a car may decide to pick up a hitchhiker on the main road and bring him further along the road for a small compensation. In April of this particular year, however, the season was still 'not going', and as a consequence we had to wait for more than a half an hour before a Malian man stopped his car and brought us uphill to the village. After he noticed the driver was a Malian man, Moustapha started a conversation in Bambara – the lingua franca of Mali. As the driver was still looking for a place to work, telephone numbers were exchanged. Maybe Moustapha could connect him to his employer.

After we had reached the village we walked to his dwelling – which Moustapha called 'his ghetto', alluding to the small groups of people who gather in the public spaces of the Gambia. Moustapha warned me that there would be 'no social life', because the season had not yet started. The village was indeed quiet. But the few villagers whom we met on our way were warmly greeted by Moustapha. He talked to a few older Spanish men, hugged a Colombian construction worker and briefly talked to the woman in the local pharmacy. Clearly, Moustapha had returned to a village that he knew well. When we reached the ghetto, the place was totally abandoned. There were no traces left of the African men sharing this dwelling when the season is 'running'. This is what Moustapha meant when he said that there would be no social life. However, it would only take a few weeks for this place to transform into a lively place. When I visited his ghetto in summertime – a time the season is flourishing – the house was shared by twelve men from different West African countries: Guinea Conakry, Senegal and the Gambia. During siestas, this house was occasionally visited by Malian itinerant traders, selling clothes and other stuff such as bottle openers, telephone chargers and work gloves. Like so many agricultural places in Europe, this village in the foothills of the Pyrenees has its own mobility rhythms. Like a Spanish siesta, the place seems to be asleep in the off-season period, to wake up again just before the harvest starts. While we sat down on a bench in the village, I raised the 'home question' to Moustapha: did he feel at home in this place? He responded: 'Yes, it is my home, for Spain, I can say this is where I feel comfortable now. The people respect me, I feel free to talk with everyone, that is it. This is my address, and I feel at home here'.

Idrissa

As son of a Pule mother and a Mandinka father, Idrissa's identity was hybrid from his birth. Like so many people in his region of origin, his life path evolved mostly in-between Senegal and the Gambia. He referred to a village in the Casamance region as his place of origin for its relationship to his father – a man who combined farming with mechanical work. Another important anchoring point was the city of Brikama in the Gambia, well known among regional travellers for its large 'garage'. In this place of movement, his mother, of Gambian nationality, runs a restaurant that I visited during my brief stay in the Gambia. This restaurant serves local inhabitants and a wide range of travellers. Besides in these meaningful places, Idrissa also spent some considerable time in Dakar – the Senegalese capital – before he embarked a 'pirogue' towards Tenerife in 2006.

He reached Tenerife and a transfer to the Spanish mainland followed. In the first three months, he lived with his uncle in Toledo. In the following years, he worked as a welder in the Spanish construction sector, which was booming before the economic crisis hit the sector hard in 2008. He continued working in the olive sector not far from Madrid and lived in Lleida to commute between the city and the nearby agricultural fields for two years. During this time, he met Xavier, a Catalan owner of a relatively small agricultural enterprise. Xavier hired Idrissa, leading to one of the most remarkable episodes in Idrissa's stay in Spain.

I waited for Xavier in a typical Catalan village bar, just where Idrissa had indicated. He had called his former employer and told him that a researcher from the Netherlands waited for him. I was excited to meet Xavier as Idrissa described their bond as much more than an employer/employee relation. Xavier was one of his close friends, who had widened his space of manoeuvrability in Catalan society. It was a hot afternoon, and the Catalan siesta just started. There were only a handful of villagers left in the bar, finishing their coffees and beers. When Xavier came in, he immediately invited me to sit next to him at the bar. He told me how he had met Idrissa, and how his Senegalese friend assisted him in transforming his conventional horticultural activities into an ecological system. According to Xavier, Idrissa had the right spirit and knowledge for this agricultural transformation. Furthermore, he told me how Idrissa had taken on the role of intermediator between him and the wider reserve of African workers. Having an intermediator is extremely important for horticulturists like Xavier. When, for instance, peaches are ready to be picked, time becomes a real pressure as there are only ten to fifteen days for harvesting. After that, the peaches are already too soft for the regular market. Consequently, Xavier was in need of a very flexible labour reserve, and during high season the numbers of workers he needed could even daily change. For many months a year, he did not hire any workers, while at the season's peaks he needed at least thirty. Only through Idrissa, and two other African men, was he able to arrange this instant labour. Xavier never made use of working contracts. Everything was arranged without the necessary paperwork.

Idrissa worked with Xavier for about nine years, first as a typical flex worker, later on even living at Xavier's home. When we arrived at Xavier's home, the Catalan man showed me the little plot that Idrissa used for the cultivation of 'African products', some vegetables and herbs. With great enthusiasm, Idrissa had told me that the plot of the cultivation was seen as a community project among African workers and that some of the products were marketed in the region. There were times that Idrissa had high hopes of expanding this activity. However, he also had very different aspirations. He is a talented reggae singer. This skill long served as an important safety net in periods of joblessness. With his talent, he regularly jumped into one of the metros of Barcelona to sing his songs for the commuters and tourists that filled the coupés. These performances yielded considerable sums of money. But as much as he loved making music, he disliked his metro performances. The constant gazing of people, the non-attentive audience, the irritations involved, formed a daily hindrance to this economic activity. He regarded his musicality as an opportunity for a more serious career path than this kind of vagabondage. His aspiration to develop a music career was one of the reasons behind his exchanging the rural place where he lived for the cosmopolitan city of Barcelona in 2013. He started to weekly sing in a coffee shop and managed to arrange several gigs a month in and around Barcelona. At the time of writing this book, his first album was available for downloading from the Internet.

However, below the surface there seemed to be another reason why he decided not to stay at Xavier's place. Notwithstanding their strong affective relation and the many opportunities that Xavier gave him, there was one major blockage: the lack of regularization. Whereas at times Idrissa emphasized the 'wonderful connection' he had with Xavier, he also called him a *coño* (cunt) for not having arranged this. During the day I spent with Xavier, I asked him whether he had ever tried to regularize Idrissa's stay by offering him a legal employment contract. He stated that this might have been possible ten years ago when the pre-contract for labourers was an easy route for their regularization. Nowadays, as he said as a way to excuse himself, one needs to have a NIE (Número de Identificación de Extranjeros, i.e. identification number for foreigners) to start the regularization procedure. Idrissa lacked this number. Thereupon I wondered what he actually paid his workers. Xavier explained he paid workers with the right documents a maximum wage of 5 euros per hour and 'illegal workers' (his words) 3 to 3.5 euros per hour. This distinction struck me since he stressed that he had never given a contract to any flex worker. When I questioned this stratified payment system, he defended himself with the following mathematical gymnastics:

> Well, you may say this indeed, if you think for one day, they only get, let's say, 35 euros for ten hours of work, you may say this is not much. But they work six days a week, ten hours per day. If you offer them work for four weeks, they earn around 1,000 to 1,500 per month. And the minimum wage in Spain is 600 per month, soooo ... They actually earn much more.

The logics of Xavier reminded me of Shakur's words: 'People can be nice to you, but they still treat you like a slave'. Idrissa considered Xavier to be one of his friends, but a friend who had exploited him. Despite Idrissa's deep irritations regarding the unwillingness of Xavier in this respect, he never considered the papers as a main priority in his daily life. He had lived in Spain without the proper documents for about twelve years. He was used to it, and in his mind, he did not see this as a major restriction. Certainly, he had tried it, and he would keep on trying when opportunities would arise, but he had long transcended the notion of fear that is so often highlighted in documents dealing with irregular migrants. He did not face major problems with the police, and he had always found work without the proper documents. He became a public figure with his music performances. He was not even scared of the media attention that also addressed his undocumented status. He seemed to feel in place in this worlding environment. He felt free – like any citizen of the city of Barcelona.

Dwelling/Moving

For Tim Ingold (2011: 148), lives are not lived *inside* places, but through, around, to and from them. Even the most rooted communities engage in cross-border mobilities (Salazar and Smart 2011: iii), and in so doing they lay trails of movement. Similarly, even the most grounded migrant in my research has engaged in cross-border mobility. Dawda – the Gambian man living in Nijmegen – is perhaps the archetypical example of this dwelling/moving dialectic. From the perspective of the state, he is one of my informants who has reached the ideal status of an *im*migrant – someone who lives a 'grounded life', who has incorporated the language, norms and values of the host society. Someone who has bought a house, has a stable address and is able to pay his mortgage and take care of his family. In spite of his settlement – or actually because of it – Dawda has built new pathways of movement through his navigating practices that help others – Yahya, Binta and Alagia, for instance – to transcend borders. He has also built paths of movement through his return visits to the Gambia, every two years, through his visits to his relatives and friends in London, Malta and elsewhere in Europe and through the containers with goods he sends to Banjul.

In this respect, my research suggests that there is often a firm discrepancy between the state's interpretation of citizenship and my interlocutors' interpretation of the granting of citizenship and residence rights. Whereas the state sees the issuing of a passport as the articulation of someone's membership,[5] many of my interlocutors framed that very same occasion as an opening to cross-border mobility. Binta thought of Canada as her next travel destination after she would have been granted Dutch citizenship, Yahya moved to the Netherlands and the Gambia as soon as he received his residence permit of Italy. The right to stay and, ideally, citizenship combine a sense of permanency with the ideal condition for comfortable mobility across borders (e.g. Della Puppa and Sredanovic 2017). These logics became particularly clear to me through my engagement with two important interlocutors, Ebou (a Gambian man whom I met in Barcelona) and Cedric (the Nigerian man who housed Sarah's family in Nijmegen for a while).

In a laundry in Barcelona – one of the most important entry points for my fieldwork in Spain – I regularly met up with Ebou (see also Introduction). Ebou is a Gambian man who passed the age of forty. In 2000, he left his country of origin for Europe and made a considerable detour all the way to Syria, Lebanon and Turkey. It took him more than three years to reach Greece, from where he reached Italy some months later. In Italy, he spent about seven years of his life as an undocumented migrant – excluding an intermediate stay of two years in the German city of Hamburg. Once back in Italy, he moved to Spain 'without any paper' and tried his luck in the agricultural sector, which finally resulted in a five-year residence permit. However, to renew this residence permit, Ebou needed to work on a contract basis, and that is why he remained in Barcelona for a year, without moving around too much. As he told me, this was quite unusual for him: 'I never sit for a long time in Barcelona, only this time I decided to stay for a longer period of time. Since September 2015 I did not move. But normally I come and go. I don't stay long'. His mobility in the last few years – to and from the Gambia, to and from Germany and to and from France – had a clear downside in the Spanish system. His employment track record had remained meagre over time. That is why he had to stay in Spain for a longer period of time. As he explained:

> You know, for the paper, to renew it, it is important you can show them something. You must show them that you had this contract, or that contract. You must show them you have worked for a long period of time. If they see that you have not done anything for the last five years, they don't like it, then they may refuse you. So you need to be able to show them something, you need to have a good profile.

Ebou had to make sure he worked with a contract, and the owner of the laundry in Barcelona was in a position to arrange this. There is an interesting mobility/locality configuration here that relates to some of the critiques I received on my work. A recurrent comment to my work so far is that in the analysis of mobile lifeworlds I simply overlook the question of people's right to stay in a place. Critical commenters claim that the movers in question actually lack the right to stay and therefore have no other option than moving around. This argument may be accurate in some cases but does not hold for Ebou. In fact, Ebou had been granted the right to stay in Spain, and this actually facilitated his cross-border mobility in various directions. However, precisely because of this mobility, his future residence became at risk. To extend the right to stay, he had 'to sit' in order to remain visible to the Spanish system. Immobility is not always a sociocultural displeasure – as in the cases of Saihou, Lamin and Shakur – it can also be a necessary condition for maintaining a mobile life. In other words, whereas some movers deliberately seek ways to escape systems, others are faced with the practical concern of how to stay and become visible within a system. After the period of 'sitting', however, Ebou's horizon was likely to shift again. He had already thought about Germany or Switzerland as his next destination.

Another illustration of a particular mobility/locality configuration with regard to citizenship comes from Cedric – a Yoruba man from western Nigeria. Between June 2014 and December 2015, I had regular contact with Cedric. We met on the campus of my university where he assisted me in preparing master's students for fieldwork activities. We also had meetings in cafés and in our homes. In January 2015, he told me he had lost his job as a cleaner, which made him reconsider (or actually re-view) Nijmegen as his place to live. He started to explore the opportunities for swapping apartments with someone in Rotterdam (the place where he lived before) or Amsterdam. During this process, he heard of job opportunities at Schiphol Airport, but the closest affordable place of residence was in Haarlem, some 30 km away from his desired domicile. During his research of possible future places to live, I semi-jokingly suggested he could maybe move to London. With a chuckling smile, he replied: 'I want to show you something, I received a letter'. He took an envelope and showed me the letter from the Dutch immigration authorities (IND) announcing that his application for Dutch citizenship had been received in good order. They also stated they would come back to him within eight weeks, of which by that time already four had passed. Then Cedric clarified why he showed me this letter right now: 'Why I show you this?! Because you said, maybe I should move to London, without this [points to the letter] I cannot move to London. Because in that place I am going to start from the grassroots. But now if I am a citizen here, I can perhaps move to London, now I am *European*'. With his reference to Europeanness he almost bypassed any national framing of citizenship – which was actually the main message of the IND letter. Furthermore, he compared his future mobility to one of the prototypical examples of EU mobility – that of mobile Polish workers: 'I just try to go there and see if I can be working there. If I can be working there, I can be working there like the Polish people, they work here, and they go back to their country'.

The freedom of mobility, in combination with permanent residence in the Netherlands, appears to be an ideal situation for Cedric. In his world, mobility and settlement are not opposite extremes of a continuum – they form a relation that allows for 'flexible citizenship' (Ong 1999). When one reaches a stable residence, new horizons are likely to emerge as one is free to leave, but also to come back (Morokvasic 2004). In this context, I have heard that many people awaited the moment they obtained citizenship or new residence rights. Interestingly, many of my interlocutors saw a passport not as an important indicator of a national identity, but rather as a travel paper. It follows that citizenship is not necessarily a condition that leads to permanent settlement, but it can be inverted into a resource for mobility (Dahinden 2010a; Moret 2017; Della Puppa and Sredanovic 2017). As the anthropologist Hage argues, 'Roots are often paradoxically experienced as an extra pair of wings' (cited by Lems 2018: 22). Thus, with this particular mobility/locality configuration, the African movers embody the notion of 'citizenship in flux' (Isin 2009) as their acts, movements and imaginaries can be seen as a rupture with dominant national frameworks of belonging and membership.[6]

In the subsequent six months, Cedric travelled twice to London. When he returned from his second visit (July 2015), he told me how he once again felt ambiguous about relocating. He said he would first look for a job in the Netherlands, and if he did not succeed, he would move to London to 'really live' there. In October of that year, he moved to Nigeria for some important family affairs, and in December he called me to tell me that he was back in the UK. As soon as he would have found a good place to live, he would invite me to London, he said. However, that was the last time we spoke to each other. Cedric is living his life somewhere in the UK, the Netherlands, Nigeria ... or elsewhere.

Moving Places: A View from Lleida

When people reground, they are not only affected by places, but they also make and remake places on a daily basis. Whereas Doreen Massey's (1991, 2005) relational sense of places is mainly based on observations in cosmopolitan London, she would probably have constructed the same theoretical lens if she was based in any provincial town in southern Europe that is driven by the seasonal rhythms of agricultural production. To illustrate this, and to dive further into the mobility/locality configurations of this chapter, I focus on the Catalan city of Lleida that borders the autonomous community of Aragón. The city of Lleida is an important node for agricultural activities for the wider region (see also Cross 2013). It is readily apparent that the city attracts flex workers at the start of the 'frutta season'. As a consequence, the number of 28,000 registered foreigners in the city appears to be an underestimation, at least for the period between April and September (Egbe 2016; Bos 2017).[7] People come from very diverse directions: among them are African workers who come from Andalusia, Milan and Lisbon, or who return from their home country. They return to the apartments that they lived in in previous years, or they find new dwellings for a cheaper price. In the fields, they often work side by side with Romanian, Chinese and Moroccan workers. Lleida is a typical meeting place – a dynamic and discontinuous entanglement of trajectories with their own temporalities.

In Lleida, seasonal workers seek ways to link up with employers, and vice versa. They come here to subscribe to one of the labour recruitment offices of the city. They often first go to the local government where they usually receive a list with labour intermediaries in the region. Many seasonal workers rely on official contracts to not violate immigration law. To spend the nights, some movers make use of a shelter – the Albergue, a place where movers can ground for two weeks. The Albergue is a node for social connection with additional services such as language classes, medical facilities and spaces for religious worship (e.g. Bos 2017). Next to these official channels, there are also more mundane infrastructures in place. Many movers head to the migrant areas in the historical city centre to hear about job opportunities and levels of payment through word of mouth. At times, especially when the frutta season is flourishing, the local infrastructures at play cannot handle the number of newcomers. Many movers then find their way to the apartments of indirect contacts. Housing co-movers in the frutta season is an opportunity to get some additional income for those workers who rent or own an apartment. Those movers who do not find shelter, sleep in public parks or at construction sites close to the city centre. The latter situation is not only a matter of a lack of social capital. Some people prefer to sleep in the open air to save money.

From his grocery shop, located at one of the gateways to the historical centre, Nelson – the Nigerian church leader – has been able to observe the mobility rhythms of Lleida for several years. He usually places one or two chairs in front of his grocery shop to socialize with people who pass by, or just observe the wanderings of people. When I sat next to him in July 2017 – the peak of the season – he shared his latest observations with me. According to him, Lleida had seen less movers coming in the last couple of years, and he told me how in 2014 African workers still used to sleep under a small roof at the opposite side of the sidewalk. He also referred to the time that the local government decided to install specific facilities – such as running water and public toilets – for the movers who spent the nights in public spaces. This led to a further concentration of African workers. According to Nelson's narrative, the authorities used this concentration also for particular forms of control (see also Egbe 2016). During controls, as he told me, the authorities found out that some people carried considerable sums of money, varying from 3,000 to 8,000 euros. It made them realize that the movers who slept in the open air were not necessarily without any financial capital. Furthermore, they also felt that they actually facilitated the housing of an informal economy – the cash people carried was interpreted as a sign of undeclared work. Soon after the facilities were put in place, Nelson observed how the toilets and water pipes were again removed. For Nelson, the incoming movements of Africans had clear positive economic effects for the city of Lleida (the agricultural sector just needed the workers) as well as for him and his family (he clearly had more customers during the season). Occasionally, however, he also expressed his disappointment regarding the mobile populations that co-created Lleida every year. He particularly found that too few movers participated in his church service. Apparently, ambivalent viewpoints regarding African mobility to Lleida are not only reserved for Lleida's government: African movers are praised for their economic contribution yet condemned for their presumed negative social effects.

Through my engagement with Moustapha, Pape and Babacar, I could further zoom in on the placemaking dynamics in Lleida. In April 2016, when I reconnected with the three men (see the opening vignette of this set of chapters), I came to realize that there was an issue going on regarding the right to inhabit the apartment. To understand this, we need to dive into the layered system of sub-renting. One year before (April 2015) the apartment was shared by the three Gambian men. Pape was at that time the 'chef of the house', meaning he was responsible for collecting the money from the different inhabitants and transferring it to 'the owner of the contract'. The owner of the contract then transferred the money (500 euros) to the owner of the apartment. This arrangement was one of continuity and change. While the configuration of inhabitants of the apartment changed constantly – or as Moustapha phrased it: 'We shift all the time' – the owner of the apartment received the rent from the same person every month. The 'chef of the house' was expected to stay for a relatively long period of time in the house in order to be able to observe who was coming and going. He arranged that empty rooms were filled and reserved beds for movers who expected to arrive soon. At times, the chef of the house moved himself, and then handed over his tasks to another person. This arrangement gave cause for tensions between Pape and Babacar. Pape (as the chef of the house) had guaranteed Babacar a place to stay once he would return from his visit to the Gambia. However, because Pape decided to spend a considerable time abroad himself – in the Netherlands, Germany and later the Gambia – he had to withdraw from the role of the chef of the house and give this responsibility to a third person. Herewith, the guaranteed stay of Babacar vanished. To Babacar's frustration and surprise, there was no place for him when he returned to Lleida in February 2016.

Whereas the apartment was fully booked in the previous months (February to August), there was a room left for me at the time of my visit in September the same year. Now, only Pape and Moustapha inhabited the house; the other movers who had grounded in the apartment for some time had departed to different places within and beyond Spain. They only had left some material traces in the form of bags, suitcases, flip-flops, clothes and toothbrushes. They had not left behind these materials permanently, because they would use them again when they returned to Lleida. They just did not take their belongings with them to their next places. Moustapha once told me that he preferred to travel light. When he moved up to the foothills of the Pyrenees, he usually only brought a small bag of clothes.

This 'Gambian apartment' can be seen as a microcosmos of Lleida as a moving place. There is some sense of permanence involved in the presence of African communities in this city. The shop and the church of Nelson are good examples of this permanence at the level of the city. In the case of the apartment, this permanence is reflected in the relatively stable connection between the owner of the contract and the owner of the house. At the same time, under this seemingly stable surface, there is a mobility wonderland to explore. The composition and number of people in both communities differ considerably according to diverse mobility rhythms. This may create some tensions in terms of facilities and infrastructures – as we have seen on both the city and apartment level. When I asked Moustapha about the extent to which the ephemeral character of community – in the sense of a limited duration of co-presence – involved practical concerns and risks, he inverted the logic of my question. He turned this ephemeral geography into a resource. He stated to have selected his current place of residence, in Pape's apartment, out of four different options in Lleida. There were even cheaper options available for him. But he deliberately chose Pape's place because Pape was his close friend. In fact, many years ago, Pape was the one who had advised him to come to Lleida in the first place. Thus, for Moustapha the dynamic character of the Gambian community in Lleida was not only a resource for its multiple options in terms of housing. The dynamic character was also an opportunity to stress a specific social bond with someone who had assisted him before.

Concluding Notes: Paths and Places

This chapter has outlined different mobility/locality configurations. It has emphasised the placemaking capacities of my interlocutors, their ambivalence towards place attachments and the harsh processes of exclusion they faced. In all these cases, I related places and groundings to mobility and trajectories. Some interlocutors – like Dawda, Binta and Tijan – actively sought ways to attach to a new place from where movement would be possible. Along their transnational pathways, they tried to build a new home, a new place to live. Others, like Moustapha, Cedric and Lamin, practised or imagined a multilocal residence where circulation and mobility between places was central. However, for all of them, mobility remained important to their social imaginaries that linked their actual residences to near and distant futures (Salazar 2011). In other words, it is indeed the path, and not the place, that is the primary condition for our being (Ingold 2011: 12).

In so doing, many of the African movers in this study reflect the image of an unknown figure who unsettles singular loyalty, identity and belonging (Isin 2009: 368). Their mobility tactics challenge us to search for a new vocabulary and interpretation of citizenship, which combines staying with moving, presence with absence and membership with deviation. At first sight, the archetype of the transmigrant transcending borders and boundaries seems to be a suitable lens through which to understand the lifeworlds of African movers in Eurospace. However, this notion is still too limiting for its bi-local demarcation – as a person who lives a connected life in-between a country of origin and a country of destination (Glick Schiller, Basch and Szanton Blanc 1995). The mobility, affective circuits and future horizons of my interlocutors introduce a sense of multi-polarity that moves beyond the logic of such here–there transnationalism. They open up new avenues to re-view conventional notions of belonging, let alone 'integration' (see also Schinkel 2018), in contemporary Europe.

NOTES

1. Literally, the phenomenologist Dastur (2000: 179) explains the phrase 'structural eventuality' with the following words: 'The word eventuality should not be taken here in its normal meaning of possibility. Speaking of the eventuality of time does not mean that time could "be" or "not be." It should, in my view, mean that time is in itself what brings contingency, unpredictability, and chance into the world'. Herewith, she distinguishes her thinking from realist and idealist philosophy by arguing that the true object of philosophy is phenomenality itself – what 'shows itself to us' (ibid.). For her, the 'eventum' (the events) arises in the becoming and deflects the temporal flow, 'as if a new world opens up through its happening' (ibid.: 182). In this respect, I see some parallels between Dastur's arguments and Ingold's work (2007, 2011) as both articulate ontological openness and prioritize dynamics over stasis. For example, Ingold (2013: 4) argues for an anthropological approach that opens up 'a space for generous, open-ended, comparative yet critical inquiry into the conditions and potentials of human life'. Dastur (2000: 183) pleads for a phenomenology that is no longer only about 'thinking of being and essence', but also about 'a thinking of the *a posteriori* and of the "after event"'. In the context of this book, it is worthwhile to note that some authors have theorized 'critical events' (Wissink, Düvell and Mazzucato 2017) and 'chance' (Gladkova and Mazzucato 2017) in order to understand how migration trajectories evolve over both time and space.
2. In specific cases, deportability is inverted to a mobility resource by the people experiencing it. See, for example, also the work of Anja K. Franck (2017) on Lesbos.
3. See Aparna et al. (2017) for a more progressive argument about the co-production of knowledge in the context of asylum.
4. This section is an extended version of a section in Schapendonk (2017b).
5. In the case of the Netherlands, the end of the *inburgeringsproces* (integration process) is a celebration that is often filled with national symbols like the flag and the national anthem.
6. In my reading, Isin's (2009) argument of citizenship in flux relates to two dimensions. First, there is his historical analysis of how the scales, sites, actors, politics and practices of citizenship have changed over centuries. Second, there is his statement that citizenship reflects an ongoing process of formation and reformation. As he (2009: 383) writes: 'To recognize that citizenship is in flux is not to lament its fluid and dynamic structure but to theorize and to account for its instability'. Following Isin, the mobility of African movers can best be interpreted as an 'act of citizenship' in the sense that it actually makes a difference in how citizenship is framed and formed (see also Balibar 2004). In so doing, Isin distinguishes acts of citizenship (as acts that make a difference by changing the order of things) from institutionalized and routinized citizenship practices such as voting and paying tax. Consequently, acts of citizenship are not necessarily founded on law, rather they are claims to justice that actually call the law into question (ibid.: 378–84).

7. It is estimated that Catalonia houses 320,000 Africans, the majority of whom come from North Africa. The city of Lleida is exceptional for the Spanish situation in that Africans form the largest migrant community. In most other parts of Spain, Europeans and Latin Americans clearly outnumber Africans (Egbe 2016).

CHAPTER
6

The Multiple

This chapter re-views the mobility tactics of African movers as a form of claim-making – a sociopolitical act. Through their mobility, the movers in question make use of Eurospace and at the same time redefine it. To make this argument, I rely on the method of re-description (Simone and Pieterse 2017) that is specifically designed to unpack the multiplicity of everyday life in order to de-essentialize the societal margins. These authors look for specific sites that have the potential to unfold 'the multiple', as they (ibid.: 11) write:

> Granted, whatever exists in the city is a manifestation of something, and that something is usually a convergence of multiple forces and backgrounds. But that something also exists in an immeasurable series of relationships with other things … The interfaces where all of these 'somethings' intersect can be the site for re-description.

While Simone and Pieterse mainly look for these sites for re-description in urban spaces on the African continent, I consider mobility itself 'a site' where different 'somethings' intersect. It is the site of the formal *and* informal, of community expectations *and* individual freedoms, of the political economy *and* transgressions. In their writing, the two urban theorists underscore that uncertainty – a key component of the previous chapters – is a double-edged sword. It indeed leads to 'material and psychic threats' but it also provides an opportunity to 'reimagine and re-enchant the world' (ibid.: 31). For this reason, they frame re-description not only as a method to find out 'what is', but also as a tool to imagine what 'might be'. The structural eventuality (see Chapter 5) of 'might be' does not point to methods of future-oriented generalizations and visualizations. Especially in discussions on African demographic growth and environmental futures, such methods of forecasting lead to unproductive, violent and neo-Malthusian world views. The notion of 'might be' rather reflects a different aspiration of 'making things different, but also of seeing in what exists something other than what we think we are seeing' (ibid.: 11). Interestingly, mobility is by definition a resource that lies at the intersection of something that *is* and something that *can be*. It is a practice that shifts grounds and changes perspectives. In so doing, mobility forms a fruitful ground to re-view Europe.

This chapter first introduces a re-described version of the economic projects of the movers in question. It unpacks the multiplicity of economic activities and pays particular attention to the intersection of formal and informal spheres in order to remain sensitive to the subtle dimensions of globalization that are seldom acknowledged in discussions of this phenomenon (e.g. Schmoll and Semi 2013). Herewith, I return to the metaphor of circuits that was central to Chapter 2. Subsequently, I re-describe the positionality of the African movers in Europe by incorporating their worlding views from Eurospace. These views from the margins challenge the notion of Europe as a centrally located homogeneous space.

In/formal Circuits

In the Gambia, as elsewhere in West Africa, it is often impossible to reduce someone's economic profile to a single profession. When Kea (2013: 107) conducted a study on farming, she found that her farmers were at the same time 'taxi drivers, traders, mechanics, shop-keepers, fishermen, marabouts, moneylenders, businessmen, factory workers, diamond miners in Sierra Leona, carpenters, metal workers, corporate farm employees, and agrarian daily wage labourers'. This combining of economic activities continues to exist in Eurospace. This can be explained by Europe's stratified labour markets. This stratification is particularly noticeable through the low-paid jobs they occupy, often based on flexible and temporary contracts – if there is a contract at all (e.g. Van Nieuwenhuyze 2009). However, this is only part of the story. As Kea (2013) illustrates, the multiplicity of activities is more the rule than the exception. That is how people are used to find ways in the Gambia and beyond (Thieme 2018). Tellingly, many of my interlocutors referred to their 'projects', a fascinating term that leaves many aspects open, including the size, level of formalization, duration and foreseen impact of the activity. Through projects, they generated extra income. Some of these projects were designed to remain invisible and unrecorded (see also Schmoll and Semi 2013), others unfolded as interesting crossovers between the formal and the informal. For instance, movers with a relatively stable job often had 'side projects' running along. Ebou's collection of 'stuff' in the Barcelonese laundry (see

Introduction) and Dawda's container business between the Netherlands and the Gambia (see Chapter 1) are insightful examples of how movers may multiply their economic profiles. Ebou combined working formally in the laundry with the informal buying, repairing and selling of stuff gathered by waste collectors from the streets of Barcelona. The laundry was his anchor place where formal and informal practices mingled. It was a node of local interaction. Through his business, Ebou connected the margins of the urban economy to the regular customers of the laundry. He saw a 'potential in the discarded' (McFarlane 2018: 14) and literally changed waste into profit. Especially during my morning visits to Ebou, I saw several waste collectors passing by. They originated from at least three continents of the world: Europe, Africa and Latin America. I witnessed Ebou's strategic negotiations with them, which reflected severe power imbalances in Barcelona's urban economy.

One day, Ebou was extremely harsh to a Romanian waste collector, who visibly struggled to make ends meet. This collector brought a couple of bicycle lights and a sound system that would connect to any iPad or iPhone (at least that is what he claimed it to be). One of the two speakers of the sound system lacked any foam and was extremely dirty. Ebou decided to involve me in this particular negotiation and asked me: 'What do you think?' I tried to be diplomatic and told him that it did not seem to be the most reliable device. But the Romanian man insisted; it worked, and it had worked for years. With an angry face, and without further testing the sound system, Ebou put it away and shouted: *'No functiona!'* In the consternation that followed, the plastic bag from the Romanian man fell from the table and batteries, lights and headphones, among other stuff, spread over the floor. On this occasion, the urban 'fragments' of the margins (McFarlane 2018) that in/formal actors attempt to reassemble showed themselves to me. The waste collector established his price: five euros for the bag with all the stuff that was now on the ground. Ebou refused and told him that he did not buy broken stuff – which was actually untrue as he had often bought stuff that was in need of repair. He checked the bicycle lights again and put them back on the table, without showing any further interest in them. But then he saw a glimpse of a leather bag that was still in the plastic bag that was offered to him and informed about the price. 'Three euros', the man replied. 'How is this possible?' Ebou yelled. After another outburst of Ebou, the Romanian man lowered the price by one euro. Ebou handed over a coin. The man left. 'How much did you pay?' I asked Ebou in the end. 'Fifty cents', he replied with very little compassion. The leather bag was put underneath the table, next to the other stuff he had collected in the last few days. The bag was not meant to be marketed in the urban circuits of Barcelona, Ebou told me. It was about to be put it in a container soon heading to the Gambia.

The laundry, thus, was not only a local node in the in/formal circuits of Barcelona, it was also a node of transnational connectivity.

Dawda used parts of his earnings from his permanent job in Nijmegen to invest in goods that he also shipped to the Gambia. He started a gym in Serekunda with the gym equipment and machines he had collected over years. In addition, he ran a shop next to the gym. The goods that were marketed there were collected in different places in the Netherlands. This shop was one of the many import/export shops along the main roads of Serekunda. Recently, Dawda had also bought two vans in the Netherlands and shipped them to the Gambia. Early 2018, he told me with pride that these two cars were changed into taxis (which involved the installation of extra seats and obtaining the taxi licence) and they were now finally 'running'. When I asked him about his next project, he said he thought about starting an import/export business in China. The connection man who had helped Yahya (Dawda's little brother) to leave Libya had moved to China and so Dawda had already a trustworthy 'trade connection' there. Interestingly, Dawda's economic activities not only created some extra earnings for himself, they were also a main source of income for his good friend Alagie – as he was the 'local agent' in all of Dawda's transnational operations. Alagie coordinated the offloading, distribution and sales of the goods and took good care of all financial issues involved. He was the manager of Dawda's gym as well as the manager of the shop next door. And then, Alagie was also involved in other activities that had nothing to do with Dawda's transnational businesses.

Ebou and Dawda were both incorporated by the formal economy in Europe. Nevertheless, they were also still engaged in the same hustling practices that shape the multiple departures of movers from West Africa. There is not just one explanation for these activities. Their in/formal practices at least illustrate that we cannot solely focus on the notion of a 'political economy' that pushes movers to the margins of EU's economy. The practices of Ebou and Dawda form a worlding circuit that is both cause and effect of transnational interconnectivity. These circuits *are* the cross-border movements that constitute a circulatory territory (Tarrius 1993).

Babacar

When Babacar returned to Spain from his six-month stay in the Gambia (February 2016), he could not stay in his previous apartment as he had expected. His friend Pape was no longer the 'chef of the house' to look after his reservations of the room (Chapter 5). Although it was rather easy for Babacar to find another place to live in Lleida, he did not stay long in the Catalan city. He first checked with his boss whether the 'frutta season' was about to start, but there was no work for him yet. Thereupon, Babacar left for Milan (with a brief transit stop in Barcelona) to visit his good friend Doudou, the owner of the guest house in Milan. Babacar and Doudou had been close friends since their youth.

In May 2016, I went to Milan to meet up with Babacar. He welcomed me at the train station and soon after he summarized his six-month stay in the Gambia. He told me how he had started a taxi business and how he enjoyed his time with his family in the Bassé area. We also discussed 'the problem' of Moustapha, who had been detained in France after a failed unauthorized border crossing, and he explained to me the friction between Pape and him about the overbooking of the Lleida apartment. The following days, Babacar showed me his 'Italian life'. He guided me to the location for his street vending activities – in the heart of a bus station. This was not just a bus station, however. It appeared to be one of the EU's main mobility hubs where all kinds of travellers through Eurospace enter or get off busses of Eurolines, FlixBus, National Express and Alsa. There are seven bus services a day from this particular place to Barcelona, six to Munich and eleven to Amsterdam. This is a nodal place for European mobility and thus for European integration. Hence, this is both literally and figuratively 'the place to be' for Afrostars like Babacar.

Babacar was an important and enthusiastic broker in my research project. In Lleida he had guided me to several important locations and connected me to various potential informants. Now in the bus station in Milan, he urged me 'to interview' the Senegalese woman who sat next to him during their workdays. I explained to him that I did not like to subject someone unannounced to a whole series of questions, as he had in mind. Babacar, however, was persistent and had already approached his neighbour. We learned from the woman that she originated from Dakar, had lived in France for eight years and had been travelling up and down to Senegal for several years now. Hearing her story, Babacar underlined the positive aspects of her mobility by enthusiastically and repeatedly stating that 'That life is *good*!'

In the bus station, we also discussed Babacar's street vending tactics. I wondered whether his customers had a specific profile. Who were his customers? Italians? People from other European countries? Babacar laughed about this question since women from 'every country in the world' showed an interest in the bags he sold. He used his Spanish, French and English language skills to attract the attention of passing travellers. His clientele was not the only worlding dimension that unfolded these days. Babacar guided me to the Chinese shops where he carefully selected his bags to sell on the streets. We had dinner in one of his favourite Chinese restaurants, and we went to one of the touristic highlights of the city: the Piazza del Duomo

(Dom Square). There we observed the preparation of the UEFA Champions League final that was hosted by the city of Milan that year. Babacar was particularly excited about this event because both clubs playing the final both originated from Madrid. Madrid was a city he felt strongly connected to, as he stated: 'Because in the Madrid area, they gave me the first paper'. He was happy that the world would soon watch the spectacle of two teams coming from 'his city'. He made photos and videos of the installation of UEFA banners, large podia and immense video screens. He stated: 'I am like a tourist now'.

During my visit to Babacar, I wondered why he had actually chosen Milan for his hustling activities. To execute this business, he could have gone to Barcelona – a city that is only a short train journey away from Lleida and which has a lively street vending sector. The first answer he gave me hinted at a rational navigation of Eurospace. If he would engage in street vending in Barcelona, he explained, he would risk interfering control by the authorities that could negatively affect his residence rights in Spain. However, his quick addition to that explanation illustrated that his choice to engage in vending activities in Milan was in fact not based on a thoroughly considered plan: 'But before I came here, I did not know I was going to do this. It is because Doudou explained to me these things'. Doudou convinced Babacar that street vending is a lucrative business. He even gave his friend five bags to start up his business. With the first disposals, Babacar had sufficient capital to buy his own bags, and so his gains accumulated. Interestingly, when he had left Lleida for Milan a couple months before he had only thought of a brief visit of about two weeks. His adaptation to the informal circuit of Milan enabled him to considerably prolong his stay. Yet, however successful he was in this business, he only saw it as a temporary side activity. During his sojourn in Milan, he was in close communication with his 'patron' in the area of Lleida to anticipate his return to Spain to resume his formal work in the frutta sector.

Vending beyond the Streets

With his economic activities in Milan, Babacar embodied a public stereotype – that of the African street vendor. This stereotype has a double and itself reinforcing connotation in European public discourses. He (it is mostly a man) is usually framed as the marginal migrant *par excellence*. Someone who has no paper, no future in Europe. Someone who is *in* society but not *of* society. His constant struggle pushes him to embody a second stereotype: the informal urban actor. Someone who is economically active in a space without a formal regulation and protection mechanism. Someone who is earning money on the basis of fraudulent products and deceptive acts. He is someone *in* and *of* the margins of our urban economies. Like most stereotypes, this portrait of the African street vendor is violently wrong. Babacar was not trapped by the margins, he actually used them to expand his space of manoeuvrability. He entangled his leisure time (visiting a friend) with productive time (selling stuff). Moreover, this activity was not a main source of income, it was one out of many sources of income, alongside his taxi business in the Gambia, the seasonal labour in Spain and other income-generating activities.

To further re-describe the image of the street vendor I now articulate the diversity of vending activities that I came across. Doudou – the good friend of Babacar and his teacher in street vending skills in Milan – had left the streets himself a long time ago, but he continued vending. He combined this economic practice with a job as a watchman in a casino. After years of street vending, he had established a regular clientele, and this provided the opportunity to give his business model a more demand-driven character. From the time he stopped selling on the streets, he received phone calls of customers who ordered specific bags. Doudou then bought these bags and delivered them to his customers. Many of them lived in Milan, but occasionally he travelled by train to bring his bags to customers in cities like Florence, Perugia and even Rome. These 'suitcase traders' (although Doudou never carried a suitcase) form less visible circuits compared to the street vendors (Schmoll and Semi 2013). Similar invisible trading circuits existed among other movers I met. Destiny and his friend Kevin, for example, always scanned shoe shops for possible sales. They purchased shoes for reduced prices in regular shops and marketed them in the Nigerian communities in Italy. Some customers were unaware of the latest sales prices, which resulted in considerable profits for the two friends. Other goods they bought (including clothes, bags and laptops) were sent to Nigeria because they expected that they would yield higher profits there. Unlike Ebou and Dawda, Kevin and Destiny did not use containers for their transnational trade. They sought out people who were about to travel to Nigeria and were willing to bring some extra baggage with them in exchange for a little bit of money. To further arrange this trade, they contacted their local brokers in Nigeria and gave them instructions on the collection and handling of the goods. Circuits like these are defined by a mix of mobility, invisibility and trust relations (ibid.).

Second-hand cars comprise another field of trade opportunities. Babacar, like many other movers, particularly sought out 'strong cars' like the Mercedes 190 (that are also used for taxi businesses in the Gambia). The actual search for these cars reflects a mingling of affective and economic circuits and unfolds a geographical complexity that is hard to reconcile with the notion of here-there transnationalism. One day, a Gambian friend who lived in Angola called Babacar and asked him to look for a Mercedes 190 in Spain. But in Spain, Babacar could not find this specific car for a good price and so he contacted a relative in Germany. This relative told Babacar that he was also unable to find the car that the man in Angola had in mind, but that he was willing to explore the market in the Netherlands. There he found one, 'collected' it and shipped it to Africa.

Second-hand cars, however, are not only shipped. Some movers personally drive them to Africa. As I learned from a Malian man called Diachari, this can almost be a full-time occupation. Diachari lived in Pamplona (Spain) with his wife and five children, but he was continuously on the move. Between 2007 and 2015 he made, on average, six 'business trips' a year to Mali. In these eight years, he bought forty-nine vehicles (cars and small trucks) in Spain, drove them to Mali and sold them there. Cars, of course, are also used as carriers of other goods – some goods are to be marketed, others are presents for beloved ones. These itinerant car trading businesses do not only operate in and from Spain. They exist everywhere in Europe, Diachari stated. He knew some 'colleagues' working from Poland. He himself, however, never explored the market outside Spain. The further the distance, the more risks involved, he explained. The anticipated risk had little to do with borders and state control, as I initially thought. The main risk involved was that a car could break down en route, which would considerably heighten the transaction costs involved.

The entrepreneurial practices of the movers under study create fruitful grounds for wider economic developments – wholesalers, travel agencies, flight operators, shipping companies and other transport companies are all happy to take a facilitating role in these circuits. Less acknowledged by studies on globalization, but equally important, are the invisible actors co-creating these circuits: the brokers, catering servants, waste collectors, informal money transfer agents and undoubtedly many other actors. It follows that these circuits are neither formal nor informal, but both. They are neither solely economic nor purely social and affective, but both. The worlding practices are a source of intermediation. Intra-urban, intra-EU and transcontinental mobilities become entangled. Movers indeed construct 'cosmopolitan socialities' (Glick Schiller, Darieva and Gruner-Domic 2011; see also Loftsdóttir 2018) though locally embedded as well as transnationally oriented activities. Or, as Uma Kothari (2008: 509) wrote about Senegalese street vendors in Barcelona: 'Peddlers mobility and economic survival produce new kinds of cosmopolitanism through invoking networks and connections and bridging boundaries with those who are different from them'. Through mobilities and connections, the in/formal circuits reach, on the one hand, the shadowed corners of the urban economies of, for instance, Milan, Barcelona and Amsterdam and lead, on the other hand, to formalized services in Europe that further connect European economies to the bustling markets of, among other places, Serekunda, Accra, Dakar and Bamako. With this position of intermediation, the movers claim a socio-economic space at the translocal edges of a worlding Europe. As we will see below, this claim at times becomes a ground for political activism.

In September 2016, a Gambian migrant association and I organized a public discussion on the position of West Africans in the city of Barcelona. One of the most powerful speakers was a representative of the so-called Sindicato Popular de Vendederos Ambulantes de Barcelona (Popular Syndicate of Street Vendors of Barcelona). This collective emerged out of a widespread frustration among street vendors in Barcelona concerning the criminalization and repressive control of their daily activities. Since 2015, street vendors could be fined with 600 euros for executing unlawful businesses. From the start, the collective has had a strong link with other activist networks, such as the Raval-based Espacio del Immigrantes (Space of Migrants) that has the objective of constructing a space to fight against migrant exclusion and institutional violence (see also Arce Bayona 2016). Through social media performances, educational campaigns, workshops and public interventions, including the collective reappropriation of spaces from which they have been expelled, the syndicate created a re-described image of themselves (see also www.manteros.org). Its narrative mingled with other critical voices that aim to construct anti-colonial knowledge regarding migrancy and informal economy. The mingling of these urban fragments has indeed turned into a political critique (McFarlane 2018). One of the latest developments in this respect was the syndicate's launch of its own clothing brand Top Manta. With this brand it inverted the frequently heard criticism regarding the marketing of counterfeit products. The brand even got a formal sales point in a bookshop in Raval (December 2017). Some months later, the entire bookshop turned into a Top Manta clothes shop. This success story of collective action is more than a story of formalizing an informal economic practice. Top Manta's profits were used to support the street vending sector. For instance, the syndicate invented an insurance mechanism for vendors whose goods are ceased by the police – who at times operate in disguise to discourage the African vendors. As such, the brand helped to bring street vending beyond the streets in order to reclaim the streets.

Transgressions

In various ways, this book is a parallel world to Favell's (2008) book on the mobility of Eurostars. Favell travelled between Brussels, Amsterdam and

London and came across middle-class European professionals who live denationalized and multilocal lives. He described these movers as urban-oriented border transgressors. They were adventurous and risk-takers. But at times, as he also vividly describes, the same Eurostars felt in doubt, 'not there yet' and disintegrated. Interestingly, one of the simple questions Favell used in his study was whether his respondents saw themselves as migrants. The most frequent reply was 'an emphatic, sometimes bemused, "No!"' (ibid.: 101). Eurostar Saskia, for example, replied to Favell's question as follows: 'No! I see myself as an expatriate – not a migrant, not at all. It depends on your perspective if your perspective is global, then you are not a migrant. You are a mover, your mobility is much higher' (ibid.: 44). The Eurostars tended to frame themselves as expats or movers since they felt that their mobility was much higher than that of a migrant. One Eurostar gave an illustrative image of a migrant, stating: 'I think of a migrant as someone who is making one big move' (ibid.: 29).

According to several scholars, however, there is an additional logic at stake that disregards the label of the migrant. Hein de Haas (2015) claims that the term migrant is more and more associated with low-skilled people from less wealthy areas. It follows that the term expat has become a class marker (see also Leinonen 2012). The label of the expat is used by privileged movers who distinguish themselves from alleged other movers – notably migrants – and is, thus, self-fulfilling. As such, the expat label reinforces the uncomfortable notion that cosmopolitan identities are reserved for a selected few: the white, Western, urban and elitist border crosser. Most African movers who were part of this study refuted this Eurocentric version of cosmopolitanism. None of their claims was as powerful as that of Mohamadou, a Senegalese man selling books in Bergamo (Italy) at the time I met him (see also Schapendonk 2017a). Mohamadou comes from Touba, a city in central Senegal known as the holy city of the Mouride brotherhood. Interestingly, the history of Mouride networks are taken as a notable counter case against Westernized versions of cosmopolitanism (Diouf and Rendall 2000; Riccio 2004). Equally so, Mohamadou's family history has a strong transnational character formed by economic, social and religious networks. His mother was a *voyageuse* (traveller) between Senegal and Saudi Arabia, before Mohamadou and his brothers started to move across borders. Mohamadou first travelled up and down to China and later to and from South Africa. He exported tea from South Africa and started a telephone shop in Dakar. Before his arrival in Bergamo, he worked in Paris and Barcelona. In the tourist season, he moved to Sardinia for some business opportunities there. From his viewpoint as a 'cosmopolitan clandestine', Europe was 'misery', especially after his residence permit expired. It was misery for its strictness and isolation. He in fact sought ways to escape

Europe, preferably with a renewed permit that would grant him the right to re-enter Europe when desired. For his next destination, he had two options in mind: Taiwan (where one of his siblings lived) and the US. Like Favell's Eurostars, Mohamadou did not frame himself as a migrant in Italy. In his life history, as well as in his anticipated future, Europe was dislocated from the centre of the world. It seemed to be just one of the places that matter in a multi-polar world.

Doudou

At the time of one of my video calls with Doudou he had just received bad news about his papers: the Italian authorities 'took everything from his hands'. Roughly a year before, he had gone to the police station to start another regularization procedure. He paid a lawyer to assist him this time, but this turned out to be of no avail. The authorities told him that he had just had too many problems in the country. Consequently, he would not get a new residence permit. After hearing the bad news, I foresaw two major problems for Doudou. First, he would enter a new episode of risk and deportability. Second, he would no longer be able to travel to his Gambian wife who lived in Leiden (the Netherlands). Doudou, however, downplayed both negative aspects. With a strong voice, but also with a lot of humour, he stated that he was not afraid of deportation. He argued that he still preferred to live in Italy, but if he would be deported he would also be happy: 'When they take me to my country, no problem. I am happy. I am there *in my home*! ... So what is the problem?! Why should I fear that they can bring me home, why?!' In a similar way, he countered the second problem I mentioned. By referring to his long stay in Italy, he claimed his right to mobility: 'I *will* travel, I will try to take something to manage. I am *Italian*, I am mafia!' We laughed about this particular claim of citizenship. Then I asked once more: 'You are not scared, huh?' He once again raised his voice and continued: 'No! I am not scared, my brother, I am illegal in Europe for about seventeen years now, what am I going to fear?'

Over the years, Doudou transgressed the notions of fear, risk and deportability that are so often related to illegality (see also Idrissa's case in Chapter 5). However, his claim of being 'illegal' for such a long time needs to be interpreted with caution. This period namely included quite some 'status mobility' (Schuster 2005) as well as multiple legal grey zones (Kubal 2013), reflecting the many ambiguities of Italian immigration law as well as the temporary nature of residence in Italy (Tuckett 2018). In 2002, for instance, Doudou actually held a residence permit that was valid for two years. This 'two-year paper' was withdrawn, however, after he was caught smoking ganja in public and a period of undocumentedness followed, lasting for approximately two years. On top of that came his arrest because of his alleged fraud with the paperwork of his guest house. During a random control, the police found out he carried the documents of an African man who had stayed in Doudou's apartment before he left to elsewhere in Europe. The police suspected Doudou of misusing someone else's documents, as Doudou stated with a sigh: 'They think I stole this document and I used it for maybe travelling or working, you see?! ... I explained to them that I kept this paper for somebody who is travelling in Europe, so I don't get anything, but they brought me to court for this'. Thus, running the guest house facilitated many people's mobility within Europe, but somehow hampered Doudou's own trajectory since it reduced his chances of long-term documentation in Italy.

When I first met Doudou (May 2016), strictly speaking he also was not undocumented. He in fact held a 'one-year soggiorno' that needed to be renewed annually. The status of this specific paper never really became clear to me. It allowed him to travel to Leiden to visit his Gambian girlfriend once in a while. However, the paper did not allow him to move to the Gambia. This is why he had always felt that his paper was 'incomplete' and why he felt being 'illegal' in Italy since the moment he lost his residence permit in the early 2000s. Interestingly, Doudou framed the impossibility to travel between Africa and Europe as an important motivation to keep moving within Europe. He reasoned: 'If I cannot travel to Africa, I told myself, I must travel in Europe'. Besides his travels to the Netherlands (he visited his girlfriend three times between May 2016 and February 2018), he travelled to Spain and France several times in the last few years.

When Doudou received the bad news about his paper, Babacar had moved again to the Gambia. He shared pictures with both Doudou and me of how he enjoyed his time in the Gambia. When Doudou saw the photos of another two taxis Babacar had recently bought, he reflected on the possibility of running a taxi himself in case he would be deported: 'I am not waiting for it to happen, but when it is happening, I don't care about it. I will try my best'. For him, deportation would mean a return to his country of origin after a long absence. He had left the Gambia already in 1997 and had spent a considerable period of time in Senegal, Mauritania, Mali and Libya. In 2000, he returned from Libya to the Gambia. This was his last visit. His physical absence did, however, not mean he was no longer involved in his country of origin. Between October and December 2016, for example, Doudou was strongly engaged in the political lobby against President Jammeh. Through live chats on Facebook and through WhatsApp group communications he mobilized diasporic groups to be politically active and advocate against Jammeh. Through numerous live videos he posted, he urged Gambian society to vote for change. Like many other Gambian movers I met in the course of this project, he felt this was a unique moment to change the political structures of his country of origin. In the aftermath of the political transition, Doudou closely monitored the practices of the new government and commented on it on social media. Like a trained journalist, he made a live report of the meeting of a delegation of the new government with the Gambian community in Milan. During the meeting he reported on, the community and government representatives discussed many issues with each other, including the lack of structural documentation of Gambian nationals in Italy. When I asked Doudou whether the government delegation included the Gambian consul in Italy, he said actually the Gambian ambassador in Spain had travelled to Milan for this meeting. Whereas the ways Gambian movers act across borders in Europe is ignored at best, and criminalized at worst, by European politics, it seems that the new Gambian administration acknowledged the social, economic and political implications of Gambian mobility in Eurospace. Political mobilization coming from the marginal and mobile spaces of Europe has proven to be a powerful source for political and societal transformation in this particular West African country (Hultin et al. 2017).

The Right to Disappear

Despite his sympathy for my project, I could not keep track of Babacar's movements. When he returned to Lleida from his prolonged stay in Italy (June 2016), I had the idea to revisit him there in September of that same year. When I contacted him two weeks before my departure to Lleida, he had already left that place to live and work in the surroundings of Gerona, another Catalan city. I initially thought I could combine my stay in Lleida with a visit to Gerona. Thus, once in Lleida, I contacted Babacar again. He, however, told me he had unexpectedly moved to Italy again, this time for a serious family affair. One of his younger brothers, who had taken the backway to Italy a while ago, had seriously fallen ill in one of Italy's reception centres. His family in the Gambia had urged Babacar to go there and take care of him. That was the last information I received from him. He disappeared from the radar, not only for me, but also for his good friend Doudou.

For several months, I heard seemingly contradictory information about Babacar. One of his friends thought he had moved to Belgium, some said he was in Italy and others thought he went back to Africa. No one, however, seemed to be entirely sure whether their information was correct. No one seemed to have spoken with Babacar directly. It all seemed to be indirect information – rumours that had travelled from country to country. When Doudou came to the Netherlands again (February 2017), we also discussed the whereabouts of Babacar. Doudou was rather relaxed about the fact he had not heard from his friend for a long time. With a touch of nonchalance, he said: 'I am sure he is fine. Otherwise I would know. Babacar can do this sometimes. He just disappears. You cannot reach him by WhatsApp or Viber, he just disappears'. When I pointed to the magical connotation of his disappearance, Doudou enthusiastically confirmed this: 'Yea! It is like magic'.

In many cases, disappearances are not magical, but caused by 'the system' instead. A disappearance may therefore lead to intense concerns in affective circuits. Pape, who had himself experienced how his temporary detention had negatively affected the well-being of his family in the Gambia, repeatedly asked me if I had heard from George, his Ghanaian friend who lived in Amsterdam and who had, in fact, connected the two of us. From May 2016, Pape's concern about George intensified. He did not hear from him for a month or so – which was very exceptional for the two friends. In fact, George had never ever been 'offline' (from Viber or WhatsApp) for such a long period of time. Possibly, he had changed his telephone number. In September, Pape was rather sure that 'something had happened'. Maybe George was sent back to his country, he thought, or maybe something worse. When they both lived in France, they had shared the contact details of their families in their countries of origin, but after some years, Pape had lost these contact details. Every time I spoke to Pape, he hoped for some good news, that his friend had reappeared, somewhere. He asked me to ask around in Amsterdam. But I did not come across any news. The silence remained.

In contrast to George's situation, no one seemed to worry about Babacar's disappearance. Pape, Moustapha, Doudou and his other friends I knew all referred to Babacar's mobility disposition as an explanation for the 'magic'. I had no other option but to accept Babacar's disappearance. Or actually, Babacar's disappearance inspired me to write a blog about the value of disconnections in a study on mobility. It gave me, so I reasoned in that blog, first-hand insights into the efforts behind social connectivity as well as the relational questions involved (where is he? Did I do something wrong? Is he OK?). However, just when I had framed the situation for myself as a lost contact, Babacar reappeared. Not in Lleida or Gerona, not through a phone call or WhatsApp message, but in Doudou's guest house in Milan.

In the beginning of May 2017, I went to see Doudou again in his place of anchorage. On a Sunday afternoon I arrived at Milan Central Station. After our mutual greetings, Doudou told me that Babacar was also around and that I would see him in the house. I was happily surprised. For about eight months, I had tried to reconnect with him, and now he just reappeared without further notice, like magic. At that moment, I also wondered why Doudou had not told me about Babacar's presence before. After all, we had repeatedly talked about Babacar's whereabouts. The answer to that question was simple. Just as Babacar's reappearance surprised me, Doudou had not expected him either. Doudou explained: 'Babacar just came last Friday, he just arrived. I even did not know he was coming. That is Babacar, you know him. I have not talked to him for like one year now, and then he just comes [starts laughing]. I did not even tell him that you are coming. Only today I told him'.

During my subsequent conversations with Babacar, it appeared that there was a lot of truth in the rumours about his whereabouts in the last eight months. He had indeed spent a short time in Belgium, from where he indeed travelled back to Spain, and now he was in Italy. Babacar's mobility reflects a form of detachment that is discussed by AbdouMaliq Simone (2019: 27) in the framework of urban informalities: 'For detachment also indicates that by the time a certain life at the margins comes to be represented, it has already moved on somewhere else'. With his movements, Babacar refused to be fixed, socially and politically. For him, disappearance – characterized by opacity – was a right to be claimed (see also Khosravi 2018). This became once more clear from his reflection on his FlixBus journey from Spain to Belgium. At the French–Belgian border, the bus was stopped, and the border police asked him some questions. One of the questions was how long he planned to stay in Belgium. Babacar replied, in all honesty: 'Maybe two days, maybe two years'.

Concluding Notes: The Europe That Is and That Which Might Be

In two chapters, this second part of this book has articulated the various ways African movers re-view Europe. It has illustrated their emplacements and their ambivalences. At the same time, it has defined their position at the margins of Europe as one of structural eventuality, which differs from precariousness. In fact, on the basis of these two chapters it is very hard to pinpoint what these margins are and what they do. This is exactly what Andrucki and Dickinson (2015) underline when they delink centres and margins from a concrete geography of places and relate them instead to mobility and performances. As they write (ibid.: 204): 'If we delink centers and margins from places and focus on bodies moving, dwelling in, and traveling through place, we can attend to the ways in which political and economic hierarchies of political space are continually reconfigured, reorganized, and reworked through emotional, affective, and material practices'. Thus, through affective and in/formal circuits, many movers not only constantly move in and out of the margins, but they redefine the ways margins relate to centres. Through the entwined character of these circuits, movers never have only one socio-economic position in only one specific society. This makes the question *where* to locate social mobility difficult to answer. That is not to say that circuits, mobilities and being in Europe are placeless phenomena. It rather means that conventional notions of success and failure become diffuse.

These circuits – as argued before – not only build transnational bridges with places of origin. They also constitute a worlding Europe (Loftsdóttir 2018); a Europe that is always multiple (Balibar 2004: 5).[1] Because these circuits never stand still, versions and interpretations of Europe also shift constantly. From the perspective of the movers, we see a Europe that *is* and *might be*. It is a Europe that is both central *and* marginal. It is a Europe that is characterized both by cross-border mobility (Schengen) and by its fight against it (Dublin). With regard to the latter, Europe aims to find the right policy measures to differentiate on the basis of deservingness (who deserves to stay?), entitlement (who is entitled to move?) and administrative emplacement (where do movers belong?). In this quest of bordering and ordering mobility (Van Houtum and Van Naerssen 2002), Europe seems to be desperately looking for transparency and clarity. The irony, however, is that when one gains more knowledge on what drives African movers to cross borders, on where they really go and on how long they intend to stay, the picture does not necessarily become clearer. This irony revealed itself in the conversation between Babacar and the border guard along the French–Belgian borderland, discussed above. When he recounted this incidence, Babacar started to laugh when he remembered the puzzled face of the border guard hearing his reply of 'Maybe two days, maybe two years'. With this reply, Babacar claimed a mobility that both *is* and *might be*.

NOTE

1. Balibar (2004: 5) writes: 'In all its points, Europe is multiple; it is always home to tensions between numerous religious, cultural, linguistic, and political affiliations, numerous readings of history, numerous modes of relations with the rest of the world, whether it is Americanism or Orientalism, the possessive individualism of "Nordic" legal systems or the "tribalism" of Mediterranean familial traditions'.

Conclusion

In September 2018, I spent my last travel budget in one of the most important anchor points for this project – the small Ligurian city where I met Yahya, Shakur and Omar for the very first time in April 2014. Through their contacts and through their navigations, my Eurospace had expanded. Through them I had met Lamin, Saihou (the Afrostar), Mamadou (the JJC), and many others. Through their movements I had ended up in very different places in, among others, Switzerland, Germany and the Gambia. Just before my departure to Italy, I called Shakur and he told me that they were 'all around'. Whereas Shakur had never left the place since April 2014 and still resided in the same Ligurian asylum shelter, several of his 'colleagues' had come back from elsewhere in Europe. Omar had just returned from his stay in Germany. Before he took off of for Italy, Omar had also spent several months in the Netherlands. He now needed to present himself to the Italian authorities to renew his papers. For him, however, staying in Italy was not easy. While he made ends meet in the raba raba way, by selling scarves and towels on the beach, his employer in Germany kept on calling to say that there was sufficient work for him in the construction sector. Also, Mamadou was back in the place from which his wanderings in Eurospace had begun. He showed me photos on his phone of Marseille, Dortmund, Strasbourg and Valencia. But now he was back in 'his town' in Italy. He felt he had come home again. He had resumed working at the dock and apologized to his employer for having disappeared so suddenly. Lamin was also in Italy and he was happy to come over from his nearby city to catch up with his friends. So, while I initially intended to visit Shakur to learn more about his place-bound life, I again found myself in the middle of a coming together of trajectories (Massey 2005).

It was almost midnight and I waited for Shakur to arrive at 'the fountain' – a public place where I used to hang out with some of my interlocutors. He approached me from behind, with his hoody over his head. He seemed to have developed more muscles over the last few months. He had shaved his head, and his little beard had grown. His friendly smile and firm hug immediately made it a very pleasant reunion. When I told him he looked good, he modestly changed this positive expression by saying: 'I am not looking good, I am just here'. Three months earlier, Shakur had informed me with a voice message that it had been 'a long journey' but he now had finally 'found the document'. In that euphoric moment, I liked his expression that he 'had found' it – as if he had finally reached the exit from a labyrinth. For Shakur, this breakthrough meant a reorientation of his future mobility, as he added: 'Let's wait and see now, what is the next step to do ... I want to change the destination, man'. What we did not know at that time was that the Italian government would soon decide to abolish the humanitarian protection status – the status that Shakur had just received. This government decision tremendously affected the future horizon of Shakur, and many others, in Eurospace.

This book started from a de-migranticized notion (Dahinden 2016) of my informants' mobility. To articulate this starting point, I preferred the term movers over migrants. That is not to say that migration research – and its related terminology – is fundamentally wrong. Nor do I argue that we should get rid of the term migrants and replace it with the term movers. On the contrary, migration research has always been an important field that helps us to position human movement in the heart of a globalizing world. Furthermore, even though the different labels that are used to categorize migrants can be well criticized on normative and empirical grounds, they still have important implications for people's being in Eurospace (Erdal and Oeppen 2018) – as the case of Shakur above illustrates. However, instead of considering bureaucratic labels as pregiven signifiers of difference or indicators for selection of research topics, I argue that we should be more sensitive to the ways labels like 'migrants', 'asylum seekers' and 'undocumented' are actually artefacts of migration policy that are reproduced and embodied, but also contested and transgressed. In other words, by following im/mobility trajectories we can actually point to moments, conditions and situations that turn movers (and stayers) into migrants and the ways they themselves move beyond that categorization.

The question then is: would this book about the lifeworlds of Africans in Eurospace have been very different had I started my project from a typical migration framework? The answer is a firm yes. I would have started from the conceptual terminology of onward migration and secondary movements. This terminology would have put the mobility dynamics in a straitjacket of residential relocation. Thus, whereas migration is generally about pinning down one's residence, mobility is not. Seen from a migration framework, this project could have been interpreted as a research endeavour that highlights the difference between settlers and sojourners. The first group are typical im-migrants, investing in integrated and place-bound lives in their destinations. The second group are the free-floaters, travellers without a destination. Logically, this migration lens would have articulated that the movers under study are the free-floaters – and, thus, one could have concluded that we dived into the lives of a different *type* of migrant. This typical framing would have invalidated my main arguments for at least two reasons. The first reason is that this migration framework opposes emplacement to movement. This book, however, claims that through different mobility/locality configurations, mobility is not in conflict with location. From stable grounds, movers start to circulate. From emplaced positions, movers start to explore possible relocations. And in their mobility, movers look for local anchorages. This argument, thus, fundamentally destabilizes the settlers/sojourners divide. Settled migrants can be highly mobile, and 'those who are displaced' may still live place-based lives (Lems 2018).

The second reason why a migration framework would have created a different narrative is that the onward migration terminology would have reproduced a rather linear story of migration – a storyline of departure/transit towards onward movement/arrival. We have seen, however, that arrivals create new forms of mobility that may fuel future relocations. With this observation, there is an insightful parallel to draw with the work of the geographers Lepawsky and Mather (2011: 245). Although they concentrate on a very different topic – e-waste – they fundamentally question the presumed linearity of economic processes, as they write:

> For us linearity is *not only* a problem of simplifying economic activity as a linear flow (cf. Hudson 2008b); nor is it *only* a problem associated with removing economic activity from the spatial, social and embodied context in which it is embedded. It is, instead, a problem related to the architecture of beginnings and endings.

Following their logic, beginnings and endings are methodological artefacts that do not necessarily match the processes we study. Instead of beginning and endings, Lepawsky and Mather propose a language of boundaries and edges. In their study on e-waste, boundaries and edges are sites where transformations take place, where materials are adjusted and where new value is made. In other words, the ending of one process is the beginning of another process. As such, boundaries and edges are the results of relations and therefore they are never fixed but always contested. Can we in a similar way imagine a pathway in migration studies that has no essential beginnings and endings?

On Beginnings and Endings

This book, thus, argues for openness. While I definitely think that the sedentarist logics – varying from securitization to humanitarianism (Nyberg Sørensen 2012; Smith and Schapendonk 2018) – behind the EU's policy approach to African mobility are counterproductive, frenetic and wrong, I do not relate the notion of openness to the utopian argument of open borders. Rather, the plea for openness relates to an intellectual reluctance to freeze migrant positionalities in Europe (or elsewhere). I have tried to do justice to the hardships, threats, risks, injustices, fears and blunt racism that many of my informants have encountered, in- and outside Eurospace. Evidently, movers may be hard hit by practices of nation states and malicious actors in the mobility industry and may endure periods of duress that a privileged ethnographer who has not experienced them can never really grasp (Cabot 2016; Khosravi 2018). These practices lead to terrible losses, devastating separations and wrecking deportations. Furthermore, there is an extremely violent politics hidden in the passivity of EU actors when it comes to not saving people who cross the Mediterranean Sea from the North African coasts (Heller 2015). In this context, I am supportive of any courageous scholar, activist or other individual who contests these injustices of the so-called 'global mobility regime' (Glick Schiller and Salazar 2013).

That said, I have yet refrained myself from falling into a terminology that frames the movers in question as subjectified actors whose spaces to manoeuvre are all too limited by some structural conditions produced by the same global mobility regime. I believe that such a positionality leads to analytical closures that produce their own violence. If one overlooks processes of transgression, resilience, navigation and escape, one easily 'fixes' the mover as a one-dimensional figure who lives a bare life. This then easily leads to a similar politics of victimization, clientization and categorization that many movers overcome in their daily lives (Aparna and Schapendonk 2018). For this reason, I have not strictly separated the experiences of the documented from the undocumented movers. Such a divide would do injustice to the dynamics of the trajectories under study, including people's status mobility (e.g. Schuster 2005). By following im/mobility trajectories, we are able to observe how 'illegality' and undocumentedness are more so phases in people's lives than a structural condition. Even in cases where this phase lasts for a considerable period of time, people may find ways to escape it (like Maggis) or else find ways to live with it (like Doudou and Idrissa). Similarly, I did not strictly separate elements of forced and voluntary migration. Instead, I related experiences of uprootedness to imaginaries of social becoming (Salazar 2011). I related irregularity to joyful mobility (in the case of Saihou), and I linked being 'grounded' in Europe to social success but also to anxiety and social isolation (in the cases of Binta and Moustapha).

There are many other intersections to identify in this book that relate to this argument of openness (borders/crossings; vulnerability/resourcefulness; dwelling/moving; individuality/sociality; place attachments/place expulsions; affective circuits/economic circuits). It follows that openness does not mean a mere celebration of agency in general, and African creativity in particular (see also Gaibazzi 2015). The structural eventuality I put forward implies that people may fall back into crisis-like situations or that they are confronted with borders in unexpected ways. Openness, in other words, does not automatically lead to progress and solutions. It does lead to frictions. As Tsing (2005: 19-20) reminds us, frictions are heterogeneous and unequal, but they also create possibilities to invent 'new arrangements of culture and power'.

Evidently, as I also stated in the Introduction, this trajectory approach comes with losses. I have built only up limited knowledge of the history, politics and daily institutional arrangements of the Dutch, German, Spanish, Italian and European-wide systems the African movers find themselves in. Furthermore, I never had the time, nor the rest, to dive into the multiple perspectives and arrangements that produce borders, margins and homes. Thus, I sacrificed some contextualization and social embeddedness for something that I highly value. These sacrifices namely provided me with a space to construct a storyline that is not written from a single location, a single setting, a single moment, or a single Europe. This plurality creates a storyline without final destinations and endings, but with multiple edges, boundaries and new beginnings.

* * *

Notes from Eurospace, July–December 2018

André – the Cameroonian man who lost Europe a while ago – called me from Greece. He told me he had left Athens and started to work in the agricultural fields outside the urban area of Athens. The money he earned was enough to pay for 'a new bet'. There was an additional advantage to his work in the open fields. It gave him some extra exposure to the sun. The sunlight made his skin colour a bit darker, and thus made him resemble better the person in the French passport he had recently bought. André asked me not to tell his girlfriend Michelle in Paris about his travel plans. It would make her nervous and he preferred to surprise her with his presence in France, one day soon.

* * *

July – the Nigerian woman who had left the Netherlands to live in London with her son – told me that she had recently reduced the number of travels to the Netherlands to focus more on life in London. She expressed her hope that her husband would relocate to London too. That was the family plan. However, July also articulated that this family plan took time since her husband was a Dutchman. She underlined that her spouse found it hard to leave his national roots behind. But above all, she was worried about how the Brexit would affect her life. She felt she tried to stay put on shifting grounds.

* * *

Idrissa – the undocumented free citizen of Barcelona – received some great news from the local authorities in October. He was granted a 'pardon'. It would not be long now for him to receive his first residence permit since he entered Spain twelve years ago. He could not wait to travel to see his mother in Brikama (the Gambia).

* * *

In October, Alagie sent me a voice message from the gym in Serekunda. He told me that his relationship with his British girlfriend had collapsed. Once again, he saw his chances to live in Europe for a longer period of time vanish.

* * *

In September, Lamin and I sat in an Italian bus and discussed home. Whereas Saihou and Yahya, among others, had visited the Gambia soon after they obtained their Italian residence permits, Lamin never really expressed the wish to travel to his country of origin. Yes, he communicated with his mother and aunty a lot, but he just did not feel the need to go back. He said he did not miss home.

Glossary

agences de courtage	brokerage services (French term)
badingya (or *badenya*)	maternal lineages; implies a sense of closeness, locality, group cohesion and stability (Madinka term)
coxeur	bus boy responsible for transfers at transport nodes (French term)
débrouillardise	hustling tactics (French term)
fadingya (or *fadenya*)	paternal lineages; implies change, conflict, innovation, self-promotion, competition and 'anything tending to spin the actor out of his established social force field' (Madinka term)
garage	bus station (popular expression in the Gambia)
illimitato	unlimited residence permit (Italian term)
inreisverbod	entry ban (Dutch term)
passeur	smuggler (French term)
permesso di soggiorno	residence permit (Italian term)
pirogue	wooden fisher boat (French term)
prefetture	provincial offices (Italian term)
questura	police station (Italian term)
raba raba	mixed connotation of hustling, struggling, rapidity and business; hustling practices (popular expression in Senegambia)
taxuu	sitting/staying put (Soninke term)
toog	to sit/to wait (Wolof term)

References

Adey, P. 2006. 'If Mobility Is Everything Then It Is Nothing: Towards a Relational Politics of (Im)mobilities', *Mobilities* 1(1): 75-94.
_____. 2010. *Mobility*. London: Routledge.
Ahrens, J., M. Kelly and I. van Liempt. 2016. 'Free Movement? The Onward Migration of EU Citizens Born in Somalia, Iran, and Nigeria', *Population, Space and Place* 22(1): 84-98.
Alioua, M. 2008. 'La Migration Transnationale – Logique Individuelle dans l'Espace National: l'Exemple des Transmigrants Subsahariens à l'Épreuve de l'Externalisation de la Gestion des Flux Migratoires au Maroc', *Social Science Information* 47(4):697-713.
Alpes, J. 2011. 'Bushfalling: How Young Cameroonians Dare to Migrate', Ph.D. dissertation. Amsterdam: University of Amsterdam.
Ambrosini, M. 2017. 'Why Irregular Migrants Arrive and Remain: The Role of Intermediaries', *Journal of Ethnic and Migration Studies* 43(11): 1813-30.
Andersson, R. 2014. *Illegality, Inc.: Clandestine Migration and the Business of Bordering Europe*. Oakland: University of California Press.
_____. 2016. 'Europe's Failed "Fight" against Irregular Migration: Ethnographic Notes on a Counterproductive Industry', *Journal of Ethnic and Migration Studies* 42(7): 1055-75.
Andrikopoulos, A. 2017. 'Argonauts of West Africa: Migration, Citizenship and Kinship Dynamics in a Changing Europe', Ph.D. dissertation. Amsterdam: University of Amsterdam.
Andrucki, M.J., and J. Dickinson. 2015. 'Rethinking Centers and Margins in Geography: Bodies, Life Course, and the Performance of Transnational Space', *Annals of the Association of American Geographers* 105(1): 203-18.
Antonopoulos, G.A. 2006. 'Greece: Policing Racist Violence in the "Fenceless Vineyard"', *Race & Class* 48(2): 92-100.
Aparna, K., et al. 2017. 'Lost Europe(s)', *Etnografia e Ricerca Qualitativa* 10(3): 435-52.
Aparna, K., and J. Schapendonk. 2018. 'Shifting Itineraries of Asylum Hospitality: Towards a Process Geographical Approach of Guest-Host Relations', *Geoforum*. Retrieved 6 April 2018 from https://doi.org/10.1016/j.geoforum.2018.03.024.
Arce Bayona, J.J. 2016. 'Surviving Is Not a Crime: The Struggles of Undocumented Migrants in Barcelona', MSc. thesis. Aalborg: Aalborg University.
Bakewell, O. 2007. 'Keeping Them in Their Place: The Ambivalent Relationship between Development and Migration in Africa', *IMI Working Papers 8*. Oxford: International Migration Institute.

Balibar, É. 2004. *We, the People of Europe? Reflections on Transnational Citizenship*. Oxford: Princeton University Press.

Bauman, Z. 1998. *Globalization: The Human Consequences*. Cambridge: Polity Press.

Belloni, M. 2016a. 'Cosmologies of Destinations: Roots and Routes of Eritrean Forced Migration towards Europe', Ph.D. dissertation. Trento: University of Trento.

―――. 2016b. '"My Uncle Cannot Say 'No' if I Reach Libya": Unpacking the Social Dynamics of Border-Crossing among Eritreans Heading to Europe', *Human Geography* 9(2): 47–56.

―――. 2016c. 'Refugees as Gamblers: Eritreans Seeking to Migrate through Italy', *Journal of Immigrant & Refugee Studies* 14(1): 104–19.

Bendixsen, S., and T.H. Eriksen. 2018. 'Time and the Other: Waiting and Hope among Irregular Migrants', in M.K. Janeja and A. Bandak (eds), *Ethnographies of Waiting: Doubt, Hope and Uncertainty*. London: Bloomsbury Publishing, pp. 87–112.

BenEzer, G., and R. Zetter. 2014. 'Searching for Directions: Conceptual and Methodological Challenges in Researching Refugee Journeys', *Journal of Refugee Studies* 28(3): 297–318.

Berger, I. 2015. 'Between Advocacy and Deception: Crafting an African Asylum Narrative', In I. Berger, et al. (eds), *African Asylum at a Crossroads: Activism, Expert Testimony, and Refugee Rights*. Ohio: Ohio University Press, pp. 163–81.

Berger, I., et al. (eds). 2015. *African Asylum at a Crossroads: Activism, Expert Testimony, and Refugee Rights*. Ohio: Ohio University Press.

Bernardt, C. 2016. 'Na de 28e Dag', *AGORA Magazine* 32(1): 10–13.

Bird, J.N. 2018. 'Death and Dying in a Karen Refugee Community: An Overlooked Challenge in the Resettlement Process', *Ethnography*. Retrieved 22 June 2018 from https://doi.org/10.1177/1466138118768624.

Bloch, A., N. Sigona and R. Zetter. 2014. *Sans Papiers: The Social and Economic Lives of Young Undocumented Migrants*. London: Pluto Press.

Boccagni, P., and L. Baldassar. 2015. 'Emotions on the Move: Mapping the Emergent Field of Emotion and Migration', *Emotion, Space and Society* 16: 73–80.

Bolay, M. 2017. 'Gold Journeys: Expulsion-Induced Mobility and the Making of Artisanal Mining Spaces in West Africa. An Ethnography of Itinerant Labour at the Bottom of the Gold Supply Chain', Ph.D. dissertation. Neuchâtel: University of Neuchâtel.

Bos, B. 2017. 'A Moving Place: A Study about the Socio-spatial Consequences of West African Mobility and Place in Lleida, Spain', MSc. thesis. Nijmegen: Radboud University.

Bourdieu, P. 1986. 'The Forms of Capital', in J.G. Richardson (ed.), *Handbook of Theory and Research for the Sociology of Education*. London: Greenwood Press, pp. 241–58.

Borri, G. 2017. 'Humanitarian Protraction Status: The Production of (Im)mobile Subjects between Turin and Berlin', *Etnografia e Ricerca Qualitativa* 10(1): 55–73.

Boyd, M. 1989. 'Family and Personal Networks in International Migration: Recent Developments and New Agendas', *International Migration Review* 23(3): 638–70.

Brachet, J. 2005. 'Constructions of Territoriality in the Sahara: The Transformation of Spaces of Transit', *Stichproben. Wiener Zeitschrift für Kritische Afrikastudien* 5(8): 239–54.

_____. 2016. 'Policing the Desert: The IOM in Libya beyond War and Peace', *Antipode* 48(2): 272-92.

_____. 2018. 'Manufacturing Smugglers: From Irregular to Clandestine Mobility in the Sahara', *The Annals of the American Academy of Political and Social Science* 676(1): 16-35.

Brachet, J., A. Choplin, and O. Pliez. 2011. 'Le Sahara entre Espace de Circulation et Frontière Migratoire de l'Europe', *Hérodote* 142(3): 163-82.

Bredeloup, S. 2008. 'L'Aventurier, une Figure de la Migration Africaine', *Cahiers Internationaux de Sociologie* 125(2): 281-306.

Büscher, M., and J. Urry. 2009. 'Mobile Methods and the Empirical', *European Journal of Social Theory* 12(1): 99-116.

Cabot, H. 2014. *On the Doorstep of Europe: Asylum and Citizenship in Greece*. Philadelphia: University of Pennsylvania Press.

_____. 2016. '"Refugee Voices": Tragedy, Ghosts, and the Anthropology of Not Knowing', *Journal of Contemporary Ethnography* 45(6): 645-72.

Calais Writers. 2017. *Voices from the 'Jungle': Stories from the Calais Refugee Camp*. London: Pluto Press.

Camenisch, A., and S. Müller. 2017. 'From (E)Migration to Mobile Lifestyles: Ethnographic and Conceptual Reflections about Mobilities and Migration', *New Diversities* 19(3): 43-57.

Campesi, G. 2015. 'Humanitarian Confinement: An Ethnography of Reception Centres for Asylum Seekers at Europe's Southern Border', *International Journal of Migration and Border Studies* 1(4): 398-418.

Carling, J. 2002. 'Migration in the Age of Involuntary Immobility: Theoretical Reflections and Cape Verdean Experiences', *Journal of Ethnic and Migration Studies* 28(1): 5-42.

Carnet, P., et al. 2012. 'Circulation Migratoire des Transmigrants', *Multitudes* 49(2): 76-88.

Casas-Cortes, M., S. Cobarrubias and J. Pickles. 2015. 'Riding Routes and Itinerant Borders: Autonomy of Migration and Border Externalization', *Antipode* 47(4): 894-914.

Casati, N. 2018. 'How Cities Shape Refugee Centres: "Deservingness" and "Good Aid" in a Sicilian Town', *Journal of Ethnic and Migration Studies* 44(5): 792-808.

Casey, E.S. 1993. *Getting Back into Place: Toward a Renewed Understanding of the Place-World*. Bloomington: Indiana University Press.

Ceesay, I. 2016. 'Aligners, Lovers and Deceptors: Aspirations and Strategies of Young Urban Hustlers in the Gambia', Ph.D. dissertation. Edinburgh: University of Edinburgh.

Chauvin, S., and B. Garcés-Mascareñas. 2014. 'Becoming Less Illegal: Deservingness Frames and Undocumented Migrant Incorporation', *Sociology Compass* 8(4): 422-32.

Choplin, A., and L. Lombard. 2010. '"Suivre la Route": Mobilités et Échanges entre Mali, Mauritanie et Sénégal', *EchoGéo* 14(September/November): 1-21.

Cole, J. 2016. 'Giving Life: Regulating Affective Circuits among Malagasy Marriage Migrants in France', in J. Cole and C. Groes (eds), *Affective Circuits: African Migrations* to Europe and the Pursuit of Social Regeneration. London: University of Chicago Press, pp. 197–222.

Cole, J., and C. Groes (eds). 2016a. *Affective Circuits: African Migrations to Europe and the Pursuit of Social Regeneration*. London: University of Chicago Press.

Cole, J., and C. Groes. 2016b. 'Introduction: Affective Circuits and Social Regeneration in African Migration', in J. Cole and C. Groes (eds), *Affective Circuits: African Migrations to Europe and the Pursuit of Social Regeneration*. London: University of Chicago Press, pp. 1–26.

Collins, F.L. 2018. 'Desire as a Theory for Migration Studies: Temporality, Assemblage and Becoming in the Narratives of Migrants', *Journal of Ethnic and Migration Studies* 44(6): 964–80.

Collyer, M. 2005. 'When Do Social Networks Fail to Explain Migration? Accounting for the Movement of Algerian Asylum-Seekers to the UK', *Journal of Ethnic and Migration Studies* 31(4): 699–718.

_____. 2007. 'In-Between Places: Trans-Saharan Transit Migrants in Morocco and the Fragmented Journey to Europe', *Antipode* 39(4): 668–90.

Cranston, S., J. Schapendonk and E. Spaan. 2018. 'New Directions in Exploring the Migration Industries: Introduction to Special Issue', *Journal of Ethnic and Migration Studies* 44(4): 543–57.

Cresswell, T. 2004. *Place: A Short Introduction*. Oxford: Blackwell Publishing.

_____. 2006. *On the Move: Mobility in the Modern Western World*. London: Routledge.

_____. 2010. 'Towards a Politics of Mobility', *Environment and Planning D: Society and Space* 28(1): 17–31.

_____. 2011. 'Mobilities I: Catching Up', *Progress in Human Geography* 35(4): 550–58.

Cross, H. 2013. *Migrants, Borders and Global Capitalism: West African Labour Mobility and EU Borders*. London: Routledge.

Cuttitta, P. 2014. '"Borderizing" the Island Setting and Narratives of the Lampedusa "Border Play"', *ACME: An International E-Journal for Critical Geographies* 13(2): 196–219.

Dahinden, J. 2010a. 'Cabaret Dancers: "Settle Down in order to Stay Mobile?" Bridging Theoretical Orientations within Transnational Migration Studies', *Social Politics* 17(3): 323–48.

_____. 2010b. 'The Dynamics of Migrants' Transnational Formations: Between Mobility and Locality', in R. Bauböck and T. Faist (eds), *Transnationalism and Diaspora: Concepts, Theories and Methods*. Amsterdam: Amsterdam University Press, pp. 51–71.

_____. 2012. 'Transnational Belonging, Non-Ethnic Forms of Identification and Diverse Mobilities: Rethinking Migrant Integration?', in M. Messer, R. Schroeder and R. Wodak (eds), *Migrations: Interdisciplinary Perspectives*. Vienna: Springer, pp. 117–28.

_____. 2016. 'A Plea for the "De-migranticization" of Research on Migration and Integration', *Ethnic and Racial Studies* 39(13): 2207–25.

Dastur, F. 2000. 'Phenomenology of the Event: Waiting and Surprise', *Hypatia* 15(4): 178–89.

De Bruijn, M., R. van Dijk and D. Foeken (eds). 2001. *Mobile Africa: Changing Patterns of Movement in Africa and Beyond*. Leiden: Brill.

De Genova, N., and N. Peutz (eds). 2010. *The Deportation Regime: Sovereignty, Space, and the Freedom of Movement*. London: Duke University Press.

De Haas, H. 2015. 'Expats', *Hein de Haas Blogspot*, 6 May. Retrieved 28 February 2017 from http://heindehaas.blogspot.nl/2015/05/expats.html.

Della Puppa, F., and D. Sredanovic. 2017. 'Citizen to Stay or Citizen to Go? Naturalization, Security, and Mobility of Migrants in Italy', *Journal of Immigrant & Refugee Studies* 15(4): 366–83.

Diouf, M., and S. Rendall. 2000. 'The Senegalese Murid Trade Diaspora and the Making of a Vernacular Cosmopolitanism', *Public Culture* 12(3): 679–702.

Drotbohm, H. 2017. 'How to Extract Hope from Papers? Classificatory Performances and Social Networking in Cape Verdean Visa Applications', in N. Kleist and D. Thorsen (eds), *Hope and Uncertainty in Contemporary African Migration*. London: Routledge, pp. 21–39.

Egbe, M.E. 2016. 'Sub-Sahara African Immigrants in the "Land of Plenty": Economic Crisis, Food Insecurity and Hunger in Tarragona and Lleida', Ph.D. dissertation. Tarragona: Universitat Rovira i Virgili.

Elliot, A., R. Norum and N.B. Salazar (eds). 2017. *Methodologies of Mobility: Ethnography and Experiment*. Oxford: Berghahn Books.

Ellis, S. 2012. *Season of Rains: Africa in the World*. Chicago: University of Chicago Press.

Engbersen, G., et al. 2013. 'On the Differential Attachments of Migrants from Central and Eastern Europe: A Typology of Labour Migration', *Journal of Ethnic and Migration Studies* 39(6): 959–81.

Erdal, M., and C. Oeppen. 2018. 'Forced to Leave? The Discursive and Analytical Significance of Describing Migration as Forced and Voluntary', *Journal of Ethnic and Migration Studies* 44(6): 981–98.

Ernste, H., H. van Houtum and A. Zoomers. 2009. 'Trans-World: Debating the Place and Borders of Places in the Age of Transnationalism', *Tijdschrift voor Economische en Sociale Geografie* 100(5): 577–86.

European Council. 2015a. *EUCAP Sahel Niger: Council Nearly Doubles Mission's Annual Budget*. Brussels: European Council, 1 March. Retrieved 1 March 2016 from https://www.consilium.europa.eu/en/press/press-releases/2015/10/05/eucap-sahel-niger-council-nearly-doubles-missions-annual-budget/.

European Council. 2015b. *EUCAP Sahel Niger to Help Prevent Irregular Migration*. Brussels: European Council, 13 May. Retrieved 1 March 2016 from http://www.consilium.europa.eu/en/press/press-releases/2015/05/13-eucap-sahel-niger/.

European Migration Network (EMN). 2013. 'EMN Synthesis Report: Intra-EU Mobility of Third Country Nationals'. Dublin. Retrieved 5 November 2018 from https://ec.europa.eu/home-affairs/sites/homeaffairs/files/doc_centre/immigration/docs/studies/emn-synthesis_report_intra_eu_mobility_final_july_2013.pdf.

Faist, T. 2000. *The Volume and Dynamics of International Migration and Transnational Social Spaces*. Oxford: Clarendon Press.

Favell, A. 2008. *Eurostars and Eurocities: Free Movement and Mobility in an Integrating Europe*. Oxford: Blackwell Publishing.

Feldman, G. 2012. *The Migration Apparatus: Security, Labor, and Policymaking in the European Union*. Stanford: Stanford University Press.

Ferguson, J. 2006. *Global Shadows: Africa in the Neoliberal World Order*. London: Duke University Press.

Ferrari, V. 2018. 'Saving Bodies, Losing Lives: Refugee Roulette in Italy', *International Migration Conference, 7–8 May*. Utrecht: Utrecht University.

Fontanari, E. 2017. 'It's My Life: The Temporalities of Refugees and Asylum-Seekers within the European Border Regime', *Etnografia e Ricerca Qualitativa* 10(1): 25-54.

Franck, A.K. 2017. 'Im/mobility and Deportability in Transit: Lesvos Island, Greece, June 2015', *Tijdschrift voor Economische en Sociale Geografie* 108(6): 879-84.

Gaibazzi, P. 2013. 'Cultivating Hustlers: The Agrarian Ethos of Soninke Migration', *Journal of Ethnic and Migration Studies* 39(2): 259-75.

———. 2014. 'Visa Problem: Certification, Kinship, and the Production of "Ineligibility" in the Gambia', *Journal of the Royal Anthropological Institute* 20(1): 38-55.

———. 2015. *Bush Bound: Young Men and Rural Permanence in Migrant West Africa*. Oxford: Berghahn Books.

Gammeltoft-Hansen, T., and N. Nyberg Sørensen (eds). 2013. *The Migration Industry and the Commercialization of International Migration*. London: Routledge.

Gammeltoft-Hansen, T., and N.F. Tan. 2017. 'The End of the Deterrence Paradigm? Future Directions for Global Refugee Policy', *Journal on Migration and Human Security* 5(1): 28-56.

Gielis, R. 2009. 'A Global Sense of Migrant Places: Towards a Place Perspective in the Study of Migrant Transnationalism', *Global Networks* 9(2): 271-87.

Giglioli, I., C. Hawthorne and A. Tiberio. 2017. 'Introduction to the Special Issue "Rethinking 'Europe' through an Ethnography of its Borderlands, Peripheries and Margins"', *Etnografia e Ricerca Qualitativa* 10(3): 335-38.

Gladkova, N., and V. Mazzucato. 2017. 'Theorising Chance: Capturing the Role of Ad Hoc Social Interactions in Migrants' Trajectories', *Population, Space and Place* 23(2): e1988.

Glick Schiller, N., and N.B. Salazar. 2013. 'Regimes of Mobility across the Globe', *Journal of Ethnic and Migration Studies* 39(2): 183-200.

Glick Schiller, N., L. Basch and C. Szanton Blanc. 1995. 'From Immigrant to Transmigrant: Theorizing Transnational Migration', *Anthropological Quarterly* 68(1): 48-63.

Glick Schiller, N., T. Darieva and S. Gruner-Domic. 2011. 'Defining Cosmopolitan Sociability in a Transnational Age: An Introduction', *Ethnic and Racial Studies* 34(3): 399-418.

Goffman, E. 1961. *Asylums: Essays on the Social Situation of Mental Patients and Other Inmates*. New York: Anchor Books.

Granovetter, M.S. 1973. 'The Strength of Weak Ties', *American Journal of Sociology* 78(6): 1360-80.

Griffiths, M. 2014. 'Out of Time: The Temporal Uncertainties of Refused Asylum Seekers and Immigration Detainees', *Journal of Ethnic and Migration Studies* 40(12): 1991-2009.

Groes, C. 2016. 'Men Come and Go, Mothers Stay: Personhood and Resisting Marriage among Mozambican Women Migrating to Europe', in J. Cole and C. Groes (eds), *Affective Circuits: African Migrations to Europe and the Pursuit of Social Regeneration*. London: University of Chicago Press, pp. 169-96.

Hahn, H.P. 2010. 'Urban Life-Worlds in Motion: In Africa and Beyond', *Africa Spectrum* 45(3): 115-29.

Hahn, H.P., and G. Klute (eds). 2007. *Cultures of Migration: African Perspectives*. Berlin: Lit Verlag.

Hathaway, J. 2018. 'A Global Solution to a Global Refugee Problem', *Asiel&Migrantenrecht* 2: 61-63.

Heller, C. 2015. 'Liquid Trajectories: Documenting Illegalised Migration and the Violence of Borders', Ph.D. dissertation. London: University of London.

Homaifar, N. 2008. 'The African Prostitute: An Everyday *Debrouillard* in Reality and African Fiction', *Journal of African Cultural Studies* 20(2): 173-82.

Hui, A. 2016. 'The Boundaries of Interdisciplinary Fields: Temporalities Shaping the Past and Future of Dialogue between Migration and Mobilities Research', *Mobilities* 11(1): 66-82.

Hultin, N., et al. 2017. 'Autocracy, Migration and the Gambia's "Unprecedented" 2016 Election', *African Affairs* 116(463): 321-40.

Hyndman, J. 1997. 'BorderCrossings', *Antipode* 29(2): 149-76.

Immigratie- en Naturalisatiedienst (IND). 2018. 'Een Familie- of Gezinslid naar Nederland Laten Komen'. Ter Apel. Retrieved 15 August 2018 from https://ind.nl/Formulieren/3076.pdf.

Ingold, T. 2007. *Lines: A Brief History*. London: Routledge.

_____. 2011. *Being Alive: Essays on Movement, Knowledge and Description*. London: Routledge.

_____. 2013. *Making: Anthropology, Archaeology, Art and Architecture*. London: Routledge.

Isin, E.F. 2009. 'Citizenship in Flux: The Figure of the Activist Citizen', *Subjectivity* 29(1): 367-88.

Jackson, M. 2013. *The Wherewithal of Life: Ethics, Migration, and the Question of Well-Being*. London: University of California Press.

Johnson, C., et al. 2011. 'Interventions on Rethinking "the Border" in Border Studies', *Political Geography* 30(2): 61-69.

Jónsson, G. 2008. 'Migration Aspirations and Immobility in a Malian Soninke Village', *IMI Working Papers 10*. Oxford: International Migration Institute.

Joosten, S. 2017. '"Survival" on the Streets of "Babylon": Ethnography of West African Migrants in Barcelona', MSc. thesis. Wageningen: Wageningen University.

Kalir, B. 2013. 'Moving Subjects, Stagnant Paradigms: Can the "Mobilities Paradigm" Transcend Methodological Nationalism?', *Journal of Ethnic and Migration Studies* 39(2): 311-27.

Kalir, B., and L. Wissink. 2016. 'The Deportation Continuum: Convergences between State Agents and NGO Workers in the Dutch Deportation Field', *Citizenship Studies* 20(1): 34–49.

Kea, P. 2013. '"The Complexity of an Enduring Relationship": Gender, Generation, and the Moral Economy of the Gambian Mandinka Household', *Journal of the Royal Anthropological Institute* 19(1): 102–19.

_____. 2016. 'Photography and Technologies of Care: Migrants in Britain and Their Children in the Gambia', in J. Cole and C. Groes (eds), *Affective Circuits: African Migrations to Europe and the Pursuit of Social Regeneration*. London: University of Chicago Press, pp. 78–100.

Khosravi, S. 2011. *'Illegal' Traveller: An Auto-ethnography of Borders*. London: Palgrave Macmillan.

_____. 2018. 'Afterword: Experiences and Stories along the Way', *Geoforum*. Retrieved 29 May 2018 from https://doi.org/10.1016/j.geoforum.2018.05.021.

King, R. 2002. 'Towards a New Map of European Migration', *International Journal of Population Geography* 8(2): 89–106.

King, R., and A. Christou. 2011. 'Of Counter-diaspora and Reverse Transnationalism: Return Mobilities to and from the Ancestral Homeland', *Mobilities* 6(4): 451–66.

Kleist, N. 2018. 'Trajectories of Involuntary Return Migration to Ghana: Forced Relocation Processes and Post-return Life', *Geoforum*. Retrieved 28 May 2018 from https://doi.org/10.1016/j.geoforum.2017.12.005.

Kleist, N., and D. Thorsen (eds). 2017. *Hope and Uncertainty in Contemporary African Migration*. London: Routledge.

Kothari, U. 2008. 'Global Peddlers and Local Networks: Migrant Cosmopolitanisms', *Environment and Planning D: Society and Space* 26(3): 500–16.

Kramsch, O., V. Mamadouh and M. van der Velde. 2004. 'Introduction: Postnational Politics in the European Union', *Geopolitics* 9(3): 531–41.

Krissman, F. 2005. 'Sin Coyote Ni Patrón: Why the "Migrant Network" Fails to Explain International Migration', *International Migration Review* 39(1): 4–44.

Kubal, A. 2013. 'Conceptualizing Semi-legality in Migration Research', *Law & Society Review* 47(3): 555–87.

Leed, E.J. 1991. *The Mind of the Traveler: From Gilgamesh to Global Tourism*. New York: Basic Books.

Leinonen, J. 2012. 'Invisible Immigrants, Visible Expats? Americans in Finnish Discourses on Immigration and Internationalization', *Nordic Journal of Migration Research* 2(3): 213–23.

Lems, A. 2016. 'Placing Displacement: Place-Making in a World of Movement', *Ethnos: Journal of Anthropology* 81(2): 315–37.

_____. 2018. *Being-Here: Placemaking in a World of Movement*. Oxford: Berghahn Books.

Lepawsky, J., and C. Mather. 2011. 'From Beginnings and Endings to Boundaries and Edges: Rethinking Circulation and Exchange through Electronic Waste', *Area* 43(3): 242–49.

Lindley, A., and N. van Hear. 2007. 'New Europeans on the Move: A Preliminary Review of the Onward Migration of Refugees within the European Union', *Compas Working Paper Series WP-07-57*. Oxford: Centre on Migration, Policy and Society.

Loftsdóttir, K. 2018. 'Global Citizens, Exotic Others, and Unwanted Migrants: Mobilities in and of Europe', *Identities: Global Studies in Culture and Power* 25(3): 302-19.

Lucht, H. 2012. *Darkness before Daybreak: African Migrants Living on the Margins in Southern Italy Today*. London: University of California Press.

Ludl, C. 2008. '"To Skip a Step": New Representation(s) of Migration, Success and Politics in Senegalese Rap and Theatre', *Stichproben: Wiener Zeitschrift für kritische Afrikastudien* 8(14): 97-122.

Mac Laughlin, J. 1999. 'Nation-Building, Social Closure and Anti-traveller Racism in Ireland', *Sociology* 33(1): 129-51.

Mainwaring, C., and N. Brigden. 2016. 'Beyond the Border: Clandestine Migration Journeys', *Geopolitics* 21(2): 243-62.

Malkki, L. 1992. 'National Geographic: The Rooting of Peoples and the Territorialization of National Identity among Scholars and Refugees', *Cultural Anthropology* 7(1): 24-44.

Marcus, G.E. 1995. 'Ethnography in/of the World System: The Emergence of Multi-sited Ethnography', *Annual Review of Anthropology* 24: 95-117.

Martiniello, M., and A. Rea. 2014. 'The Concept of Migratory Careers: Elements for a New Theoretical Perspective of Contemporary Human Mobility', *Current Sociology* 62(7): 1079-96.

Massa, A. 2018. 'Borders and Boundaries as Resources for Mobility: Multiple Regimes of Mobility and Incoherent Trajectories on the Ethiopian-Eritrean Border', *Geoforum*. Retrieved 28 May 2018 from https://doi.org/10.1016/j.geoforum.2018.01.007.

Massey, D. 1991. 'A Global Sense of Place', *Marxism Today*, June: 24-29.

_____. 2005. *For Space*. London: Sage Publishing.

Mazzucato, V., et al. 2015. 'Transnational Families between Africa and Europe', *International Migration Review* 49(1): 142-72.

Mazzucato, V., M. Kabki and L. Smith. 2006. 'Transnational Migration and the Economy of Funerals: Changing Practices in Ghana', *Development and Change* 37(5): 1047-72.

McFarlane, C. 2018. 'Fragment Urbanism: Politics at the Margins of the City', *Environment and Planning D: Society and Space* 36(6): 1007-25.

McMahon, S., and N. Sigona. 2018. 'Navigating the Central Mediterranean in a Time of "Crisis": Disentangling Migration Governance and Migrant Journeys', *Sociology* 52(3): 497-514.

Meeus, B. 2012. 'How to "Catch" Floating Populations? Research and the Fixing of Migration in Space and Time', *Ethnic and Racial Studies* 35(10): 1775-93.

Merriman, P. 2014. 'Rethinking Mobile Methods', *Mobilities* 9(2): 167-87.

Molenaar, F., et al. 2017. *A Line in the Sand: Roadmap for Sustainable Management in Agadez*. The Hague: Clingendael.

Moret, J. 2017. 'Mobility Capital: Somali Migrants' Trajectories of (Im)mobilities and the Negotiation of Social Inequalities across Borders', *Geoforum*. Retrieved 5 January 2018 from https://doi.org/10.1016/j.geoforum.2018.01.007.

Morokvasic, M. 2004. '"Settled in Mobility": Engendering Post-wall Migration in Europe', *Feminist Review* 77: 7-25.

Mountz, A. 2011. 'The Enforcement Archipelago: Detention, Haunting, and Asylum on Islands', *Political Geography* 30(3): 118-28.

Neveu Kringelbach, H. 2016. 'The Paradox of Parallel Lives: Immigration Policy and Transnational Polygyny between Senegal and France', in J. Cole and C. Groes (eds), *Affective Circuits: African Migrations to Europe and the Pursuit of Social Regeneration*. London: University of Chicago Press, pp. 146-68.

Noten, T. 2016. 'Providing Hospitality to Undocumented Migrants in the City of Nijmegen', MSc. thesis. Nijmegen: Radboud University.

Nyanzi, S., et al. 2005. 'Bumsters, Big Black Organs and Old White Gold: Embodied Racial Myths in Sexual Relationships of Gambian Beach Boys', *Culture, Health & Sexuality: An International Journal for Research, Intervention and Care* 7(6): 557-69.

Nyberg Sørensen, N. 2012. 'Revisiting the Migration–Development Nexus: From Social Networks and Remittances to Markets for Migration Control', *International Migration* 50(3): 61-76.

Olwig, K.F. 2007. *Caribbean Journeys: An Ethnography of Migration and Home in Three Family Networks*. Durham: Duke University Press.

Ong, A. 1999. *Flexible Citizenship: The Cultural Logics of Transnationality*. London: Duke University Press.

Ortensi, L.E., and E. Barbiano di Belgiojoso. 2018. 'Moving On? Gender, Education, and Citizenship as Key Factors among Short-Term Onward Migration Planners', *Population, Space and Place* 24(5): e2135.

Papadopoulos, D., N. Stephenson and V. Tsianos. 2008. *Escape Routes: Control and Subversion in the Twenty-First Century*. London: Pluto Press.

Papageorgopoulous, S. 2018. 'Asylum Seekers in Samos: An Unreasonable Reality', *Border Criminologies*, 12 April. Retrieved 11 June 2018 from https://www.law.ox.ac.uk/research-subject-groups/centre-criminology/centreborder-criminologies/blog/2018/04/asylum-seekers.

Papataxiarchis, E. 2016. 'Being "There": At the Front Line of the "European Refugee Crisis" -Part 1', *Anthropology Today* 32(2): 5-9.

Parr, H., C. Philo and N. Burns. 2003. '"That Awful Place Was Home": Reflections on the Contested Meanings of Craig Dunain Asylum', *Scottish Geographical Journal* 119(4): 341-60.

Pascual-de-Sans, À. 2004. 'Sense of Place and Migration Histories Idiotopy and Idiotope', *Area* 36(4): 348-57.

Pathirage, J., and M. Collyer. 2011. 'Capitalizing Social Networks: Sri Lankan Migration to Italy', *Ethnography* 12(3): 315-33.

Pelckmans, L. 2012. '"Having a Road": Social and Spatial Mobility of Persons of Slave and Mixed Descent in Post-independence Central Mali', *Journal of African History* 53(2): 235-55.

Piot, C. 2010. *Nostalgia for the Future: West Africa after the Cold War*. London: University of Chicago Press.

Poeze, M., and V. Mazzucato. 2014. 'Ghanaian Children in Transnational Families: Understanding the Experiences of Left-Behind Children through Local Parenting Norms', in L. Baldassar and L. Merla (eds), *Transnational Families, Migration and the Circulation of Care: Understanding Mobility and Absence in Family Life*. London: Routledge, pp. 149-69.

Portes, A. 1998. 'Social Capital: Its Origins and Applications in Modern Sociology', *Annual Review of Sociology* 24: 1-24.

Prothmann, S. 2018. 'Migration, Masculinity and Social Class: Insights from Pikine, Senegal', *International Migration* 56(4): 96-108.

Rajaram, P.K., and C. Grundy-Warr. 2004. 'The Irregular Migrant as Homo Sacer: Migration and Detention in Australia, Malaysia, and Thailand', *International Migration* 42(1): 33-64.

Ramos, C. 2018. 'Onward Migration from Spain to London in Times of Crisis: The Importance of Life-Course Junctures in Secondary Migrations', *Journal of Ethnic and Migration Studies* 44(11): 1841-57.

Ramsøy, I.J. 2014. *Embedded Movement: Senegalese Transcontinental Migration and Gender Identity*. Malmö: Malmö University.

Riccio, B. 2001. 'From "Ethnic Group" to "Transnational Community"? Senegalese Migrants' Ambivalent Experiences and Multiple Trajectories', *Journal of Ethnic and Migration Studies* 27(4): 583-99.

———. 2004. 'Transnational Mouridism and the Afro-Muslim Critique of Italy', *Journal of Ethnic and Migration Studies* 30(5): 929-44.

———. 2008. 'West African Transnationalisms Compared: Ghanaians and Senegalese in Italy', *Journal of Ethnic and Migration Studies* 34(2): 217-34.

Rytter, M. 2012. 'Semi-legal Family Life: Pakistani Couples in the Borderlands of Denmark and Sweden', *Global Networks* 12(1): 91-108.

Salazar, N.B. 2011. 'The Power of Imagination in Transnational Mobilities', *Identities: Global Studies in Culture and Power* 18(6): 576-98.

Salazar, N.B., and A. Smart. 2011. 'Anthropological Takes on (Im)mobility', *Identities: Global Studies in Culture and Power* 18(6): i-ix.

Sanò, G. 2017. 'Inside and Outside the Reception System: The Case of Unaccompanied Minors in Eastern Sicily', *Etnografia e Ricerca Qualitativa* 10(1): 121-42.

Schapendonk, J. 2015. 'What if Networks Move? Dynamic Social Networking in the Context of African Migration to Europe', *Population, Space and Place* 21(8): 809-19.

———. 2017a. 'Afrostars and Eurospaces: West African Movers Re-viewing "Destination Europe" from the Inside', *Etnografia e Ricerca Qualitativa* 10(3): 393-414.

———. 2017b. 'The Multiplicity of Transit: The Waiting and Onward Mobility of African Migrants in the European Union', *International Journal of Migration and Border Studies* 3(2-3): 208-27.

———. 2018a. 'Navigating the Migration Industry: Migrants Moving through an African-European Web of Facilitation/Control', *Journal of Ethnic and Migration Studies* 44(4): 663-79.

_____. 2018b. 'On Wayfaring and Transporting: Understanding the Mobility Trajectories of African Migrants in Europe', in F. Hillmann, T. van Naerssen and E. Spaan (eds), *Trajectories and Imaginaries in Migration: The Migrant Actor in Transnational Space*. London: Routledge, pp. 17-33.

_____. 2018c. 'The Geography of a Global Refugee System', *Asiel&Migrantenrecht* 2: 64-67.

Schapendonk, J., and G. Steel. 2014. 'Following Migrant Trajectories: The Im/mobility of Sub-Saharan Africans en Route to the European Union', *Annals of the Association of American Geographers* 104(2): 262-70.

Schapendonk, J., et al. 2018. 'Re-routing Migration Geographies: Migrants, Trajectories and Mobility Regimes', *Geoforum*. Retrieved 9 September 2018 from https://doi.org/10.1016/j.geoforum.2018.06.007.

Schinkel, W. 2018. 'Against "Immigrant Integration": For an End to Neocolonial Knowledge Production', *Comparative Migration Studies*. Retrieved 6 July 2019 from https://doi.org/10.1186/s40878-018-0095-1.

Schmoll, C., and G. Semi. 2013. 'Shadow Circuits: Urban Spaces and Mobilities across the Mediterranean', *Identities: Global Studies in Culture and Power* 20(4): 377-92.

Schuster, L. 2005. 'The Continuing Mobility of Migrants in Italy: Sifting between Places and Statuses', *Journal of Ethnic and Migration Studies* 31(4): 757-74.

Schwarz, I. 2018. 'Migrants Moving through Mobility Regimes: The Trajectory Approach as a Tool to Reveal Migratory Processes', *Geoforum*. Retrieved 27 May 2018 from https://doi.org/10.1016/j.geoforum.2018.03.007.

Sheller, M., and J. Urry. 2006. 'The New Mobilities Paradigm', *Environment and Planning A: Economy and Space* 38(2): 207-26.

Sigona, N. 2005. 'Locating "the Gypsy Problem": The Roma in Italy: Stereotyping, Labelling and "Nomad Camps"', *Journal of Ethnic and Migration Studies* 31(4): 741-56.

Simone, A. 2001. 'On the Worlding of African Cities', *African Studies Review* 44(2): 15-41.

_____. 2004. *For the City Yet to Come: Changing African Life in Four Cities*. London: Duke University Press.

_____. 2014. 'Just the City', *Opening Lecture of Human Geography Master Programme 2014–2015 of Radboud University Nijmegen, 8 September*. Retrieved 15 August 2018 from https://www.youtube.com/watch?v=pw0Ml8RKphg.

_____. 2019. *Improvised Lives: Rhythms of Endurance in an Urban South*. Cambridge: Polity Press.

Simone, A., and E. Pieterse. 2017. *New Urban Worlds: Inhabiting Dissonant Times*. Cambridge: Polity Press.

Sinatti, G. 2011. '"Mobile Transmigrants" or "Unsettled Returnees"? Myth of Return and Permanent Resettlement among Senegalese Migrants', *Population, Space and Place* 17(2): 153-66.

Skov, G. 2016. 'Transfer Back to Malta: Refugees' Secondary Movement within the European Union', *Journal of Immigrant & Refugee Studies* 14(1): 66-82.

Smith, L., and J. Schapendonk. 2018. 'Whose Agenda? Bottom Up Positionalities of West African Migrants in the Framework of European Union Migration Management', *African Human Mobility Review* 4: 1175-1204.

Somerville, K. 2015. 'Strategic Migrant Network Building and Information Sharing: Understanding 'Migrant Pioneers' in Canada', *International Migration* 53(4): 135-54.

Spierings, B., and M. van der Velde. 2013. 'Cross-Border Differences and Unfamiliarity: Shopping Mobility in the Dutch-German Rhine-Waal Euroregion', *European Planning Studies* 21(1): 5-23.

Steinberg, J. 2015. *A Man of Good Hope: One Man's Extraordinary Journey from Mogadishu to Tin Can Town*. London: Jonathan Cape.

Tagaris, K. 2018. 'Greek Port on Edge as More Migrants Try to Stow Away to Italy', *Reuters*, 13 March. Retrieved 9 June 2018 from https://www.reuters.com/article/us-europe-migrants-greece-port/greek-port-on-edge-as-more-migrants-try-to-stow-away-to-italy-idUSKCN1GP1IS.

Tarrius, A. 1993. 'Territoires Circulatoires et Espaces Urbains: Différentiation des Groupes Migrants', *Les Annales de la Recherche Urbaine* 59-60: 51-60.

⸺. A. 1995. 'Territoires Circulatoires des Entrepreneurs Commerciaux Maghrébins de Marseille: Du Commerce Communautaire aux Réseaux de l'Économie Souterraine Mondiale', *Journal des Anthropologues* 59: 15-35.

Teunissen, P. 2018. 'Border Crossing Assemblages: Differentiated Travelers and the Viapolitics of FlixBus', *Journal of Borderlands Studies*. Retrieved 13 June 2018 from https://doi.org/10.1080/08865655.2018.1452165.

Thieme, T.A. 2018. 'The Hustle Economy: Informality, Uncertainty and the Geographies of Getting By', *Progress in Human Geography* 42(4): 529-48.

Toma, S., and E. Castagnone. 2015. 'What Drives Onward Mobility within Europe? The Case of Senegalese Migrations between France, Italy and Spain', *Population* 70(1): 65-95.

Triulzi, A. 2012. '"Like a Plate of Spaghetti": Migrant Narratives from the Libya-Lampedusa Route', in A. Triulzi and R.L. McKenzie (eds), *Long Journeys: African Migrants on the Road*. Leiden: Brill, pp. 213-32.

Tsing, A. 2005. *Friction: An Ethnography of Global Connection*. Oxford: Princeton University Press.

Tsoni, I. 2013. 'African Border-Crossings in a "City of Others": Constellations of Irregular Im/mobility and In/equality in the Everyday Urban Environment of Athens', *Journal of Mediterranean Studies* 22(1): 141-69.

Tuckett, A. 2015. 'Strategies of Navigation: Migrants' Everyday Encounters with Italian Immigration Bureaucracy', *Cambridge Journal of Anthropology* 33(1): 113-28.

⸺. 2018. *Rules, Papers, Status: Migrants and Precarious Bureaucracy in Contemporary Italy*. Stanford: Stanford University Press.

Van Doorn, M., P. Scheepers and J. Dagevos. 2013. 'Explaining the Integration Paradox among Small Immigrant Groups in the Netherlands', *Journal of International Migration and Integration* 14(2): 381-400.

Van Houtum, H., and T. van Naerssen. 2002. 'Bordering, Ordering and Othering', *Tijdschrift voor Economische en Sociale Geografie* 93(2): 125-36.

Van Nieuwenhuyze, I. 2009. *Getting By in Europe's Urban Labour Markets: Senegambian Migrants' Strategies for Survival, Documentation and Mobility*. Amsterdam: University of Amsterdam Press.

Van Ooijen, S. 2016. 'Hustling Your Way Forward: A Study on the Trajectories and Social Networks of West African Migrants Moving towards and within the European Union', MSc. thesis. Nijmegen: Radboud University.

Vermeulen, B. 2016. 'De Veermannen van de Sahara', *NRC Handelsblad*, 20 February. Retrieved 7 March 2017 from http://www.nrc.nl/handelsblad/2016/02/20/de-veermannen-van-de-sahara-1589973.

Verstraete, G. 2001. 'Technological Frontiers and the Politics of Mobility in the European Union', *New Formations* 43: 26–43.

Vianelli, L. 2017. 'Europe's Uneven Geographies of Reception: Excess, Differentiation, and Struggles in the Government of Asylum Seekers', *Etnografia e Ricerca Qualitativa* 10(3): 363–92.

Vigh, H.E. 2006. 'Social Death and Violent Life Chances', in C. Christiansen, M. Utas and H.E. Vigh (eds), *Navigating Youth, Generating Adulthood: Social Becoming in an African Context*. Uppsala: Nordiska Afrikainstitutet, pp. 31–60.

———. 2009. 'Motion Squared: A Second Look at the Concept of Social Navigation', *Anthropological Theory* 9(4): 419–38.

Waage, T. 2006. 'Coping with Unpredictability: "Preparing for Life" in Ngaoundéré, Cameroon', in C. Christiansen, M. Utas and H.E. Vigh (eds), *Navigating Youth, Generating Adulthood: Social Becoming in an African Context*. Uppsala: Nordiska Afrikainstitutet, pp. 61–87.

Wagner, U., and B. Yamba. 1986. 'Going North and Getting Attached: The Case of the Gambians', *Ethnos: Journal of Anthropology* 51(3-4): 199–222.

Wilson Janssens, M.C. 2018. 'Spatial Mobility and Social Becoming: The Journeys of Four Central African Students in Congo-Kinshasa', *Geoforum*. Retrieved 19 August 2018 from https://doi.org/10.1016/j.geoforum.2018.05.018.

Wimmer, A., and N. Glick Schiller. 2002. 'Methodological Nationalism and Beyond: Nation-State Building, Migration and the Social Sciences', *Global Networks* 2(4): 301–34.

Wissink, M., F. Düvell and V. Mazzucato. 2017. 'The Evolution of Migration Trajectories of Sub-Saharan African Migrants in Turkey and Greece: The Role of Changing Social Networks and Critical Events', *Geoforum*. Retrieved 20 May 2018 from https://doi.org/10.1016/j.geoforum.2017.12.004.

Zhang, V. 2018. 'Im/mobilising the Migration Decision', *Environment and Planning D: Society and Space* 36(2): 199–216.

Index

abjection, 25, 27
Afrostar, 21, 153-54, 182, 194
Agadez. *See under* Niger
agriculture
   agricultural fields, 74, 166, 198
   agricultural season, 141-42
   agricultural sector, 126, 141-43, 169, 173
   agricultural spaces, 142, 148
Alpes, Jill, 10n1, 19, 27, 30, 89
ambivalence, 145-49, 153, 175, 192
Amsterdam. *See under* Netherlands
Andalusia. *See under* Spain
Andersson, Ruben, 89-90, 93, 103, 115, 123, 162
Andrikopoulos, Apostolos, 11n5, 68, 71-72, 87n2, 87n8, 124
Aparna, Kolar, 72, 161, 176n3, 197
Asylheim, 23-24, 64, 153. *See also* asylum: shelter
asylum, 2, 22-24, 33, 39, 45, 77, 103, 145, 156, 176n3
   bureaucracy, 35 (*see also* migration: bureaucracy)
   centre, 21, 36, 58, 63-66 (*see also* asylum: shelter)
   claim, 51n9, 110, 134
   European approach to, 111
   policy, 24
   procedures, 19, 22, 35-37, 47, 66, 91, 104, 122-25, 146-48
   seeker, 4, 8, 22, 45, 51n9, 63-66, 104, 110-15, 120, 123, 147, 153-56, 162-65, 196
   shelter, 32, 38, 78, 158, 162-64, 194
   space, 23, 33, 58, 78, 99, 155, 158, 162-64
   system, 21, 34, 36, 117-18, 121, 123-24, 153
Athens. *See under* Greece

Babylon, 27, 111
backway, the, 15, 25-28, 33, 56, 62, 110, 150, 190
Balibar, Étienne, 128, 152, 176n6, 193
Banjul. *See under* Gambia
Barcelona. *See under* Spain
beginnings and endings, 196-98
Belloni, Milena, 19, 30, 50n4, 57, 89, 94, 96, 108
belonging, 2, 4, 38, 90, 149, 171, 175
   multiple, 3
   non-belonging, 145, 148, 156
Bergamo. *See under* Italy
Bern. *See under* Switzerland
Bolay, Matthieu, 10n1, 11n2, 26, 28, 92, 145, 150
border, 2, 4-5, 9, 11n4, 11n7, 18, 22, 34, 36, 47-49, 57-58, 86, 87n4, 92-95, 107-8, 123, 134-39, 142, 147-48, 153, 158-59, 169, 175, 187, 190, 192-93, 197-98
   commuter, 136, 153, 162
   control, 23, 37, 102, 127-30, 144
   crossing, 8, 41, 45, 63, 77, 85, 97, 136, 144, 182, 198
   game, 89, 102
   guards, 19, 40, 56, 70, 89, 90, 95, 102, 107, 129-130, 137-138, 158, 193
   intra-EU, 21
   police, 48, 129, 130-131, 136, 192
bordering, 10, 22, 89, 111, 115, 130, 133-38, 193
Brachet, Julien, 26, 27, 94, 107
broker, 30, 184-85. *See also* mobility: facilitator
bumster, 28, 69, 157

Cabot, Heath, 6, 35, 85, 159, 161, 164, 197
Cameroon, 6, 41-45, 62, 84-85, 118

camp, the, 22, 32, 35, 37, 64, 69, 102–3, 112–14, 154–55, 162, 164
encampment, 102, 146
Canary Islands. *See under* Spain
Caritas, 32, 58, 91, 112–18, 120–21, 162
Casati, Noemi, 113, 115, 117
Ceesay, Ismaila, 27–29, 69
Ceuta. *See under* Spain
China, 58, 99, 181, 187
circuits
  affective, 4, 9, 53–54, 57, 59–62, 64, 75–76, 81, 86, 96–97, 121, 139, 175, 191, 198
  informal, 2, 67, 183
circulations, 4–5, 10, 11n1, 26, 80, 94, 134, 147, 150, 175
citizenship, 55, 68, 76, 128, 169–71, 175, 176n6, 188
  acts of, 152, 176n6
  EU citizen, 6, 21, 38, 68
  flexible, 171
  in flux, 171, 176n6
Coconut Island, 156–58, 160
Cole, Jennifer, 4, 9, 42, 53–54, 57, 78
connection man, 33, 54, 56–58, 60–61, 98–102, 105–6, 118–19, 181. *See also* mobility: facilitator
cosmopolitanism, 5, 167, 172, 185–87
coxeur, 27, 95

Dahinden, Janine, 2, 4, 6, 11n2, 65, 90, 128, 145, 148, 171, 195
Dakar. *See under* Senegal
Dastur, Françoise, 152, 176n1
débrouillardise, 28, 56, 71. *See also* hustling
de-migranticization, 4, 31, 90, 128, 195
departure, 3, 11n7, 19, 20, 33, 38, 45–46, 48, 56, 74–75, 85, 196
  multiple, 9, 20, 31–33, 38, 41, 45, 49, 181
  worlding, 9, 17
deportability, 139, 152, 163, 176n2, 188
deportation, 34, 45–49, 76, 123, 132–33, 152, 162, 188–89, 197
  continuum, 46
  regime, 45
deserving, 113, 117, 138
deservingness, 112–17, 139n2, 193
detention, 22, 27, 47, 65, 88n8, 95, 130, 132, 134–37, 144, 191
  centre, 26, 70, 97, 131–32, 134, 162–64

disappearing, 45, 52, 191–92, 194
  the right to disappear, 190–192
Dublin Regulation, 22, 35, 132, 135–136, 194
Dutch Repatriation and Departure Service (DT&V), 134–35, 164
dwelling/moving, 168, 198

ECOWAS (Economic Community of West African States), 93, 108
edges, 186, 196, 198
Ellis, Stephen, 27–28, 50n1
endings. *See* beginnings and endings
entry ban, 133, 136
escape, 10, 34, 48, 71–79, 90–92, 95–97, 103, 107, 108n5, 109, 112, 121–22, 152, 158, 161, 170, 187, 197
  politics of, 97
  route, 27, 138, 152
EU (European Union), 3, 11n2, 21–22, 45, 59, 87, 93, 97, 102–3, 110, 122–23
  borders, 21, 36, 38, 47, 93–94, 107
  member states, 22, 35, 37, 45–46, 68, 110–11, 115, 117, 123, 124
Europe
  lost, 83–86, 107, 159–62, 198
  real, 85, 105–6
  worlding, 2, 10, 186, 193
Europeanness, 3, 171
European policy, 45–46, 68, 90, 93, 123, 193, 197
Eurospace, 2, 4, 6–7, 10, 11n4, 38, 62–63, 65–67, 69, 71, 79, 81, 83, 90, 97, 101–4, 108–9, 123, 130–33, 138, 148, 152–53, 160, 175, 178–79, 182–83, 190, 194–95, 197–98
Eurostars, 2, 11n2, 21, 70, 148, 186–88
  Eurostars in Eurocities (Favell), 21
exclusion, 146, 175, 186
  politics of, 2, 6, 108
  spaces of, 158–59
  system of, 156
exploitation, 57, 94, 107, 115–16

facilitation/control, 89–90, 103, 109, 138
Favell, Adrian, 2, 4, 6, 11n2, 21, 70, 90, 148, 186–88
  Eurostars in Eurocities, 21
Feldman, Gregory, 6, 54, 76, 89–90, 93, 109, 111

finding ways, 7, 10, 26, 50, 52, 57, 59–60, 86, 91, 108, 138–39, 164, 179, 197
fingerprints, 34–35, 100, 130, 136, 154
  fingerprinting, 47, 122
France, 31, 33, 47–49, 67, 72, 80, 103–7, 153, 169, 182, 189, 191
  Paris, 70–71, 107, 143, 187, 198
funniness, 120–23

Gaibazzi, Paolo, 10n1, 17, 19, 26, 28, 32, 46, 49, 50n3, 51n6, 51n10, 141, 145, 148, 150, 198
Gambia, 2, 6–8, 13–14, 17, 20–21, 24, 26–33, 35, 50nn2–3, 50n5, 51nn6–7, 51n10, 55–57, 59–65, 69, 73–75, 79–80, 87n3, 87n8, 98–101, 120, 141–42, 144n1, 149–151, 154, 158, 165–66, 168–69, 174, 179–82, 184, 189–91, 194
  Banjul, 7, 33–34, 57, 61, 99, 169
  Serekunda, 2, 17–18, 29–30, 43, 55, 58–59, 87n7, 150, 181, 186, 199
  Serekunda Market, 17, 20, 28, 33, 50n5, 56
gambling, 20, 29–31, 35, 47, 70, 152
ganja, 18, 144, 154, 188
Germany, 2, 8, 14, 23–24, 32, 34–39, 64, 66–73, 78, 81, 88n8, 90, 92, 117–18, 122, 124–27, 129, 134–38, 153, 158, 161, 169–70, 174, 185, 194
Ghadaffi (former Libyan president), 17, 108n1
ghetto, 50n3, 94, 96–97, 165
  youth, 18, 21, 50n3
globalization, 9, 25, 27, 30, 179, 185
Greece, 7, 35, 37, 46–48, 72, 85, 98, 102, 131, 134, 169
  Athens, 3, 8, 85, 103–7, 158, 161, 198
  Lesbos, 103, 176n2
  Samos, 46, 103, 105
Groes, Christian, 4, 9, 42, 53–54, 57, 76–78
grounding, 145, 156, 165, 175
  regrounding, 2, 32, 49, 82, 172
guest house, 13–14, 35, 40, 86, 100, 141, 182, 189, 191

homesickness, 79–80
hope, 5, 26–28, 30, 31, 51n7, 59, 75, 101, 104, 107, 123, 132, 153, 159, 167, 199

horizon, 25, 38–40, 132, 149, 170–71, 175, 195
Hui, Allison, 3
humanitarianism, 89, 115, 124, 197
humanitarian crisis, 85, 102–3, 161
humanitarian protection, 34–35, 66, 91, 113, 115, 195
hustlers, 27–29, 32
hustling, 19–21, 29, 31–32, 48, 56, 70, 104, 131, 138, 181
  hustling tactics of connectivity, 28, 69

imaginaries, 18, 86, 171, 175, 197
imagination, 2, 5, 11, 50n3, 97
immigrant, 4, 90, 168, 196
Immigratie- en Naturalisatiedienst (IND), 31, 44, 76, 134–37, 155, 171
immobility, 19, 24, 31, 76, 112, 170
  immobilization, 102
  involuntary, 24, 25, 45, 51n6, 91 (*see also* sitting)
  See also im/mobility
im/mobility, 4–6, 8–10, 32, 41, 51, 145
  politics of, 10, 22, 81
  processes, 8, 19
  trajectories, 5, 19, 32–33, 36, 53, 153, 195, 197
IND. *See* Immigratie- en Naturalisatiedienst
informality, 10, 20
  informal businesses, 2, 151
  informal labour, 117
  informal practices, 2, 151, 180
Ingold, Tim, 11n3, 52, 159, 168, 175, 176n1
integration, 4–5, 110, 117, 124, 175, 176n5
  European, 2, 10, 134, 182
  paradox, 148
  test, 42–44, 51n8, 74, 79, 151
irregularity, 154, 197
  irregular migrants, 46, 132, 136, 168
  irregular migration, 17, 51n10, 93–94, 101–2
  See also undocumentedness
Isin, Engin F., 152, 171, 175–76
Istanbul. *See under* Turkey

Italy, 5, 14, 17, 19, 21–25, 33–37, 46–49, 56–58, 60, 63–67, 88n8, 90, 101–2, 104, 106, 110–12, 115–17, 120, 122–23, 126–27, 130–33, 138, 141–42, 146–50, 152, 169, 184, 187–88, 190, 192
  authorities, 14, 47, 100, 131–32, 188, 194
  Bergamo, 5, 7, 128, 187
  Lampedusa, 19, 21, 57, 63, 92, 100–2
  Liguria, 7, 32, 35–36, 38, 58, 66–67, 91, 99, 112–13, 121, 147, 149, 194
  Milan, 2, 13–14, 16, 21–22, 35, 40, 61, 100–1, 141–43, 172, 182–85, 190–91
  Naples, 8, 19, 21–22, 25, 34, 36, 46, 58, 63, 91, 112, 117, 130, 132, 154
  Rome, 15, 22, 29, 63, 102, 128, 130, 132, 159–60, 184
  Sicily, 15, 33, 66, 113

Jammeh (former Gambian president), 17–18, 50nn1–3, 65, 95, 189
Journey Just Come (JJC), 65–66, 91, 117, 194

Kea, Pamela, 17, 26, 87n3, 179
Khosravi, Shahram, 6, 8, 11nn7–8, 123, 128, 136, 139n3, 147, 153, 159, 162, 192, 197
Kleist, Nauja, 3–5, 46, 75, 153

labour contract, 7, 115, 124–25
labyrinth, 43, 121, 133, 144, 195
Lampedusa. *See under* Italy
lawyer, 24, 43, 104, 111, 125, 130–33, 135, 143, 188
Leiden. *See under* Netherlands
Lems, Annika, 10, 11n7, 145, 156, 171, 196
Lepawsky, Josh, 196
Lesbos. *See under* Greece
Libya, 19, 21, 27, 32–33, 36, 56–58, 61, 66, 91–99, 101, 107–8, 116, 159, 161, 181, 189
  Sabha, 26, 56, 96
  Tripoli, 26, 56, 58, 61, 97, 98–99, 101
Liguria. *See under* Italy
Lleida. *See under* Spain
local anchorage, 145, 196. *See also* place: attachment

local footholds, 65, 148. *See also* place: attachment
locality, 26, 57, 145. *See also* mobility/locality configuration
London. *See under* United Kingdom (UK)
Lucht, Hans, 11n7, 22, 25, 56, 100–1, 139n1
luck, 22, 24, 27, 29–31, 34–35, 40–41, 45–46, 49, 70, 75, 98, 121–22, 127, 138–39, 169

madness, 161–62. *See also* wickedness
Mali, 26, 48–49, 66, 70, 91, 93, 95, 123, 165, 185, 189
Malkki, Liisa, 46, 51n10
Malta, 37, 60–61, 87n4, 100–1, 169
Mandinka, 17, 21, 26, 50n2, 64, 146, 166
margins, 10, 22, 111, 152, 178–81, 184, 192–93, 198
  marginalization, 2, 28, 146, 153
  of Eurospace, 2, 10, 152, 192
massage of relations, 32, 59, 61, 83, 86, 135–36
Massey, Doreen, 24, 53, 172, 194
Mather, Charles, 196
Mauritania, 33, 48, 60, 93, 100–1, 189
Mazzucato, Valentina, 57, 80, 84, 176n1
Mediterranean, 19, 125, 193n1
  city, 67
  passage, 61, 97–98
  route, 101
  Sea, 97–98, 101, 111, 154, 197
migrancy, 4, 90, 128, 186
migranticization, 4, 90, 94–95. *See also* de-migranticization
migration, 2–5, 46, 49, 50n2, 51n10, 53, 55, 62, 70, 87n4, 93, 123, 128, 195–97
  apparatus, 6, 9, 54, 76, 90, 109, 111, 115, 139 (*see also* system, the)
  broker, 27, 30, 31, 46, 89 (*see also* mobility: facilitator)
  bureaucracy, 4, 109, 111, 136 (*see also* system, the)
  forced, 50n4, 113, 197
  industry, 9, 30, 57, 89
  irregular, 17, 51n10, 93–94, 101–2
  journey, 3, 41, 52
  onward, 3, 87n4, 195
  policy, 24, 45, 46, 51n10, 11, 195

return, 4, 46
studies, 3, 9-11, 19, 53, 57, 62, 71-72, 80, 152, 195-96
transit, 3
Milan. *See under* Italy
mobilities, 4-6, 10, 11n7, 38, 45, 57, 63, 71, 89, 145, 168, 185, 193
flexible, 4, 41, 127
mobility
African, 3-4, 18, 31, 49, 56, 90, 115, 173, 197
capital, 7, 150
control, 9, 107
controllers, 9, 90
cross-border, 4, 10, 49, 89, 93, 95, 107, 123, 168-70, 193
culture of, 5, 10n1, 46, 51n6, 92
facilitation, 9, 90, 103, 107
facilitator, 9, 57, 89-91, 94, 96, 101, 103-4, 107, 108n1, 134
industry, 27, 47, 56, 98, 106-7, 197
mobile lifeworld, 3, 5, 32, 81, 131, 170
mobile livelihood, 26, 49, 65, 147
mobile space, 102, 190
politics of, 60, 83-84, 98
processes, 2-3, 9, 21, 52-53, 61, 64-65, 69, 71, 79, 86, 89, 138
production of, 107
regimes, 4-6, 22, 46, 84, 89, 93, 103, 128, 138, 146, 197
rhythms, 20, 65, 165, 173-74
tactics, 175, 178
wonderland, 16, 174
mobility/locality configuration, 10, 145-46, 170-72, 175, 196. *See also* im/mobility
more or less holiday, 38-41, 101, 127
Moret, Joëlle, 3-4, 7, 53, 150, 171
Morocco, 6, 47-49, 62, 70, 75, 84, 93, 98, 101, 103
movement
cross-border, 21, 22, 63, 181
flexible, 41, 127 (*see also* mobilities: flexible)
free, 68, 93, 108n2
moving places, 172-74
non-movement, 25
secondary, 3, 195
See also mobility
multiple, the, 10, 178
multi-polarity, 175, 188

Naples. *See under* Italy
nation state, 2, 4, 57, 84, 90, 127, 130, 197
navigation, 2, 4-5, 7-9, 13-14, 20-21, 26, 33-34, 50n5, 53-54, 57, 61-62, 71, 73, 89, 98, 101-3, 109, 112, 115, 117, 123-25, 138-39, 146, 148, 152, 183, 194, 197
social, 9, 39, 52, 86
Netherlands, 1-2, 5-6, 8, 13-14, 20, 29-32, 40-44, 51n9, 56, 59, 61-64, 72-76, 78-79, 82-84, 87n6, 90, 98, 124-26, 130-36, 138, 150-51, 153, 162-63, 166, 169, 171-72, 174, 176n5, 180-81, 185, 194, 199
Amsterdam, 1, 7, 14, 22, 68, 72, 88n10, 101, 125, 141, 155-56, 170, 182, 185-86, 191
Leiden, 8, 13-14, 101, 188-89
Nijmegen, 1, 3, 6, 20, 33, 55-56, 77, 134-35, 137, 151, 155-56, 169-70, 181
network
networking, 30, 62, 64, 142, 151
network work, 54, 59, 61-62, 69, 83, 142
social, 9, 19, 53-54, 57, 60, 62, 70-71, 73, 121, 139
NGO, 29, 46, 110, 115, 124
Niger, 26, 91-95
Agadez, 26-27, 33, 56-58, 62, 93-96, 108n3
Nigeria, 6, 40, 46, 62, 81, 128, 131-32, 170-72, 184
Nijmegen. *See under* Netherlands

obedient, 117. *See also* deservingness
opacity, 8, 192
openness, 176n1, 197-98
ordering, 10, 22, 111, 193. *See also* bordering; othering
Oslo, 32-34, 38, 62
othering, 10, 111, 148, 153. *See also* bordering; ordering

papers, 13-15, 24, 30, 34, 36, 39, 41-42, 44, 47, 64, 70, 78, 80, 87, 120, 124, 126, 128, 133, 136-37, 146, 168, 188, 194
paperwork, 30, 35, 43, 125, 133-34, 136, 143, 167, 189
Paris. *See under* France

passeur, 104–5. *See also* mobility: facilitator; smuggler
permanence, 141, 145, 174
Pieterse, Edgar, 178
Piot, Charles, 10n1, 25, 27, 30, 43
place
 attachment, 10, 145, 146, 149, 153–54, 175, 198
 expulsion, 198
 gymnastics, 156, 158
 placemaking, 146, 148, 155, 160, 173, 175
postnational Europe, 2, 21, 37–38, 134. *See also* worlding: Europe
postnational lives, 38
precariousness, 152, 192
 precarity, 5, 28, 152–53
 See also vulnerability
project, 4, 33, 55, 61–62, 85, 179

raba raba, 21, 28, 34, 67, 138, 194. *See also* hustling
racism, 25, 146, , 161, 197. *See also* xenophobic aggression
reception system, 110, 117, 120, 124. *See also* asylum: system
Red Cross, 118
refugee, 4, 36, 45, 50n4, 72, 108, 110, 120, 122, 138–39, 148–49, 162
 reception crisis, 23, 34, 102, 110, 115, 127–28
 paper, 24, 39, 139n2 (*see also* papers)
 status, 113, 155 (*see also* papers)
residence, 3, 19, 24, 64, 68, 74, 97, 114, 123, 38, 153, 170–71, 175, 188, 195
 permit, 14–15, 34, 36–38, 42, 44, 63, 65, 70, 74–76, 78–79, 87n6, 115, 126–27, 129–33, 136–37, 169, 187–89, 199 (*see also* papers)
 rights, 87n8, 141, 169, 171, 183
re-viewing Europe, 3, 10, 141, 146, 161, 179, 192
Riccio, Bruno, 5, 80, 187
Rome. *See under* Italy
routines, 154, 159–60
rumours, 18, 49, 190, 192

Sabha. *See under* Libya
Salazar, Noel B., 2, 4–5, 8, 11n6, 18, 22, 84, 89, 107, 168, 175, 197
Samos. *See under* Greece

Schengen, 132, 147, 193
 Agreement, 102
 space, 11n4, 34, 47, 87, 128, 130
 visa, 136
sedentarism, 3, 51n10, 145, 197
 sedentarist metaphysics, 46, 51n10
 sedentary lifestyle, 10, 46, 156
Senegal, 6–7, 31, 33, 47–49, 51n6, 51n10, 55–56, 74–75, 87n7, 100–1, 149, 165–66, 182, 187, 189
 Dakar, 45, 48–49, 74, 166, 182, 186–87
Senegambia, 17, 19, 21, 24, 28, 79, 98, 109, 138
Serekunda. *See under* Gambia
Serekunda Market. *See under* Gambia
Sicily. *See under* Italy
Simone, AbdouMaliq, 2, 7, 9, 18–20, 50n5, 86, 138, 178, 192
sitting, 20, 25–27, 37, 49, 51n6, 91, 149, 154, 170
slavery, 116–17, 168
smuggler, 57, 89, 94, 96, 99, 104
social navigation. *See under* navigation
Spain, 1–2, 5, 8, 24, 30, 33, 48–49, 61, 65–66, 70, 72, 80, 87n8, 123–24, 126, 139n2, 141, 143–44, 153, 161, 166, 174, 177n7, 181, 183–85, 192, 199
 Andalusia, 48, 65, 172
 Barcelona, 2, 5–7, 47, 49, 70–71, 124–25, 167–70, 180–83, 186–87, 199
 Canary Islands, 33, 37, 60, 93, 97
 Ceuta, 1, 97, 103
 Lleida, 1, 5, 7, 14, 30, 65, 80–81, 100, 141–43, 166, 172–75, 177n7, 181–83, 190–91
 Tenerife, 8, 166
stability, 5, 26, 38, 152–53
 instability, 52, 87n1, 176n6
Steinberg, Jonny, 11n7
street vending, 5, 22, 131, 182–86. *See also* informality
structural eventuality, 152–53, 176n1, 178, 192, 198
Sweden, 24, 38, 51n7, 63, 125, 162
Switzerland, 8, 17, 22, 25, 29, 36–37, 63–64, 76, 91, 129–31, 146–48, 170, 194
 Bern, 8, 39, 146–47, 159
Syria, 7, 169

system, the, 9–10, 35, 37, 47, 103, 109–13, 115–16, 118, 120–26, 137–38, 146–47, 156, 162, 191

Tenerife. *See under* Spain
Thieme, Tatiana A., 20, 28, 179
third-country nationals, 3
Top Manta, 186
tourism industry, 28, 55
tourist, 7, 17, 28, 51n7, 55, 121, 167, 183
  guide, 28, 69, 157
  visa: 20, 24, 41, 43, 74, 75, 97
trajectory
  approach, 5, 7, 8, 97, 198
  ethnography, 5–6
  im/mobility trajectories, 5, 7, 19, 24, 32–33, 36, 46, 53, 142, 153, 195, 197
incoherent trajectories, 153
transgression, 2, 4–5, 54, 147–48, 152–53, 186–88, 195, 197
transnationalism
  transmigrant, 175
  transmigration, 11n1
  transnational business, 41, 49, 81, 181, 184
  transnational community, 61, 88n10
  transnational connectivity, 5, 80, 85, 181
  transnational lifeworld, 57–58, 81
  transnational movement, 2
trans-Saharan space, 108
  journey, 33, 57, 62
  mobility, 27, 33, 93–94
  pathway, 33, 57, 91–92, 107
Tripoli. *See under* Libya
Tsing, Anna, 198
Tsoni, Ionna, W., 153, 158–59
Tuckett, Anna, 109, 188
Turkey, 6–7, 32–33, 46–48, 84, 98, 161, 169
  Istanbul, 3, 46, 84–85, 103, 105, 130–31, 161
  Turkey-EU deal, 102

uncertainty, 28, 52, 132, 139, 146, 153, 178
uncertain terrains, 5, 9, 53–54

undocumentedness, 121, 136, 152–53, 168, 188–89, 195, 197
undocumented move, 35
undocumented people, 107, 116, 128, 132, 135–36, 147, 152, 169, 197, 199
United Kingdom (UK), 24, 40–41, 66, 72, 81–83, 171–72
  London, 40–41, 60, 62, 81–83, 153, 169–72, 187, 199
university, 40–41, 84, 127, 170
unknowable spaces, 158–59, 164

victimhood, 117
victimization, 197
Vigh, Henrik E., 5, 9, 28, 39, 52, 54, 57, 83, 86, 87n1, 88n12, 139, 152
violence, 91, 95, 97–98, 107–9, 146, 159, 161, 197
  institutional, 164, 186
visa, 20, 24, 40–46, 48, 55, 74–75, 87n8, 88n9, 97, 125–26, 136
  lottery, 25, 30–31, 41, 57, 120
  Schengen, 136
  student, 40, 126
  system, 30, 45, 121
  tourist, 20, 24, 41, 43, 74, 75, 97
  trouble, 41
vulnerability, 10, 152, 198

wayfarer, 11n3, 94
wayfaring, 11n3, 31, 52. *See also* wayfinding
wayfinding, 9, 52, 57, 62, 70, 90
West Africa, 10n1, 19–20, 25, 27, 33, 46, 49, 80, 84, 92–94, 150, 179, 190
wickedness, 100, 133, 158. *See also* madness
worlding, 9, 17–19, 33, 49, 130, 160, 168, 179, 182, 185
  circuit, 57, 181
  connection, 20, 56
  departures, 9, 17
  Europe, 2, 10, 186, 193
  place, 20
  travel, 33, 54

xenophobic aggression, 146, 160–61

Zodiac, 48, 98

www.ingramcontent.com/pod-product-compliance
Lightning Source LLC
Chambersburg PA
CBHW051540020426
42333CB00016B/2028